EVOLVE

STUDENT'S BOOK

with Digital Pack

Leslie Anne Hendra, Mark Ibbotson,
and Kathryn O'Dell

5

CAMBRIDGE
UNIVERSITY PRESS

CAMBRIDGE
UNIVERSITY PRESS & ASSESSMENT

Shaftesbury Road, Cambridge CB2 8EA, United Kingdom

One Liberty Plaza, 20th Floor, New York, NY 10006, USA

477 Williamstown Road, Port Melbourne, VIC 3207, Australia

314–321, 3rd Floor, Plot 3, Splendor Forum, Jasola District Centre, New Delhi – 110025, India

103 Penang Road, #05–06/07, Visioncrest Commercial, Singapore 238467

Cambridge University Press & Assessment is a department of the University of Cambridge.

We share the University's mission to contribute to society through the pursuit of education, learning and research at the highest international levels of excellence.

www.cambridge.org
Information on this title: www.cambridge.org/9781009235518

First published with Digital Pack 2022

20 19 18 17 16 15 14 13 12 11

Printed in Poland by Opolgraf

A catalogue record for this publication is available from the British Library

ISBN 978-1-009-23085-8 Student's Book with eBook
ISBN 978-1-009-23551-8 Student's Book with Digital Pack
ISBN 978-1-009-23552-5 Student's Book with Digital Pack A
ISBN 978-1-009-23553-2 Student's Book with Digital Pack B
ISBN 978-1-108-40907-0 Workbook with Audio
ISBN 978-1-108-40881-3 Workbook with Audio A
ISBN 978-1-108-41195-0 Workbook with Audio B
ISBN 978-1-108-40519-5 Teacher's Edition with Test Generator
ISBN 978-1-108-41074-8 Presentation Plus
ISBN 978-1-108-41205-6 Class Audio CDs
ISBN 978-1-108-40800-4 Video Resource Book with DVD
ISBN 978-1-009-23185-5 Full Contact with Digital Pack

Additional resources for this publication at www.cambridge.org/evolve

ACKNOWLEDGMENTS

The *Evolve* publishers would like to thank the following individuals and institutions who have contributed their time and insights into the development of the course:

Asli Derin Anaç, **Istanbul Bilgi University**, Turkey; Claudia Piccoli Díaz, **Harmon Hall**, Mexico; Daniel Martin, **CELLEP**, Brazil; Daniel Nowatnick, USA; Devon Derksen, **Myongji University**, South Korea; Diego Ribeiro Santos, **Universidade Anhembri Morumbi**, São Paulo, Brazil; Esther Carolina Euceda Garcia, **UNITEC (Universidad Tecnologica Centroamericana)**, Honduras; Gloria González Meza, **Instituto Politecnico Nacional, ESCA (University)**, Mexico; Heidi Vande Voort Nam, **Chongshin University**, South Korea; Isabela Villas Boas, **Casa Thomas Jefferson**, Brasilia, Brazil; Ivanova Monteros, **Universidad Tecnológica Equinoccial**, Ecuador; Lenise Butler, **Laureate Languages**, Mexico; Luz Libia Rey G, **Centro Colombo Americano Bogotá**, Colombia; Maria Araceli Hernández Tovar, **Instituto Tecnológico Superior de San Luis Potosí**, Capital, Mexico; Monica Frenzel, **Universidad Andres Bello**, Chile; Ray Purdey, **ELS Educational Services**, USA; Roberta Freitas, **IBEU**, Rio de Janeiro, Brazil; Rosario Aste Rentería, **Instituto De Emprendedores USIL**, Peru; Verónica Nolivos Arellano, **Centro Ecuatoriano Norteamericano**, Quito, Equador.

To our speaking competition winners, who have contributed their ideas:

Alejandra Manriquez Chavez, Mexico; Bianca Kinoshita Arai Kurtz, Brazil; Gabriel Santos Hernández, Mexico; Gerardo Torres, Mexico; Giulia Gamba, Brazil; Hector Enrique Cruz Mejia, Honduras; Jorge, Honduras; Ruben, Honduras; Stephany Ramírez Ortiz, Mexico; Veronica, Ecuador.

To our expert speakers, who have contributed their time:

Bojan Andric, Carolina Hakopian, Jacqueline Castañeda Nuñez, Lucia D'Anna, Odil Odilov, Wendy Sanchez-Vaynshteyn.

And special thanks to Wayne Rimmer for writing the Pronunciation sections, and to Laura Patsko for her expert input.

Authors' Acknowledgments

The authors would like to extend their warmest thanks to the team at Cambridge University Press. They'd particularly like to thank Gillian Lowe and Nino Chelidze for their kind, thorough, and encouraging support.

Leslie Anne Hendra would like to thank Michael Stuart Clark, as always.

Mark Ibbotson would like to thank Nathalie, Aimy, and Tom.

Kathryn O'Dell would like to thank Kevin Hurdman for his support throughout the project and for his contribution to this level.

The authors and publishers acknowledge the following sources of copyright material and are grateful for the permissions granted. While every effort has been made, it has not always been possible to identify the sources of all the material used, or to trace all copyright holders. If any omissions are brought to our notice, we will be happy to include the appropriate acknowledgements on reprinting and in the next update to the digital edition, as applicable.

Key: REV = Review, U = Unit.

Text

U1: Text from 'The Maker Movement Taking Over America. Here's How.' by Zara Stone, 11.12.2015. Copyright © Zara Stone. Reproduced with permission; **U3:** Adapted text from 'Quiet Revolution'. Copyright © Susan Cain. Reproduced with kind permission; **U5**: Wareable Ltd. for the adapted text from 'I tried VR therapy to cure my fear of flying' by Luke Johnson. Copyright © Wareable Ltd. Reproduced with kind permission; **U6:** The Moth for the text from 'Storytelling Tips & Tricks'. Copyright © The Moth. Reproduced with kind permission; MailOnline for the adapted text from 'Man trades up from a paperclip to a house', *MailOnline,* 11.07.2006. Copyright © MailOnline. Reproduced with permission; **U7:** Interview text of 'Sofian and Nathalie'. Copyright © Nathalie Grandjean and Sofian Rahmani. Reproduced with kind permission of Mark Ibbotson; TalentSmart Inc. for the text from 'Why You Should Spend Your Money on Experiences, Not Things' by Travis Bradberry, Ph.D. Copyright © TalentSmart and Dr. Travis Bradberry. Reproduced with kind permission; **U8:** The Guardian for the adapted text from 'How to complain effectively' by Anna Tims, *The Guardian,* 18.02.2010. Copyright Guardian News & Media Ltd 2018. Reproduced with permission; **U9:** The Art of Manliness for the text from 'How to Make Small Talk with Strangers: My 21-Day Happiness Experiment' by John Corcoran, https://smartbusinessrevolution.com/. Copyright © Art of Manliness. Reproduced with kind permission;

U10: Telegraph Media Group Limited and Michal Ben-Josef Hirsch for text 'Can you find your doppelganger in a day?' by Maxine Frith. Copyright © Telegraph Media Group Limited 2015 and Michal Ben-Josef Hirsch. Reprinted by permission of Telegraph Media Group Limited and Michal Ben-Josef Hirsch. All rights reserved; Monster Worldwide for the text from '8 ways to make your social media profile an employer magnet' by Mack Gelber. Copyright 2018 - Monster Worldwide, Inc. All Rights Reserved. **U11:** SiteSell Inc. for the text from 'Fake Reviews: Spot 'em and Stop 'em!' by Ken Envoy. Copyright © Ken Evoy, Founder & CEO of SiteSell. Reproduced with kind permission; **U12:** Interview text of 'Kevin Hurdman'. Copyright © Kathryn O'Dell with Kevin Hurdman. Reproduced with kind permission.

Photography

The following photographs are sourced from Getty Images.

U1–U12: Tom Merton/Caiaimage; **U1:** Alex Trautwig/Major League Baseball; xavierarnau/E+; Mathisa_s/iStock/Getty Images Plus; MajchrzakMorel/DigitalVision; Spin12/iStock/Getty Images Plus; Steven Puetzer/Corbis/Getty Images Plus; RyanJLane/E+; stocksnapper/iStock/Getty Images Plus; Halfdark; Morsa Images/DigitalVision; Emma Farrer/Moment; TommL/E+; Hero Images; Pacific Press/LightRocket; JGI/Jamie Grill; alexsl/E+; Pekic/E+; Halfdark; kozak_kadr/iStock/Getty Images Plus; Images Of Our Lives/Archive Photos/Getty Images Plus; TonyBaggett/iStock/Getty Images Plus; SuperStock/Getty Images Plus; Michelle Bennett/Lonely Planet Images/Getty Images Plus; RyanJLane/E+; George Marks/Retrofile RF; **U2:** Tunatura/iStock/Getty Images Plus; frentusha/iStock/Getty Images Plus; Science Photo Library - NASA/ESA/STSCI/J.HESTER & A.LOLL, ASU/Brand X Pictures; Rodolfo Parulan Jr/Moment; Martín Damian Monterisi/iStock/Getty Images Plus; Jonathan Therrien/500px Prime; robas/iStock/Getty Images Plus; PeopleImages/E+; damircudic/E+; Emilija Manevska/Moment; AFP/Stringer; Wolfgang Kaehler/LightRocket; Wildroze/E+; THEPALMER/iStock/Getty Images Plus; tdub_video/E+; swissmediavision/E+; **U3:** andresr/E+; Roger Hunt/500px; Lisa Barber/Photolibrary/Getty Images Plus; sergoua/iStock/Getty Images Plus; Ekaterina Gorskikh/EyeEm; Franziska Uhlmann/EyeEm; Svetlana Zhukova/Moment; Sisoje/E+; Noah Clayton; Tara Moore/Taxi/Getty Images Plus; Ronnie Kaufman/DigitalVision; Martin Beck/arabianEye; Anthony Charles/Cultura; Jon Feingersh Photography Inc/DigitalVision; Jose Luis Pelaez Inc/DigitalVision; Francesco Carta fotografo/Moment; Seth Joel/The Image Bank/Getty Images Plus; Blair_witch/iStock/Getty Images Plus; Reinhardt Dallgass/EyeEm; kali9/E+; Patrick Frischknecht/robertharding/Getty Images Plus; H. Armstrong Roberts/ClassicStock/Archive Photos/Getty Images Plus; FG Trade/E+; Cris Cantón Photography/Moment; Ippei Naoi/Moment; Mawardi Bahar/EyeEm; Emmanuel Nalli/iStock/Getty Images Plus; Putra Kurniawan/EyeEm; Angela Bax/EyeEm; ajr_images/iStock/Getty Images Plus; Delmaine Donson/E+; **REV1:** fotoVoyager/iStock Unreleased; **U4:** Graiki/Moment Unreleased; GeorgePeters/E+; Pete Saloutos/Image Source; Klaus Vedfelt/DigitalVision; Vesnaandjic/E+; Emilija Manevska/Moment; PeopleImages/E+; Sean Gladwell/Moment; Hinterhaus Productions/DigitalVision; South_agency/E+; Michel Dória/Moment; Caiaimage/Chris Ryan; **U5:** Visual China Group; Ariel Skelley/DigitalVision; real444/E+; Luis Alvarez/DigitalVision; Asia-Pacific Images Studio/E+; FREDERIC J. BROWN/AFP; SOPA Images/LightRocket; Brent Olson/Moment; John Lamb/The Image Bank/Getty Images Plus; pbombaert/Moment; 10'000 Hours/DigitalVision; SolStock/E+; Django/E+; Hero Images; **U6:** SAFIN HAMED/AFP; Michel PONOMAREFF/PONOPRESSE/Gamma-Rapho; Idaho Statesman/Tribune News Service; Bryn Hughes Photography/DigitalVision; 5m3photos/Moment; Caiaimage/Chris Ryan/OJO+; Daniele Carotenuto Photography/Moment; kozmoat98/iStock/Getty Images Plus; Chayapon Bootboonneam/EyeEm; by wildestanimal/Moment Open; ADRIAN DENNIS/AFP; Caiaimage/Sam Edwards; Butsaya/iStock/Getty Images Plus; WHL; ilbusca/E+; Hiroshi Watanabe/Stone/Getty Images Plus; Chris Tobin/DigitalVision; Simon Winnall/Stone/Getty Images Plus; Martin Barraud/The Image Bank/Getty Images Plus; **REV2:** selimaksan/E+; **U7:** Barcroft Media; Flying Colours Ltd/DigitalVision; Ariel Skelley/Photodisc; Nancy Honey/Cultura; Sophie Powell/EyeEm; wanderluster/iStock/Getty Images Plus; kolderal/Moment; Bread and Butter/DigitalVision; Erik Isakson; Franz Pritz/Picture Press/Getty Images Plus; Elizabeth Beard/Moment; maurizio siani/Moment; maurizio siani/Moment; Barry Winiker/Stockbyte; **U8:** 10'000 Hours/DigitalVision; momentimages; Louis Turner; Alexander Walter/DigitalVision; Abraham/Moment; Mikael Dubois/Publisher Mix; Igor Golovniov/EyeEm; aluxum/iStock/Getty Images Plus; PhotoAlto/Frederic Cirou; 3alexd/iStock/Getty Images Plus; TokioMarineLife/iStock/Getty Images Plus; PhonlamaiPhoto/iStock/Getty Images Plus; RapidEye/E+; Suparat Malipoom/EyeEm; frema/iStock/Getty Images Plus; monkeybusinessimages/iStock/Getty Images Plus; **U9:** Boston Globe; Andrew Brookes/Cultura; 10'000 Hours/DigitalVision; Rubberball/Mike Kemp; Michael Blann/DigitalVision; Dan Dalton/Caiaimage; GoodLifeStudio/DigitalVision Vectors; Fentino/E+; The AGE/Fairfax Media; miodrag ignjatovic/E+; fstop123/E+; **REV3:** Sky Noir Photography by Bill Dickinson/Moment; **U10:** Trevor Williams/DigitalVision; Juanmonino/E+; Fuse/Corbis; Ken Reid/The Image Bank/Getty Images Plus; xavierarnau/E+; maxicake/iStock/Getty Images Plus; Junior Gonzalez; YinYang/E+; kupicoo/E+; Jose Luis Pelaez/Photodisc; Maskot; sturti/E+; twomeows/Moment; **U11:**

VCG/Visual China Group; TANG CHHIN SOTHY/AFP; PHILIPPE LOPEZ/AFP; anilakkus/iStock/Getty Images Plus; Donald Bowers/Stringer/Getty Images Entertainment; NASA/Handout/Getty Images News; SeppFriedhuber/E+; JohnnyGreig/E+; Stephen Marks/The Image Bank/Getty Images Plus; cglade/iStock/Getty Images Plus; KatarzynaBialasiewicz/iStock/Getty Images Plus; Nataba/iStock/Getty Images Plus; AndreyPopov/iStock/Getty Images Plus; **U12:** ANDY BUCHANAN/AFP; Devon Strong/The Image Bank/Getty Images Plus; Roberto Ricciuti/GettyImages Entertainment; FabianCode/DigitalVision Vectors; mrPliskin/iStock/Getty Images Plus; sal73it/iStock/Getty Images Plus; Tetra Images; Carlos Alvarez/Stringer/Getty Images Entertainment; DenKuvaiev/iStock/Getty Images Plus; Nick Dolding/DigitalVision; Westend61; Indeed; Flashpop/DigitalVision; trinetuzun/iStock/Getty Images Plus; **REV4:** Stephan Zirwes; gawrav/E+.

The following photographs are source from other libraries/sources.

U1: Copyright © Hailey Dawson. Reproduced with kind permission of Yong Dawson; **U6:** Dinodia Photos/Alamy Stock Photo; Copyright © Kyle MacDonald. Reproduced with kind permission; **U10:** Copyright © Telegraph Media Group Limited 2015; **U12:** Copyright © JD Dworkow.

Front cover photography by Bernhard Lang/Stone/Getty Images Plus/Getty Images.

Illustrations

U1, U3: Alessandra Ceriani (Sylvie Poggio Artists Agency); **U4:** Denis Cristo (Sylvie Poggio Artists Agency); **U9:** Ana Djordjevic (Astound US); **U12:** Lyn Dylan (Sylvie Poggio Artists Agency).

Audio production by CityVox, New York.

EVOLVE

SPEAKING MATTERS

EVOLVE is a six-level American English course for adults and young adults, taking students from beginner to advanced levels (CEFR A1 to C1).

Drawing on insights from language teaching experts and real students, EVOLVE is a general English course that gets students speaking with confidence.

This student-centered course covers all skills and focuses on the most effective and efficient ways to make progress in English.

Confidence in teaching.
Joy in learning.

Better Learning WITH EVOLVE

Better Learning is our simple approach where insights we've gained from research have helped shape content that drives results. Language evolves, and so does the way we learn. This course takes a flexible, student-centered approach to English language teaching.

Meet our expert speakers

Our expert speakers are highly proficient non-native speakers of English living and working in the New York City area.

Videos and ideas from our expert speakers feature throughout the Student's Book for you to respond and react to.

Scan the QR codes below to listen to their stories.

Wendy Sanchez-Vaynshteyn
from Bolivia
Data scientist

Bojan Andric
from Serbia
Interpreter

Carolina Hakopian
from Brazil
Dentist

Jacqueline Castañeda Nuñez
from Mexico
Urbanist

Lucia D'Anna
from Italy
Lead Promotion Specialist

Odil Odilov
from Tajikistan
Finance Assistant

INSIGHT

Research shows that achievable speaking role models can be a powerful motivator.

CONTENT

Bite-sized videos feature expert speakers talking about topics in the Student's Book.

RESULT

Students are motivated to speak and share their ideas.

Student-generated content

EVOLVE is the first course of its kind to feature real student-generated content. We spoke to over 2,000 students from all over the world about the topics they would like to discuss in English and in what situations they would like to be able to speak more confidently. Their ideas are included throughout the Student's Book.

"It's important to provide learners with interesting or stimulating topics."

Teacher, Mexico (Global Teacher Survey, 2017)

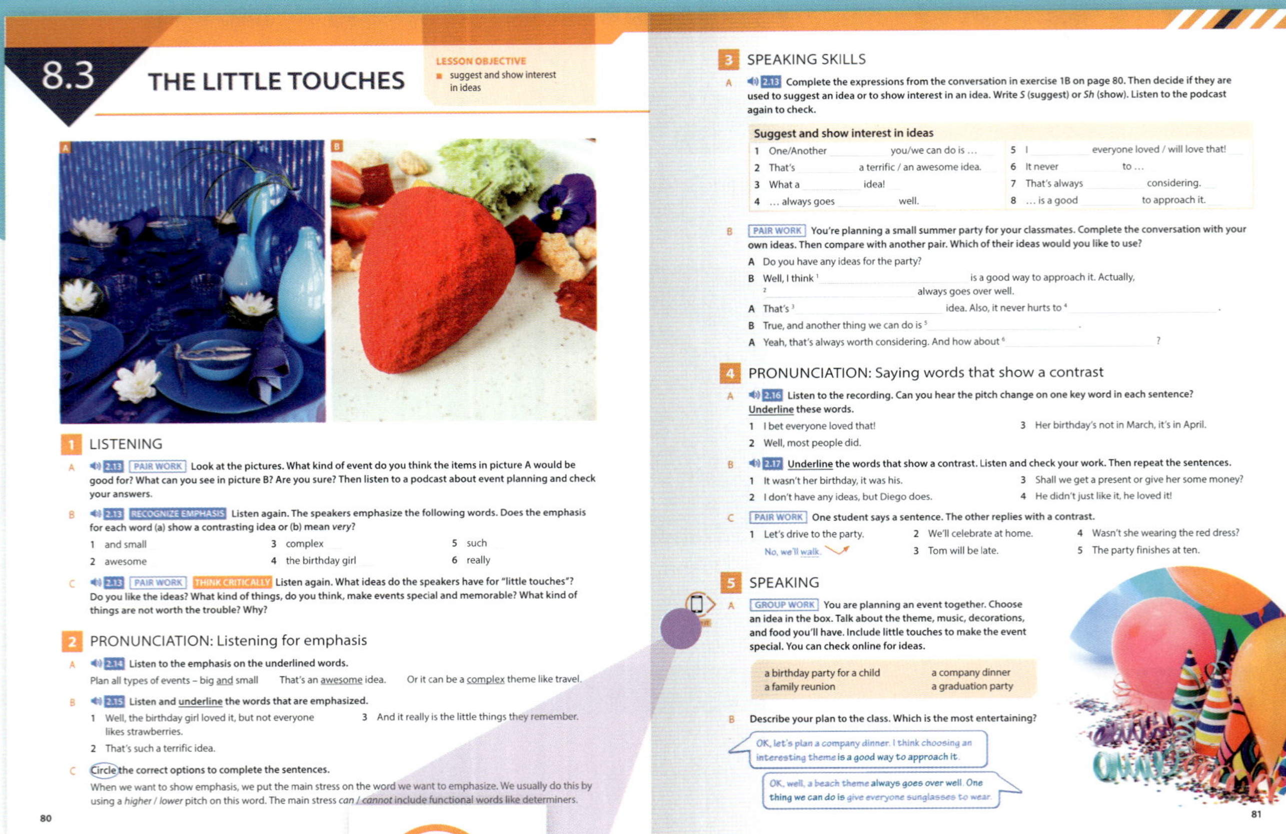

8.3 THE LITTLE TOUCHES

LESSON OBJECTIVE
- suggest and show interest in ideas

1 LISTENING

A 2.13 PAIR WORK Look at the pictures. What kind of event do you think the items in picture A would be good for? What can you see in picture B? Are you sure? Then listen to a podcast about event planning and check your answers.

B 2.13 RECOGNIZE EMPHASIS Listen again. The speakers emphasize the following words. Does the emphasis for each word (a) show a contrasting idea or (b) mean *very*?

1 and small ___ 3 complex ___ 5 such ___
2 awesome ___ 4 the birthday girl ___ 6 really ___

C 2.13 PAIR WORK THINK CRITICALLY Listen again. What ideas do the speakers have for "little touches"? Do you like the ideas? What kind of things, do you think, make events special and memorable? What kind of things are not worth the trouble? Why?

2 PRONUNCIATION: Listening for emphasis

A 2.14 Listen to the emphasis on the underlined words.

Plan all types of events – big and small. That's an awesome idea. Or it can be a complex theme like travel.

B 2.15 Listen and underline the words that are emphasized.

1 Well, the birthday girl loved it, but not everyone likes strawberries.
2 That's such a terrific idea.
3 And it really is the little things they remember.

C Circle the correct options to complete the sentences.

When we want to show emphasis, we put the main stress on the word we want to emphasize. We usually do this by using a *higher / lower* pitch on this word. The main stress *can / cannot* include functional words like determiners.

80

3 SPEAKING SKILLS

A 2.13 Complete the expressions from the conversation in exercise 1B on page 80. Then decide if they are used to suggest an idea or to show interest in an idea. Write *S* (suggest) or *Sh* (show). Listen to the podcast again to check.

Suggest and show interest in ideas	
1 One/Another ___ you/we can do is … ___	5 I ___ everyone loved / will love that! ___
2 That's ___ a terrific / an awesome idea. ___	6 It never ___ to … ___
3 What a ___ idea! ___	7 That's always ___ considering. ___
4 … always goes ___ well. ___	8 … is a good ___ to approach it. ___

B PAIR WORK You're planning a small summer party for your classmates. Complete the conversation with your own ideas. Then compare with another pair. Which of their ideas would you like to use?

A Do you have any ideas for the party?
B Well, I think [1] ___ is a good way to approach it. Actually, [2] ___ always goes over well.
A That's [3] ___ idea. Also, it never hurts to [4] ___.
B True, and another thing we can do is [5] ___.
A Yeah, that's always worth considering. And how about [6] ___?

4 PRONUNCIATION: Saying words that show a contrast

A 2.16 Listen to the recording. Can you hear the pitch change on one key word in each sentence? Underline these words.

1 I bet everyone loved that!
2 Well, most people did.
3 Her birthday's not in March, it's in April.

B 2.17 Underline the words that show a contrast. Listen and check your work. Then repeat the sentences.

1 It wasn't her birthday, it was his.
2 I don't have any ideas, but Diego does.
3 Shall we get a present or give her some money?
4 He didn't just like it, he loved it!

C PAIR WORK One student says a sentence. The other replies with a contrast.

1 Let's drive to the party.
No, we'll walk.
2 We'll celebrate at home.
3 Tom will be late.
4 Wasn't she wearing the red dress?
5 The party finishes at ten.

5 SPEAKING

A GROUP WORK You are planning an event together. Choose an idea in the box. Talk about the theme, music, decorations, and food you'll have. Include little touches to make the event special. You can check online for ideas.

a birthday party for a child
a family reunion
a company dinner
a graduation party

B Describe your plan to the class. Which is the most entertaining?

OK, let's plan a company dinner. I think choosing an interesting theme is a good way to approach it.

OK, well, a beach theme always goes over well. One thing we can do is give everyone sunglasses to wear.

81

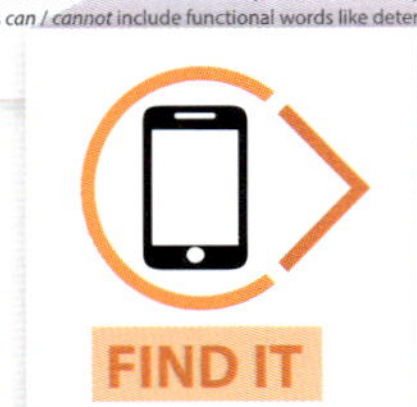

Find it

INSIGHT

Research with hundreds of teachers and students across the globe revealed a desire to expand the classroom and bring the real world in.

CONTENT

Find it are smartphone activities that allow students to bring live content into the class and personalize the learning experience with research and group activities.

RESULT

Students engage in the lesson because it is meaningful to them.

Designed for success

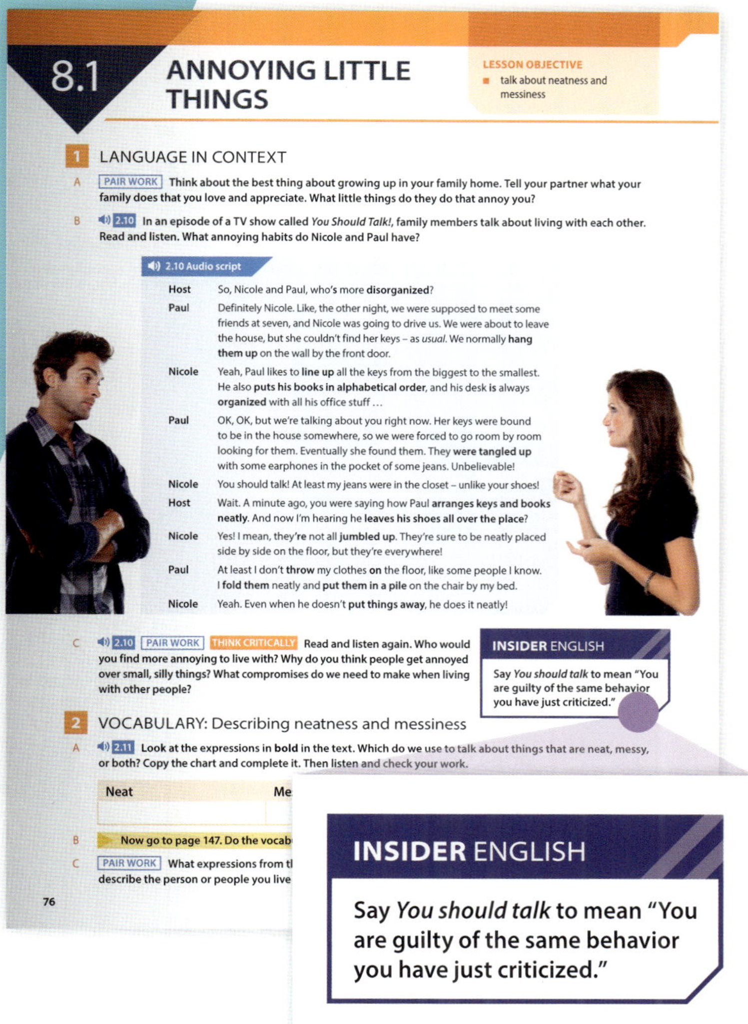

8.1 ANNOYING LITTLE THINGS

LESSON OBJECTIVE
- talk about neatness and messiness

1 LANGUAGE IN CONTEXT

A PAIR WORK **Think about the best thing about growing up in your family home. Tell your partner what your family does that you love and appreciate. What little things do they do that annoy you?**

B 2.10 **In an episode of a TV show called *You Should Talk!*, family members talk about living with each other. Read and listen. What annoying habits do Nicole and Paul have?**

2.10 Audio script

Host So, Nicole and Paul, who's more **disorganized**?

Paul Definitely Nicole. Like, the other night, we were supposed to meet some friends at seven, and Nicole was going to drive us. We were about to leave the house, but she couldn't find her keys – as *usual*. We normally **hang them up** on the wall by the front door.

Nicole Yeah, Paul likes to **line up** all the keys from the biggest to the smallest. He also **puts his books in alphabetical order**, and his desk **is** always **organized** with all his office stuff …

Paul OK, OK, but we're talking about you right now. Her keys were bound to be in the house somewhere, so we were forced to go room by room looking for them. Eventually she found them. They **were tangled up** with some earphones in the pocket of some jeans. Unbelievable!

Nicole You should talk! At least my jeans were in the closet – unlike your shoes!

Host Wait. A minute ago, you were saying how Paul **arranges keys and books neatly**. And now I'm hearing he **leaves his shoes all over the place**?

Nicole Yes! I mean, they**'re** not all **jumbled up**. They're sure to be neatly placed side by side on the floor, but they're everywhere!

Paul At least I don't **throw** my clothes **on** the floor, like some people I know. I **fold them** neatly and **put them in a pile** on the chair by my bed.

Nicole Yeah. Even when he doesn't **put things away**, he does it neatly!

C 2.10 PAIR WORK THINK CRITICALLY **Read and listen again. Who would you find more annoying to live with? Why do you think people get annoyed over small, silly things? What compromises do we need to make when living with other people?**

INSIDER ENGLISH

Say *You should talk* to mean "You are guilty of the same behavior you have just criticized."

2 VOCABULARY: Describing neatness and messiness

A 2.11 **Look at the expressions in bold in the text. Which do we use to talk about things that are neat, messy, or both? Copy the chart and complete it. Then listen and check your work.**

Neat	Me

B Now go to page 147. Do the vocab

C PAIR WORK What expressions from t describe the person or people you live

76

INSIDER ENGLISH

Say *You should talk* to mean "You are guilty of the same behavior you have just criticized."

Pronunciation

INSIGHT

Research shows that only certain aspects of pronunciation actually affect comprehensibility and inhibit communication.

CONTENT

EVOLVE focuses on the aspects of pronunciation that most affect communication.

RESULT

Students understand more when listening and can be clearly understood when they speak.

Insider English

INSIGHT

Even in a short exchange, idiomatic language can inhibit understanding.

CONTENT

Insider English focuses on the informal language and colloquial expressions frequently found in everyday situations.

RESULT

Students are confident in the real world.

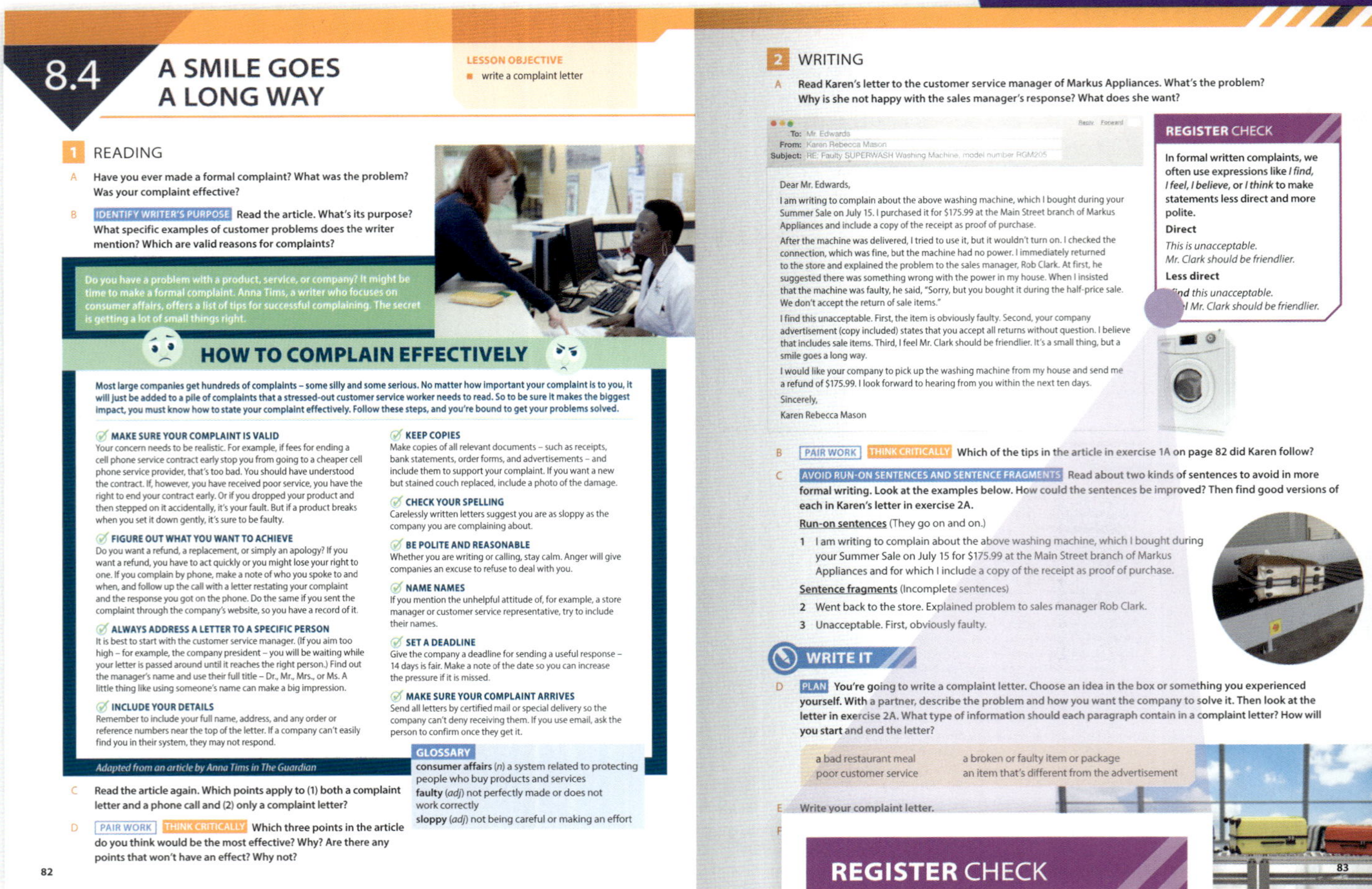

8.4 A SMILE GOES A LONG WAY

LESSON OBJECTIVE
- write a complaint letter

1 READING

A Have you ever made a formal complaint? What was the problem? Was your complaint effective?

B IDENTIFY WRITER'S PURPOSE Read the article. What's its purpose? What specific examples of customer problems does the writer mention? Which are valid reasons for complaints?

Do you have a problem with a product, service, or company? It might be time to make a formal complaint. Anna Tims, a writer who focuses on consumer affairs, offers a list of tips for successful complaining. The secret is getting a lot of small things right.

HOW TO COMPLAIN EFFECTIVELY

Most large companies get hundreds of complaints – some silly and some serious. No matter how important your complaint is to you, it will just be added to a pile of complaints that a stressed-out customer service worker needs to read. So to be sure it makes the biggest impact, you must know how to state your complaint effectively. Follow these steps, and you're bound to get your problems solved.

MAKE SURE YOUR COMPLAINT IS VALID
Your concern needs to be realistic. For example, if fees for ending a cell phone service contract early stop you from going to a cheaper cell phone service provider, that's too bad. You should have understood the contract. If, however, you have received poor service, you have the right to end your contract early. Or if you dropped your product and then stepped on it accidentally, it's your fault. But if a product breaks when you set it down gently, it's sure to be faulty.

FIGURE OUT WHAT YOU WANT TO ACHIEVE
Do you want a refund, a replacement, or simply an apology? If you want a refund, you have to act quickly or you might lose your right to one. If you complain by phone, make a note of who you spoke to and when, and follow up the call with a letter restating your complaint and the response you got on the phone. Do the same if you sent the complaint through the company's website, so you have a record of it.

ALWAYS ADDRESS A LETTER TO A SPECIFIC PERSON
It is best to start with the customer service manager. (If you aim too high – for example, the company president – you will be waiting while your letter is passed around until it reaches the right person.) Find out the manager's name and use their full title – Dr., Mr., Mrs., or Ms. A little thing like using someone's name can make a big impression.

INCLUDE YOUR DETAILS
Remember to include your full name, address, and any order or reference numbers near the top of the letter. If a company can't easily find you in their system, they may not respond.

KEEP COPIES
Make copies of all relevant documents – such as receipts, bank statements, order forms, and advertisements – and include them to support your complaint. If you want a new but stained couch replaced, include a photo of the damage.

CHECK YOUR SPELLING
Carelessly written letters suggest you are as sloppy as the company you are complaining about.

BE POLITE AND REASONABLE
Whether you are writing or calling, stay calm. Anger will give companies an excuse to refuse to deal with you.

NAME NAMES
If you mention the unhelpful attitude of, for example, a store manager or customer service representative, try to include their names.

SET A DEADLINE
Give the company a deadline for sending a useful response – 14 days is fair. Make a note of the date so you can increase the pressure if it is missed.

MAKE SURE YOUR COMPLAINT ARRIVES
Send all letters by certified mail or special delivery so the company can't deny receiving them. If you use email, ask the person to confirm once they get it.

Adapted from an article by Anna Tims in The Guardian

GLOSSARY
consumer affairs (*n*) a system related to protecting people who buy products and services
faulty (*adj*) not perfectly made or does not work correctly
sloppy (*adj*) not being careful or making an effort

C Read the article again. Which points apply to (1) both a complaint letter and a phone call and (2) only a complaint letter?

D PAIR WORK THINK CRITICALLY Which three points in the article do you think would be the most effective? Why? Are there any points that won't have an effect? Why not?

82

2 WRITING

A Read Karen's letter to the customer service manager of Markus Appliances. What's the problem? Why is she not happy with the sales manager's response? What does she want?

Reply Forward
To: Mr. Edwards
From: Karen Rebecca Mason
Subject: RE: Faulty SUPERWASH Washing Machine, model number RGM205

Dear Mr. Edwards,

I am writing to complain about the above washing machine, which I bought during your Summer Sale on July 15. I purchased it for $175.99 at the Main Street branch of Markus Appliances and include a copy of the receipt as proof of purchase.

After the machine was delivered, I tried to use it, but it wouldn't turn on. I checked the connection, which was fine, but the machine had no power. I immediately returned to the store and explained the problem to the sales manager, Rob Clark. At first, he suggested there was something wrong with the power in my house. When I insisted that the machine was faulty, he said, "Sorry, but you bought it during the half-price sale. We don't accept the return of sale items."

I find this unacceptable. First, the item is obviously faulty. Second, your company advertisement (copy included) states that you accept all returns without question. I believe that includes sale items. Third, I feel Mr. Clark should be friendlier. It's a small thing, but a smile goes a long way.

I would like your company to pick up the washing machine from my house and send me a refund of $175.99. I look forward to hearing from you within the next ten days.

Sincerely,
Karen Rebecca Mason

REGISTER CHECK
In formal written complaints, we often use expressions like *I find*, *I feel*, *I believe*, or *I think* to make statements less direct and more polite.
Direct
This is unacceptable.
Mr. Clark should be friendlier.
Less direct
I find this unacceptable.
I feel Mr. Clark should be friendlier.

B PAIR WORK THINK CRITICALLY Which of the tips in the article in exercise 1A on page 82 did Karen follow?

C AVOID RUN-ON SENTENCES AND SENTENCE FRAGMENTS Read about two kinds of sentences to avoid in more formal writing. Look at the examples below. How could the sentences be improved? Then find good versions of each in Karen's letter in exercise 2A.

Run-on sentences (They go on and on.)
1 I am writing to complain about the above washing machine, which I bought during your Summer Sale on July 15 for $175.99 at the Main Street branch of Markus Appliances and for which I include a copy of the receipt as proof of purchase.

Sentence fragments (Incomplete sentences)
2 Went back to the store. Explained problem to sales manager Rob Clark.
3 Unacceptable. First, obviously faulty.

WRITE IT

D PLAN You're going to write a complaint letter. Choose an idea in the box or something you experienced yourself. With a partner, describe the problem and how you want the company to solve it. Then look at the letter in exercise 2A. What type of information should each paragraph contain in a complaint letter? How will you start and end the letter?

a bad restaurant meal | a broken or faulty item or package
poor customer service | an item that's different from the advertisement

E Write your complaint letter.

83

REGISTER CHECK

In formal written complaints, we often use expressions like *I find*, *I feel*, *I believe*, or *I think* to make statements less direct and more polite.

Direct

This is unacceptable.
Mr. Clark should be friendlier.

Less direct

***I find** this unacceptable.*
***I feel** Mr. Clark should be friendlier.*

Register check

INSIGHT

Teachers report that their students often struggle to master the differences between written and spoken English.

CONTENT

Register check draws on research into the Cambridge English Corpus and highlights potential problem areas for learners.

RESULT

Students transition confidently between written and spoken English and recognize different levels of formality as well as when to use them appropriately.

"The presentation is very clear, and there are plenty of opportunities for student practice and production."

Jason Williams, Teacher, Notre Dame Seishin University, Japan

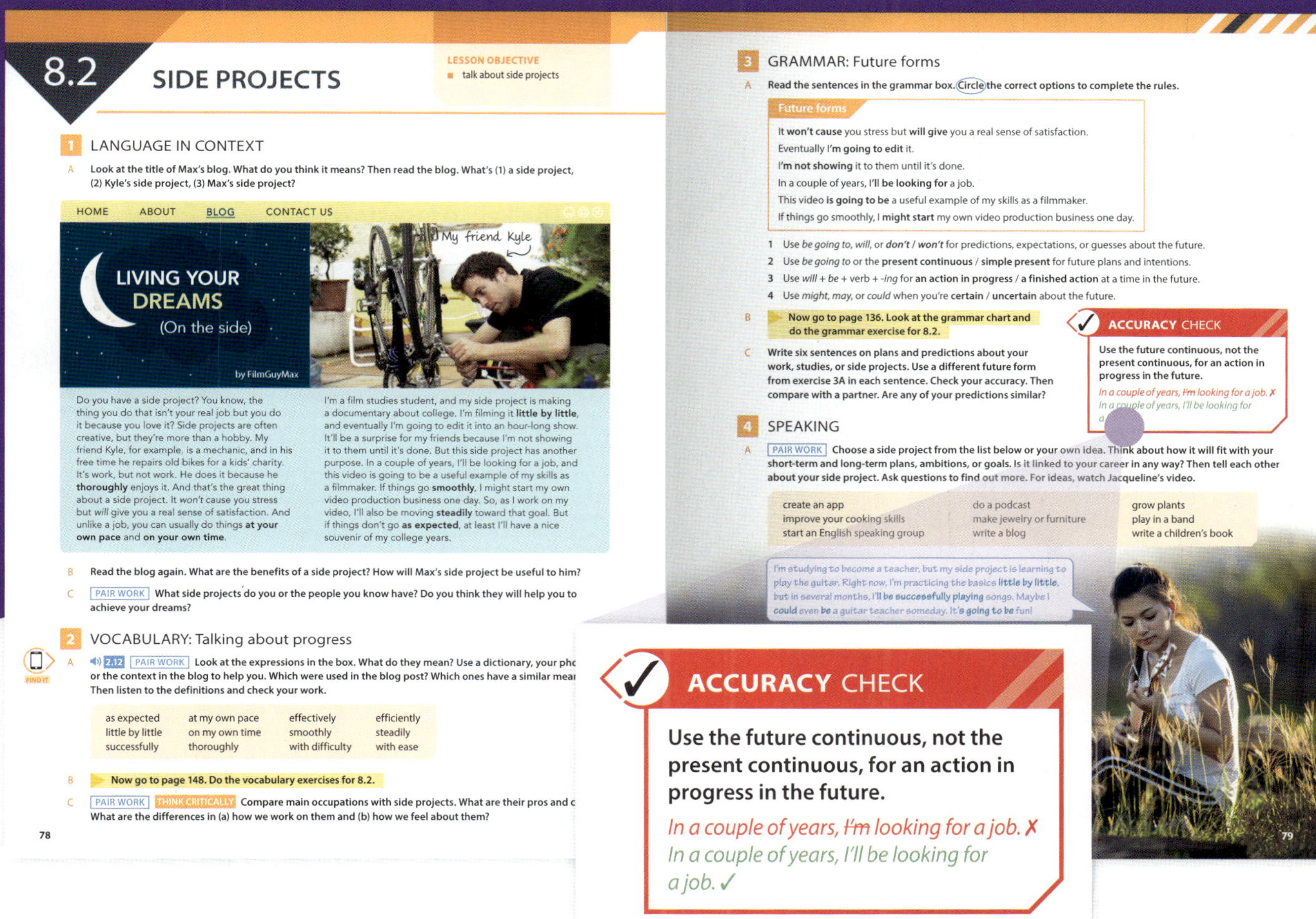

8.2 SIDE PROJECTS

LESSON OBJECTIVE
- talk about side projects

1 LANGUAGE IN CONTEXT

A Look at the title of Max's blog. What do you think it means? Then read the blog. What's (1) a side project, (2) Kyle's side project, (3) Max's side project?

HOME ABOUT BLOG CONTACT US

LIVING YOUR DREAMS (On the side)

by FilmGuyMax

My friend Kyle

Do you have a side project? You know, the thing you do that isn't your real job but you do it because you love it? Side projects are often creative, but they're more than a hobby. My friend Kyle, for example, is a mechanic, and in his free time he repairs old bikes for a kids' charity. It's work, but not work. He does it because he **thoroughly** enjoys it. And that's the great thing about a side project. It *won't* cause you stress but *will* give you a real sense of satisfaction. And unlike a job, you can usually do things **at your own pace** and **on your own time**.

I'm a film studies student, and my side project is making a documentary about college. I'm filming it **little by little**, and eventually I'm going to edit it into an hour-long show. It'll be a surprise for my friends because I'm not showing it to them until it's done. But this side project has another purpose. In a couple of years, I'll be looking for a job, and this video is going to be a useful example of my skills as a filmmaker. If things go **smoothly**, I might start my own video production business one day. So, as I work on my video, I'll also be moving **steadily** toward that goal. But if things don't go **as expected**, at least I'll have a nice souvenir of my college years.

B Read the blog again. What are the benefits of a side project? How will Max's side project be useful to him?

C PAIR WORK What side projects do you or the people you know have? Do you think they will help you to achieve your dreams?

2 VOCABULARY: Talking about progress

A 2.12 PAIR WORK Look at the expressions in the box. What do they mean? Use a dictionary, your pho… or the context in the blog to help you. Which were used in the blog post? Which ones have a similar mea… Then listen to the definitions and check your work.

as expected	at my own pace	effectively	efficiently
little by little	on my own time	smoothly	steadily
successfully	thoroughly	with difficulty	with ease

B Now go to page 148. Do the vocabulary exercises for 8.2.

C PAIR WORK THINK CRITICALLY Compare main occupations with side projects. What are their pros and c… What are the differences in (a) how we work on them and (b) how we feel about them?

78

3 GRAMMAR: Future forms

A Read the sentences in the grammar box. Circle the correct options to complete the rules.

Future forms
- It **won't cause** you stress but **will give** you a real sense of satisfaction.
- Eventually **I'm going to edit** it.
- **I'm not showing** it to them until it's done.
- In a couple of years, **I'll be looking for** a job.
- This video **is going to be** a useful example of my skills as a filmmaker.
- If things go smoothly, I **might start** my own video production business one day.

1 Use *be going to*, *will*, or *don't* / *won't* for predictions, expectations, or guesses about the future.
2 Use *be going to* or the **present continuous** / **simple present** for future plans and intentions.
3 Use *will* + *be* + verb + *-ing* for **an action in progress** / **a finished action** at a time in the future.
4 Use *might*, *may*, or *could* when you're **certain** / **uncertain** about the future.

B Now go to page 136. Look at the grammar chart and do the grammar exercise for 8.2.

C Write six sentences on plans and predictions about your work, studies, or side projects. Use a different future form from exercise 3A in each sentence. Check your accuracy. Then compare with a partner. Are any of your predictions similar?

ACCURACY CHECK
Use the future continuous, not the present continuous, for an action in progress in the future.
In a couple of years, ~~I'm~~ looking for a job. ✗
In a couple of years, I'll be looking for a job. ✓

4 SPEAKING

A PAIR WORK Choose a side project from the list below or your own idea. Think about how it will fit with your short-term and long-term plans, ambitions, or goals. Is it linked to your career in any way? Then tell each other about your side project. Ask questions to find out more. For ideas, watch Jacqueline's video.

create an app	do a podcast	grow plants
improve your cooking skills	make jewelry or furniture	play in a band
start an English speaking group	write a blog	write a children's book

I'm studying to become a teacher, but my side project is learning to play the guitar. Right now, I'm practicing the basics **little by little**, but in several months, I'll **be successfully playing** songs. Maybe I **could** even **be** a guitar teacher someday. It's **going to be** fun!

79

ACCURACY CHECK

Use the future continuous, not the present continuous, for an action in progress in the future.

In a couple of years, ~~I'm~~ looking for a job. ✗
In a couple of years, I'll be looking for a job. ✓

Accuracy check

INSIGHT

Some common errors can become fossilized if not addressed early on in the learning process.

CONTENT

Accuracy check highlights common learner errors (based on unique research into the Cambridge Learner Corpus) and can be used for self-editing.

RESULT

Students avoid common errors in their written and spoken English.

You spoke. We listened.

Students told us that speaking is the most important skill for them to master, while teachers told us that finding speaking activities which engage their students and work in the classroom can be challenging.

That's why EVOLVE has a whole lesson dedicated to speaking: Lesson 5, *Time to speak*.

Time to speak

INSIGHT

Speaking ability is how students most commonly measure their own progress, but is also the area where they feel most insecure. To be able to fully exploit speaking opportunities in the classroom, students need a safe speaking environment where they can feel confident, supported, and able to experiment with language.

CONTENT

Time to speak is a unique lesson dedicated to developing speaking skills and is based around immersive tasks which involve information sharing and decision making.

RESULT

Time to speak lessons create a buzz in the classroom where speaking can really thrive, evolve, and take off, resulting in more confident speakers of English.

8.5

TIME TO SPEAK

The key to less stress

LESSON OBJECTIVE

- make a podcast on ways to reduce stress

NOT STRESSED AT ALL — VERY STRESSED

A DISCUSS How stressed are you? Where would you put yourself on the scale above? Would you say most of your stress is caused by one or two big things or a number of small things? In pairs, discuss examples of big and small things that can make you feel stressed. For ideas look at the pictures. Add four ideas of your own.

B Compare your ideas with other pairs. Find out common causes of stress.

C DECIDE Which of the causes of stress from part B can be reduced by taking simple actions? What actions can be taken? With your partner from part A, discuss the ideas in the box and your own ideas. Then choose your top three effective and simple actions.

SIMPLE ACTIONS TO REDUCE STRESS:

Delete it.	Don't read it.	Don't reply.
Make "to-do" lists.	Do it right away.	Get up earlier.
Go to bed later.	Say "No!"	Discuss the problem.

D PREPARE You're going to present your actions in a short podcast. Plan: (1) the introduction, (2) your actions and the reasons why you think they're simple and effective (give some examples), and (3) the conclusion. You can take notes.

E PRESENT Present your podcast to the class. Answer any questions about it.

F AGREE The class compares the podcasts and chooses two that have the best ideas and are well presented.

To check your progress, go to page 155.

USEFUL PHRASES

DECIDE

One/Another thing you could do is …

It never hurts to …

… is always worth considering.

… is a good way to approach it.

PREPARE

If you do this, you're bound to / sure to …

You're going to …

You might …

You'll be + verb + *-ing* …

84

Experience Better Learning with EVOLVE: a course that helps both teachers and students on every step of the language learning journey.

Speaking matters. Find out more about creating safe speaking environments in the classroom.

EVOLVE unit structure

Unit opening page

Each unit opening page activates prior knowledge and vocabulary and immediately gets students speaking.

Lessons 1 and 2

These lessons present and practice the unit vocabulary and grammar in context, helping students discover language rules for themselves. Students then have the opportunity to use this language in well-scaffolded, personalized speaking tasks.

Lesson 3

This lesson is built around an off-the-page dialogue that practices listening skills. It also models and contextualizes useful speaking skills. The final speaking task draws on the language and strategies from the lesson.

Lesson 4

This is a skills lesson based around an engaging reading text. Each lesson asks students to think critically and ends with a practical writing task.

Lesson 5

Time to speak is an entire lesson dedicated to developing speaking skills. Students work on collaborative, immersive tasks which involve information sharing and decision making.

CONTENTS

Listening	Speaking skills	Reading	Writing	Speaking
Upgrade ▪ A conversation between two coworkers	▪ Discuss issues and agree strongly	**Back to basics** ▪ An article about the Maker Movement	**An opinion essay** ▪ Organize information	▪ Talk about your attitude toward change ▪ Talk about things from when you were younger that aren't around anymore ▪ Compare things in your past and present life ▪ Talk about the Maker Movement **Time to speak** ▪ Talk about what life was like in a past decade
Finding out ▪ A conversation between a guide and a tourist	▪ Exchange information	**Extreme living** ▪ An interview about living in Antarctica	**A description of an area** ▪ Use numerical words and phrases	▪ Talk about the most important areas of research and exploration ▪ Talk about life forms in difficult environments ▪ Give advice on doing a free-time activity you enjoy ▪ Talk about living in an extreme environment **Time to speak** ▪ Plan an outdoor vacation
Asking for favors ▪ Conversations between an intern, an employee, and their bosses	▪ Make and respond to requests	**The right job for me** ▪ An advertisement for jobs in a zoo	**A personal statement** ▪ Compose and evaluate a personal statement	▪ Talk about introverts and extroverts ▪ Talk about how different things or experiences make you feel ▪ Make and respond to requests ▪ Talk about a job you would like to do and a job you would be best at **Time to speak** ▪ Interview a job candidate
Two people, one job ▪ A counseling session on job sharing	▪ Discuss advantages and disadvantages	**The me team** ▪ An article about disadvantages of teamwork	**Summary of an article** ▪ Summarize main points	▪ Talk about an experience of coordinating a group of people ▪ Talk about making group decisions ▪ Discuss advantages and disadvantages of job sharing ▪ Talk about your attitude toward teamwork **Time to speak** ▪ Discuss organizing a fund-raising event
Stop blaming gaming ▪ A TV debate about video games	▪ Consider and contrast ideas	**What language barrier?** ▪ An article about translation apps	**Online comments** ▪ State opinion and give examples	▪ Discuss how VR programs can help people in different areas of life ▪ Discuss how the development of technology can affect the way we communicate with different people ▪ Discuss benefits of video games ▪ Discuss translation apps **Time to speak** ▪ Plan a community improvement campaign
Something in the water ▪ An interview with a couple who thought they saw a shark	▪ Make, contradict, and clarify assumptions	**Getting it wrong** ▪ Posts about being in the wrong place at the wrong time	**A story** ▪ Make a story interesting	▪ Tell a story about someone who went viral ▪ Talk about managing expectations ▪ Describe an interesting experience ▪ Talk about unexpected situations resulting from small mistakes **Time to speak** ▪ Tell a story for a contest

	Learning objectives	Grammar	Vocabulary	Pronunciation
Unit 7 Priorities	■ Discuss worthwhile experiences ■ Talk about purchases ■ Bargain for a purchase ■ Write a for-and-against essay ■ Negotiate a boat trip	■ Gerunds and infinitives after adjectives, nouns, and pronouns ■ Infinitives after verbs with and without objects	■ Positive experiences ■ Making purchases	■ Listening for vowel linking between words ■ Saying /ŋ/
Unit 8 Small things matter	■ Talk about neatness and messiness ■ Talk about side projects ■ Suggest and show interest in ideas ■ Write a complaint letter ■ Make a podcast on ways to reduce stress	■ Modal-like expressions with *be* ■ Future forms	■ Describing neatness and messiness ■ Talking about progress	■ Listening for emphasis ■ Saying words that show a contrast
Unit 9 Things happen	■ Talk about how your life might be different ■ Talk about mistakes ■ Reassure someone about a problem ■ Write an article giving tips ■ Talk about key events in your life	■ Unreal conditionals ■ Wishes and regrets	■ Luck and choice ■ Commenting on mistakes	■ Listening for different word groups ■ Using intonation in conditional sentences
	Review 3 (Review of Units 7–9)			
Unit 10 People, profiles	■ Talk about people's characteristics ■ Talk about customer research ■ Give your impressions ■ Write a professional profile ■ Develop a plan to improve a company website	■ Gerunds after prepositions ■ Causative verbs	■ Describing characteristics ■ Describing research	■ Quoting from a text ■ Recognizing /eɪ/, /aɪ/, and /ɔɪ/
Unit 11 Really?	■ Talk about fake goods ■ Talk about untrue information ■ Express belief and disbelief ■ Write a persuasive essay ■ Share tips on solutions	■ Passive forms ■ Passives with modals and modal-like expressions; passive infinitives	■ Describing consumer goods ■ Degrees of truth	■ Listening for intonation on exclamations and imperatives ■ Saying /oʊ/ and /aʊ/
Unit 12 Got what it takes?	■ Talk about talent ■ Discuss how to make life better ■ Describe your ambitions ■ Write a review of a performance ■ Give a presentation about yourself	■ Adverbs with adjectives and adverbs ■ Making non-count nouns countable	■ Skill and performance ■ Describing emotional impact	■ Listening for sounds that change ■ Using syllable stress in words
	Review 4 (Review of Units 10–12)			
	Grammar charts and practice, pages 129–140	**Vocabulary exercises, pages 141–152**		

Listening	Speaking skills	Reading	Writing	Speaking
A good bargain ■ Price negotiation for a purchase	■ Negotiate a price	**Money's worth** ■ An article about spending money on experiences vs. things	**A for-and-against essay** ■ Organize an essay	■ Talk about your job or a job you would like to do ■ Talk about purchases ■ Talk about bargaining ■ Discuss spending money on experiences vs. things **Time to speak** ■ Negotiate features of a boat trip
The little touches ■ A podcast about event planning	■ Suggest and show interest in ideas	**A smile goes a long way** ■ An article about complaining effectively	**A complaint** ■ Avoid run-on sentences and sentence fragments	■ Talk about qualities of a good roommate ■ Talk about side projects ■ Plan an event ■ Discuss effective ways to complain **Time to speak** ■ Discuss ways to reduce stress
My mistake ■ A radio phone-in about an embarrassing situation	■ Give reassurance	**Good conversations** ■ An online article about making small talk with strangers	**An article** ■ Parallel structures	■ Talk about how your life might be different if you'd made different choices ■ Talk about small regrets and make wishes ■ Describe a problem and offer reassurance ■ Discuss what makes a good conversationalist **Time to speak** ■ Talk about your news at a school reunion
A careful choice ■ A conversation between two friends discussing which company to order a cake from	■ Give your impressions	**A professional profile** ■ An article about rewriting your professional profile	**A professional profile** ■ Use professional language	■ Talk about the ways we like to be similar to or different from others ■ Talk about your customer profile ■ Choose a gym based on its online profile ■ Give advice on writing a professional profile **Time to speak** ■ Come up with tips on making the career section of a website attractive to potential employees
Believe it or not … ■ Two conversations about a NASA probe sent to the sun	■ Express belief and disbelief	**Convince me** ■ An article with tips on identifying fake product reviews	**Persuasive essay** ■ Use persuasive language	■ Talk about counterfeit goods ■ Talk about false stories you've read online ■ Talk about rumors ■ Discuss how to identify fake information **Time to speak** ■ Talk about common problems people search for online and solutions for them
Maybe one day … ■ A college interview for a theater program	■ Describe ambitions; express optimism and caution	**Success behind the scenes** ■ A personal narrative by a guitar tech	**A concert review** ■ Show reason and result	■ Talk about being good at something due to practice or natural talent ■ Talk about small things you can do to make people happy ■ Talk about your ambitions ■ Talk about what contributes to success in a job **Time to speak** ■ Make a presentation about yourself

Hailey Dawson, seven,
throwing out the ceremonial first pitch wearing a 3D-printed robotic hand at Minute Maid Park for the 2017 World Series Game 4 between the Houston Astros and Los Angeles Dodgers.

UNIT OBJECTIVES

- talk about how we deal with change
- talk about past difficulties
- discuss issues and agree strongly
- write an opinion essay
- talk about daily life in the past

STEP FORWARD

1

START SPEAKING

A **Describe what you see in this picture. What do you think is special about the girl's right hand? Read the caption and check.**

B **In what ways can 3D-printed objects improve our lives? How might a 3D-printed object cause us problems?**

C **Talk about something you often use or do that has improved your life. This could be an app, a gadget, or something else.**

D **With a partner, list some other helpful inventions. How can they help us? For ideas, watch Jacqueline's video.**

EXPERT SPEAKER

What do you think of Jacqueline's example?

1.1 LIFE CHANGES

LESSON OBJECTIVE

- talk about how we deal with change

1 LANGUAGE IN CONTEXT

A **What are some of the biggest changes that people experience in life? Are they positive or negative?**

B 1.02 **Read and listen to an episode from Christa Garcia's podcast "No Fear." What life changes does she mention?**

1.02 Audio script

Ten months ago, as regular listeners will know, I made two big life changes: I moved to a new city, and I changed jobs. My work situation wasn't great: I'd just lost a job, and I couldn't find a single engineering position anywhere in Florida. Then this job in Chicago came up. It was perfect and too good to refuse. But … but … but … .

I'd lived in Florida all my life. My family was here, and my friends. And I **was frightened of tackling** a new job. Plus, it's really cold in Chicago, and this girl is 100% Florida. You know what I mean?

I said to my brother, "I **can't take** all this change!" He just said, "**Get a grip**, Christa. You**'re** perfectly **capable of** handling all this."

After I stopped being mad at him for not being more understanding, I realized that I'm always looking for an excuse to avoid change, and I'll do anything to keep my life simple. And I'm not alone. We often talk negatively about the future, don't we? We tend to fear change. And when we're feeling scared, we **underestimate** our ability to **cope with** things. But actually, we **adapt** to new situations extremely well. Think about huge changes like starting college, getting your first job, having a baby – people **get through** challenges like this all the time. We should **accept** that we're terrific at **surviving**, and instead of **resisting** change, we should **welcome** it. That's what I did, and now life is good, and that**'s a** real **step forward**!

C 1.02 **Read and listen again. What did Christa realize about people's ability to change? How did her own attitude change?**

2 VOCABULARY: Facing challenges

FIND IT

A 1.03 PAIR WORK **Look at the expressions in the box. Look at how they're used in the podcast and describe each one using other words. Use a dictionary or your phone to help you. Then listen and check.**

accept	adapt	be a step forward	be capable of	be frightened of
can't take	cope with	get a grip	get through	resist
survive	tackle	underestimate	welcome	

B **Now go to page 141. Do the vocabulary exercises for 1.1.**

C PAIR WORK **Do you agree with Christa's thoughts about our ability to change? Tell your partner, and use examples if you can. Use the words in exercise 2A.**

3 GRAMMAR: Present habits

A **Read the sentences in the grammar box. Circle the correct options to complete the rules.**

Present habits

I'**m always looking for** an excuse to avoid change, and I'**ll do** anything to keep my life simple.
We **often talk** negatively about the future, don't we?
We **tend to fear** change.
When we'**re feeling** scared, we underestimate our ability to cope with things.

1 For a habit that is more noticeable or frequent than usual, you can use *always* or *constantly* with the **simple present / present continuous**.
2 You can use the modal *will* for **present / past** habits.
3 You can use the verb **tend to / keep** + a verb to talk about present habits.
4 You can use the **simple present / present continuous** for a continuing activity that happens at the same time as another habit.

B **Now go to page 129. Look at the grammar chart and do the grammar exercise for 1.1.**

C PAIR WORK **Think of something you do regularly, such as going to the gym, meeting friends, studying, or working. Describe your present habits using the prompts below. Then compare your sentences with a partner. How different or similar are your regular habits?**

1 I tend to …
2 My friends and I often …
3 When I'm feeling …
4 I'm always …
5 When I'm tired, I'll …

D **Think of one thing you'd like to change about your life. What habits do you have that prevent you from moving forward? How can you tackle these habits?**

4 SPEAKING

A GROUP WORK THINK CRITICALLY **Do you welcome change, or do you prefer to stick to your habits? Explain your answers. Is it easier to adapt to changes that you decide to make or ones that are outside your control? Think of some examples.**

I **tend to worry** about big changes. I**'ll follow** the same routine every day and be perfectly happy about it. I think things outside our control, like losing your job or your best friend moving away, are harder to **cope with** because you can't plan and prepare for them.

1.2 MEMORY LANE

LESSON OBJECTIVE
- talk about past difficulties

1 LANGUAGE IN CONTEXT

A **PAIR WORK** **Look at the pictures. When were the items popular? When did people stop using these items? Why?**

B **Read Amy's blog post. What time period does she describe? How old do you think she was then? How old is she now?**

banana seat bike

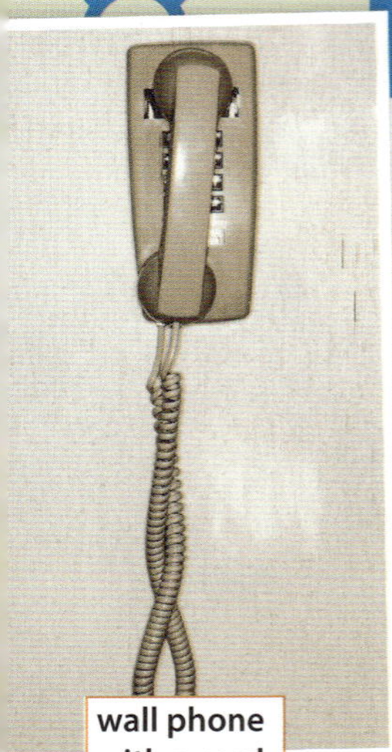
wall phone with a cord

The TIME MACHINE in my living room

Do you ever binge-watch TV shows and feel like you've taken a time machine to a different place and time? I just watched *Stranger Things*, which takes place in the 1980s. It was like going back in time to my childhood.

Remember those bikes with banana-shaped seats? One of the boys in the series rides one, just like the one I used to ride to school every day. I wouldn't even lock it – I'd just leave it outside all day. In many ways, life was simple then. But some things were **frustrating** …

When you're on the phone, do you move around a lot, like me? Well, in the 1980s, we could only walk as far as the cord reached. And with only one phone in the house, we didn't use to have any privacy. I'd **drive** my brother **crazy** because I talked to my friends for hours. Making calls away from home was **tricky**, too. Have you ever used a pay phone? I never used to have enough coins with me – it was **infuriating**! And how about sharing music? You probably use a music app, right? My older sister used to make me mixtapes with different songs she liked. I realize now how **complex** and **time-consuming** it was. Even watching TV was more difficult then. It **got on my nerves** to have to get up and change the channel all the time because there was no such thing as a remote control. Now I just push the "off" button from the couch to travel back to the present and take a break from binge-watching!

TV with no remote control

cassette tape

GLOSSARY
binge-watch (*v*) to watch many or all episodes of a TV show in one session

2 VOCABULARY: Describing annoying things

A **Cover the blog post. Can you remember which seven words and phrases from the box below Amy uses? What does she describe with the words?**

awkward	be a waste of time	be hard to operate	clumsy
complex	drive sb crazy	frustrating	get on sb's nerves
infuriating	lose patience	time-consuming	tricky

! *sb* = somebody

FIND IT

B 1.04 **Look at the words in the box again. Which ones are adjectives, and which ones are verb phrases? Use a dictionary or your phone to help you. Then listen and check. Which words mean *annoying*? Which mean *difficult, uncomfortable, takes a lot of or too much time*?**

C **Now go to page 141. Do the vocabulary exercises for 1.2.**

D **PAIR WORK** **THINK CRITICALLY** **Describe some present-day everyday objects using words from exercise 2A. Which of them do you think will still be used in ten years' time? How might they change?**

3 GRAMMAR: Past habits

A **Read the sentences in the grammar box. Circle the correct options to complete the rules. Can you find more examples in the text in exercise 1B on page 4?**

Past habits

We **didn't use to have** any privacy. **I never used to have** enough coins.

I'**d drive** my brother crazy.

It **got** on my nerves to have to get up and change the channel all the time.

! **Use the simple past for single completed past actions:**

*I just **watched** the last episode of* Stranger Things.

1 *Used to, didn't use to,* and *never used to* can show past habits, **single** / **repeated** past actions, and past states.

2 *Would* (*not*) can mean the same thing as (***not***) ***used to*** / ***could*** (***not***) for past habits and repeated actions. Do not use *would* (*not*) for past states.

3 You **can** / **can't** use the simple past for past habits, repeated past actions, and past states.

B **Now go to page 129. Look at the grammar chart and do the grammar exercise for 1.2.**

C **Change the sentences so they're true for you. Use (*not/never*) *used to* or *would* (*not*). Then check your accuracy. Compare your statements with a partner.**

1 When I was a child, I rode my bike without a helmet.
2 My parents cooked with a microwave.
3 I didn't stream music in the 1990s.
4 When I was a kid, I texted my friends every day.
5 Before cell phones, I had to memorize my friends' phone numbers.

✓ ACCURACY CHECK

Do not use *be* before *used to* when talking about past habits.

I ~~am~~ used to cycle to school. ✗
I used to cycle to school. ✓

4 SPEAKING

A PAIR WORK **Think of objects from when you were younger that aren't around anymore. Why aren't they around anymore? Do you miss those objects? Why or why not? For ideas, watch Jacqueline's video.**

I **used to have** this game console that fit in my pocket. It only had one game, but **I'd carry** it around everywhere and play the game all the time. It was really **frustrating** if I forgot to bring it with me. Now I simply play games on my phone …

EXPERT SPEAKER

How similar are Jacqueline's memories to yours?

1.3 UPGRADE

LESSON OBJECTIVE

- discuss issues and agree strongly

1 LISTENING

A PAIR WORK **In what situations do you send or receive emails? Do you think it's an effective way to communicate? Why or why not?**

B 1.05 **Listen to coworkers Shawn and Lorena talk about problems with email. What other ways of communication do they mention?**

C 1.05 LISTEN FOR OPINIONS **Listen again. What does Lorena think the problems with email are? Do you agree with her? What does Shawn think about the alternative that Lorena mentions? Do you agree with him?**

D PAIR WORK THINK CRITICALLY **Compare different ways of communication, such as face-to-face conversations, texts, IMs, video calls, etc. What are their advantages and disadvantages? Which ways of communication do you find most effective in which situations?**

2 PRONUNCIATION: Listening for main stress

A 1.06 **Listen. What do you notice about the underlined words?**

1 … I can get some <u>real</u> work done.

2 … people usually choose the <u>easy</u> option.

3 All this technology was supposed to help us be more <u>efficient</u> …

B 1.07 **<u>Underline</u> the word in each item that you think has the main stress. Listen and check.**

1 When it comes to technology, …

2 … waiting to use the single fax machine we had in our office.

3 And don't forget about all that paper!

C **Circle the correct words to complete the sentences.**

One word / *Several words* in each word group will have the main stress. Words with the main stress are usually near the *beginning* / *end* of the word group, and they give information that is *new* (*and important*) / *old* (*and not so important*) to listeners.

INSIDER ENGLISH

When something used to connect to the internet isn't working, it's "down."

*It looks like the server is **down**.*

*My Wi-Fi is **down** again!*

3 SPEAKING SKILLS

A 1.05 **Look at the sentences from the conversation in exercise 1B on page 6. Are the speakers discussing issues (D) or agreeing strongly (A)? Write *D* or *A*. Where, do you think, is the main stress in each sentence? Listen to the conversation again to check.**

Discuss issues and agree strongly

1. **When it comes to** technology, you can rely on the server to be unreliable. ___
2. **That's so true!** ___
3. **You can say that again.** ___
4. **I couldn't agree more.** ___
5. **Looking at the big picture,** I think email isn't that bad. ___
6. **Overall,** if I had to choose … ___
7. **Have it your way!** ___

B PAIR WORK **With your partner, take turns making and responding to statements using the prompts below and bold expressions from exercise 3A.**

1. writing / easier / laptop / tablet
2. texting / the best way to communicate with …
3. video calls / for work / personal communication
4. face-to-face / most important for …

C PAIR WORK **Student A: Go to page 157. Student B: Go to page 159. Follow the instructions.**

4 PRONUNCIATION: Saying /ʧ/

A 1.08 **Listen to the /ʧ/ sound in these words and then repeat the words.**

picture cheap suggestion achieve touch question

B **Underline the /ʧ/ sound in each pair of words.**

status statue stomach watch actual action nature major

1.09 **Listen and check. Then repeat the words with the /ʧ/ sound.**

C **Underline the /ʧ/ sounds in the conversation below. Then take turns practicing the conversation with a partner.**

A Looking at the bigger picture, we've got more of a chance now.

B Actually, I don't think we're going to achieve very much. We need to make some big changes.

5 SPEAKING

A GROUP WORK **Compare something from your past with something in your present life. Look at the ideas below. Discuss your views on the issues.**

last job / current job
last home / current home
high school / college
old device / current device

Generally speaking, I think the atmosphere in college is more relaxed than in high school.

I couldn't agree more.

*So, **overall,** do you think college is easier?*

1.4 BACK TO BASICS

LESSON OBJECTIVE

- write an opinion essay

1 READING

A **IDENTIFY MAIN IDEAS** **What skills or knowledge have your grandparents and parents passed on to you? Can you tell your partner something that you do or make that they taught you? Read the article and say what Barbara's grandparents passed on to her. What is the Maker Movement?**

COMING AROUND AGAIN

When I was a kid, I used to spend weekdays with my grandpa and grandma while my mom was at work. I'd sometimes help my grandma make her special oatmeal cookies. To be honest, I used to be better at eating them than I was at baking them. They were so good! But in those days, more often than not, I'd watch my grandfather in his workshop – actually their garage – where he spent most mornings. He was an amateur inventor, and he would take old pieces of metal or wood and make something new and practical that he or my grandmother could use around the house. He once gave me a wallet to hold dollar bills that he had made out of flat cardboard, leather, and elastic. It was a magic wallet – you opened the wallet, placed the bill on top of the elastic inside, closed the wallet, opened it again from the other side and – lo and behold – the bills were behind the elastic and held securely. He had put a ten dollar bill in there, "just in case you need it." Every time I use it I think of my grandfather, and I know it's the only wallet in the world like it.

Fast forward to earlier this year. I went to a Maker Faire with my friend. "What's a Maker Faire?" I hear you ask. Well, first I need to tell you about the Maker Movement. This was founded way back in 2005 as a way to encourage DIY through art, electronics, and craft projects. Since then, it's gone from strength to strength around the world. There are about 135 million makers in the U.S. alone – that's over half the population. Maker Faires are basically festivals which celebrate and promote these skills. The 2015 Maker Faire had over 1.1 million visitors – the same audience size as Taylor Swift's *1989 World Tour*.

So, how is the Maker Movement different to what my grandpa was doing in his workshop all those years ago? It's hard to define, but a lot of it is about individuals using new technologies – technologies that are accessible to you and me, like 3D printers – so that they can create unique items and projects that have a use beyond their original intention. A maker is anyone who is creating, and if you're building or adapting something or trying to make something new, that means you.

The future could be pretty exciting for all makers out there. Dale Dougherty, founder of Maker Media which published *Maker: Magazine* back in 2005, and that kicked off the movement, believes the future of makers depends on education. He says young people need help to develop their creative and technical abilities. "When kids play *Minecraft* they expect not just to play, but also to evolve," Dougherty said. It's fun, and everyone tackles projects and learns skills together.

My grandparents are gone now, but I'd love to think that if they were around today they would be makers, too. I've inherited my grandfather's love of finding out how things work, and I've just sold my first handmade lamp that I made from recycled glass and other materials. By using the creative skills they passed down to me, in my own way I've joined the maker movement.

By Barbara Cohen

GLOSSARY

amateur (*adj*) doing something as a hobby
craft (*n*) an activity in which you make something using a lot of skill, especially with your hands
DIY (do-it-yourself) (*n*) repairing and making things yourself instead of paying someone to do it

B **IDENTIFY SPECIFIC INFORMATION** **Read the article. What's the significance of these numbers?**

a 2005 **b** 135,000,000 **c** 2015 **d** 1,100,000

C **THINK CRITICALLY** **Why do you think the Maker Movement has become so popular around the world? What do you think of this movement? Would you be interested in becoming a maker?**

2 WRITING

A Read Carmen's essay about forgotten skills. Which ones does she mention? What was good about them?

Reviving forgotten skills

Recently, there has been some discussion about reviving skills from the past, such as repairing mechanical items like watches and raising animals. These skills are good for the environment, save money, and can be extremely enjoyable. I think this is an excellent trend and would like to share two almost-forgotten skills that my grandmother used to have.

The first is sewing. Most of us buy our clothes at the store, and we throw them away when they're worn. My grandmother, however, used to make clothes for my father, and later in life for my sisters and me. She would fix holes and small tears in our clothes, too, so they would last until we grew out of them.

The second skill is preserving food. My grandmother used to preserve all kinds of fruit and vegetables in the fall and store them in jars. Then, in the middle of the winter, she'd bring out a jar of raspberries or cucumbers, and it would immediately bring back a wonderful feeling of summer. It also cost less than buying them in the store.

I think bringing back skills like these is a fantastic idea. In fact, I'm planning to research how to raise chickens so I can have fresh eggs.

GLOSSARY

revive (*v*) to make something from the past exist again

preserve (*v*) to treat food in a particular way so it can be kept for a long time

B **ORGANIZE INFORMATION** Read about organizing an opinion essay. Then check if Carmen's essay has all these features.

1st paragraph: Introduce the topic and state your opinion.

2nd paragraph: Use a topic sentence to introduce your example and give the main idea of the paragraph; describe the example.

3rd paragraph: (same as second paragraph)

4th paragraph: Restate your opinion but with different words than before.

WRITE IT

FIND IT

C **PLAN** You're going to write a formal opinion essay about skills from the past. With your partner, discuss two or three forgotten skills and what you would like to say about them. Choose from the skills in the pictures below or use your phone to find other ideas. Then think how you will organize your essay, using the structure described in exercise 2B. What points are you going to include in each paragraph?

D Write your opinion essay. You can write a similar introduction and conclusion to Carmen's.

knitting

baking

beekeeping

making pottery

E **PAIR WORK** Read your partner's essay. What do you think of the skills he or she describes?

1.5 TIME TO SPEAK
Blast from the past

LESSON OBJECTIVE
- talk about daily life in the past

1910	1920	1930	1940	1950	1960	1970	1980	1990

A **PREPARE** Look at the pictures. In pairs, discuss which decade you think each picture is from. Then work with another pair and discuss your ideas. How else was life different in each time period?

B **DECIDE** Imagine you are on a reality TV show where you have to live for a week the way people did in the past. In groups, say which decade you want to live in, from 1910 to 1990, and why. Then decide on one decade together.

FIND IT

C **RESEARCH** In your group, answer the questions about what life was like in the decade you chose. You can go online to research ideas.

1 How did people use to do everyday chores?
2 What transportation did they use?
3 What styles of clothes did they wear?
4 What tech items did they have?
5 How did they entertain themselves?

D Imagine you just finished your week on the TV show. In your group, talk about your imagined experiences. How does living in that decade compare to life today? What was better? Worse? What did you enjoy about the experience? What difficulties did you have?

E **DISCUSS** You are going to debate whether it's better to live now or in the decade you discussed. Make two teams within your group. Team A: Think of reasons why life was better then. Team B: Brainstorm the reasons why it's better to live in the present day. Each team has two minutes to present their points to the other team.

F Report the results of your debate to the class. Would most people prefer to live in the past or now?

To check your progress, go to page 153.

USEFUL PHRASES

PREPARE
It was very awkward.
It was hard to operate.
It used to drive … crazy
It was really tricky.

DISCUSS
It was a step forward from …
We shouldn't underestimate …
It helped to cope with …
It was a waste of time.
It used to be so time-consuming.

Generally speaking, …
Looking at the big picture …
Overall …
When it came to …

UNIT OBJECTIVES

- talk about exploration and research
- talk about life forms in different environments
- exchange important information
- write a description of an area
- plan an outdoor experience

NATURAL LIMITS

2

START SPEAKING

A What can you see in the picture? What effect do you think it has on the fish and other wildlife in the ocean?

B In what other ways does human activity affect wildlife? Can you think of examples from your area or country?

C What are the benefits and drawbacks of human activity you discussed in exercise B? Do you think the activity is justified? For ideas, watch Odil's video.

EXPERT SPEAKER

What do you think of Odil's ideas?

2.1 DEEP OCEAN OR DEEP SPACE?

LESSON OBJECTIVE

- talk about exploration and research

1 VOCABULARY: Space and ocean exploration

A **Look at the pictures. Which one is in space? Which is in the ocean? Which do you think most people would want to learn about?**

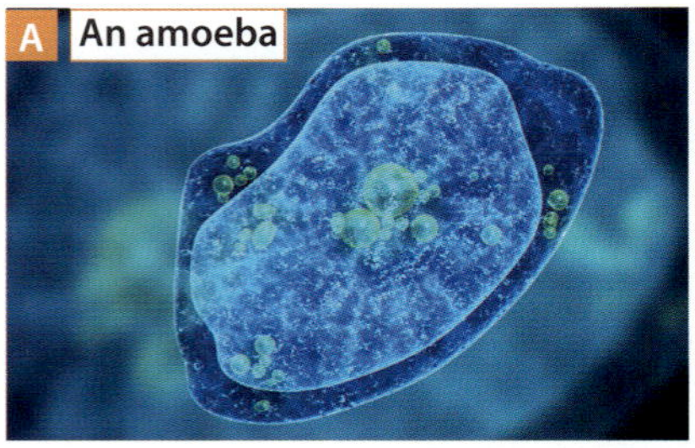

A An amoeba

B A supernova

FIND IT

B 1.10 PAIR WORK **Look at the words and phrases in the box and discuss their meanings. Use a dictionary or your phone to help you. Then listen and check your work. Which words and phrases could you use to talk about space, which about the ocean, and which about both?**

atmosphere	come across	exploration	investigation
launch	monitor	observe	preserve
resources	satellite	species	surface
use up			

C **Now go to page 142. Do the vocabulary exercises for 2.1.**

D PAIR WORK THINK CRITICALLY **Why do we explore space and the ocean? What effect can it have on our daily lives? Are there other issues we should be using our resources on instead?**

2 LANGUAGE IN CONTEXT

A 1.11 PAIR WORK **Read and listen to the podcast. What are the advantages and disadvantages of space and ocean exploration according to the speakers? Which speaker do you agree with more. Why?**

1.11 Audio script

Host Today's guests on *Discovery Now*, Ronnie Jones and Johanna Flores, are here to discuss the question: Which is more important, space or ocean **exploration**? Ronnie?

Ronnie I would definitely prefer to explore space rather than study the ocean. There's so much mystery beyond Earth's **atmosphere**. And we can learn more from research into space than most people realize. Without it we would probably never have inventions like phone cameras, ear thermometers, wireless headsets, and even clean energy technology.

Johanna I disagree. How about the benefits of underwater research for industry, for medicine, for technology? And it's much less expensive and a lot safer than space travel. Space exploration just isn't useful enough to justify the cost.

Host Good point. Can you justify the cost, Ronnie?

Ronnie Of course. The earth is getting overcrowded, and it won't be long before we'll need other places to live. Solving future problems on Earth is worth any price.

Johanna It's less important to fix future problems than to fix current ones. People depend on the ocean for jobs, food, and even breathing! Ocean plants produce about 70 percent of Earth's oxygen. Maybe we should find ways to **preserve** our oceans' **resources** instead of **using** them **up** – which is a lot easier than trying to live in space.

Ronnie But what about life in space? On Mars, for example, there's water, and where there's water, there could be life!

Johanna But we don't know for sure if any other planets support life. However, there's definitely life below the **surface** of the ocean we still know almost nothing about. We keep discovering amazing **species** deep under the water. Only about five to ten percent of the deep ocean has been explored. Overall, it is obvious to me that there are fewer benefits to space exploration.

3 GRAMMAR: Comparative structures

A **Read the sentences in the grammar box. Circle the correct options to complete the rules.**

Comparative structures

I would definitely prefer to explore space **rather than study** the ocean.

We can **learn more** from research into space **than** most people realize.

Space exploration just **isn't useful enough** to justify the cost.

It's **less important to fix** future problems **than** (it is) **to fix** current ones.

There are **fewer benefits** to space exploration.

1 When comparing, put the thing you like less after ***prefer*** / ***rather than***. To compare actions, use a gerund or the **base form of the verb** / **past participle** after *rather than*.
2 When using *more* or *less* as a pronoun, put it **after** / **before** a verb.
3 Use **a gerund** / **an infinitive** after an adjective + *enough*.
4 Use *less* with **count** / **non-count** nouns. Use *fewer* with **count** / **non-count** nouns.
5 You **always have to** / **don't always have to** repeat the first subject + verb in comparative structures.

B **Now go to page 130. Look at the grammar chart and do the grammar exercise for 2.1.**

C **Complete the sentences with your own ideas using the constructions in parentheses. Then check your accuracy. Compare ideas with a partner.**

1 Ocean exploration is … (adjective + *enough* + infinitive)
Ocean exploration is not important enough to justify the risks.
2 Space travel is … (adjective + *enough* + infinitive)
3 Space exploration is … (comparative adjective + *than*)
4 I prefer … (verb/gerund + *rather than* + verb/gerund)
5 We can learn … (*more* or *less* as a pronoun)
6 It's less important … (infinitive *than* infinitive)

✓ ACCURACY CHECK

Use *than*, not *then*, with comparative structures.

There is less oxygen on Mars ~~then~~ on Earth. ✗

There is less oxygen on Mars than on Earth. ✓

4 SPEAKING

A THINK CRITICALLY **What environments do people explore? What do you think are the top areas of research and exploration that can help us and the planet? Why? For ideas, watch Odil's video.**

People explore the natural world around them and also their own biology. It may be ***easier to solve*** *our most urgent issues by* ***observing*** *the results of human activity or studying our DNA,* ***rather than trying*** *to* ***investigate*** *…*

EXPERT SPEAKER

Do you think Odil's suggestions are good? Why or why not?

2.2 EXTREME LIFE

LESSON OBJECTIVE
- talk about life forms in different environments

1 LANGUAGE IN CONTEXT

A PAIR WORK **Make a list of ten wild animals in your country. Where can you usually find them? Does your country have an official national animal?**

B **Read the article about four unusual animals. What are they? Where do they live?**

NATURE'S "TOUGH COOKIES"

We often discuss how to preserve **endangered** species of wildlife but rarely talk about the opposite side of nature: **creatures** that can survive in extremely difficult **environments**. So here are four examples of nature's "tough cookies."

Nicaragua's Masaya Volcano is one of the most active **volcanoes** in Central America. **Poisonous** gas rises from the volcano. It's an absolutely awful place to live. Yet hundreds of small, green parrots have made it their home. Experts aren't sure how they survive in a **habitat** that would kill other **forms of life**, but somehow they've managed to adapt to it.

In Alaska, where temperatures remain below zero for several months, wood frogs survive by freezing. Almost two-thirds of their body water turns to ice. They become very hard and appear to be dead. But in the spring, they thaw out and head straight for the nearest **pond**.

Super-hot water and poisonous gases boil up from holes in the ocean floor off the coast of Ecuador. This is surely the least suitable environment for anything to live. Yet in and around these holes, various forms of **sea life** exist. The tiniest and most common are microbes called "extremophiles." Their existence may help explain the **origins** of life on earth.

The final "tough cookie" has few limits to its **territory**. Rats are the most **adaptable** mammal that we know of. They live almost everywhere and recover fast from whatever we do to them. They won't win a popularity contest, but they definitely get the first prize for being super **survivors**.

GLOSSARY
head (straight) for (*v*) go toward something
microbe (*n*) a very small living thing that can only be seen with a microscope
mammal (*n*) an animal that feeds its babies milk

C **Read the article again. What makes each living thing a "tough cookie"? Which one do you think is the toughest? Why?**

INSIDER ENGLISH

Someone is a *tough cookie* if they are not easily hurt emotionally or physically.

*You don't need to worry about Rachel. She is a really **tough cookie.***

2 VOCABULARY: The natural world

A 1.12 **Look at the words in the box. Which two are not in the article? Which ones are nouns or noun phrases, and which are adjectives? Listen and check your work.**

adaptable	animal life	creature	endangered	environment
form of life	habitat	origin	plant life	poisonous
pond	sea life	survivor	territory	volcano

B **Now go to page 142. Do the vocabulary exercises for 2.2.**

C THINK CRITICALLY **What are some endangered animals that you know of? What do you think can be done to protect them?**

3 GRAMMAR: Superlative structures; ungradable adjectives

A **Read the sentences in the grammar boxes. Circle the correct options to complete the rules.**

Superlative structures

Nicaragua's Masaya Volcano is **one of the most active** volcanoes in Central America.

Yet in and around these holes, various forms of sea life exist. **The tiniest and most common** are microbes.

Rats are **the most adaptable** mammal (that) we know of.

Ungradable adjectives

It's an **absolutely awful** place to live.

They become very hard and appear to be **dead**.

The **final** "tough cookie" has few limits to its territory.

1 After *one of the most* + adjective, use a **singular** / **plural** noun.

2 Nouns are not always repeated after superlative adjectives. After "the tiniest and most common," the missing words are ***holes*** / ***forms of sea life***.

3 For superlative structures with *that* clauses, *that* is **always** / **not always** needed.

4 You **can** / **can't** use ungradable adjectives with *absolutely* and *completely*.

B **Now go to page 130. Look at the grammar chart and do the grammar exercises for 2.2.**

C **Complete the sentences about the natural world. Compare with a partner. Answers are at the bottom of the page.**

1 The black mamba is one of the most poisonous ____________________ .

2 The dwarf lantern shark is one of the ____________________ animals in the ocean.

3 Out of all the planets in the solar system, Neptune and Uranus are the ____________________ .

4 The water in the geysers can be very hot or even absolutely ____________________ .

4 SPEAKING

FIND IT

A PAIR WORK **Choose one of the topics below. Where can these life forms be found? How difficult is life for them? You can check online if you want. Then tell another pair about the topic you chose.**

- wild animals that have adapted to life in your city
- the rarest animals, birds, or plants in your country / the world
- the most beautiful or the most dangerous forms of life you know of

*One of the most common wild animals in our city is the raccoon. A common **habitat** of urban raccoons are people's sheds and attics. Raccoons come out into the streets to find food, but city life is **extremely dangerous** for them ...*

Answers: 1 snakes 2 smallest 3 coldest or farthest from the sun 4 boiling

2.3 FINDING OUT

LESSON OBJECTIVE
- exchange important information

1 LISTENING

A PAIR WORK **Do you think hiking is a fun activity? Why or why not? Tina is preparing to go hiking in the mountains of Peru. She calls her guide to ask about things she needs to take with her. Imagine you're Tina. Think of some important questions to ask.**

B 1.13 **Listen. What are the four different problems with water and sweat that the guide discusses?**

C 1.13 LISTEN FOR DETAILS **Listen again. Complete the information that the guide provides.**

1 Type of coat to bring: ____________
2 Type of T-shirt not to bring: ____________
3 Minimum size of backpack: ____________ liters
4 Weight of backpack without water: ____________ kilos
5 Weight of water: ____________ kilos

D **In your opinion, which of the water problems described by the guide is the most dangerous? Explain why.**

2 PRONUNCIATION: Listening for weak forms and rhythm

A 1.14 **Listen to the phrase *a couple of questions*. What pattern does it have?**

1 ● ● ● ● a couple of questions

2 • ● • ● a couple of questions

3 ● • ● • a couple of questions

B 1.15 **Put the phrases into the columns. Then listen and check your answers.**

at least 50 liters
what sort of coat
a risk of snow
prepare for the worst
I'm sure you know
a good waterproof coat

Pattern 1 • ● • ●	Pattern 2 ● • • ●	Pattern 3 • ● ● ●

C **Are these statements true or false?**

1 Phrases usually have a rhythm where there is a combination of stressed and unstressed words.
2 Words that carry the main meaning, like nouns and verbs, are usually stressed.
3 Functional words, like prepositions and articles, are also usually stressed.

3 SPEAKING SKILLS

A 1.13 **Look at these sentences from the conversation in exercise 1B on page 16. Find two expressions that indicate danger (D), and two expressions that indicate essential information (E). Write *D* or *E*. Which words in these sentences are unstressed? Listen again to check.**

Asking for information

Is there any danger of really bad weather? ___

What exactly do you mean by "the worst"? ___

Is there a risk of snow? ___

What sort of coat **would you recommend** taking? ___

Providing information

The most important thing to consider is that mountain weather is unpredictable. ___

First and foremost, you need a good waterproof coat. ___

One thing to keep in mind is that you don't want a thick coat. ___

Another thing to consider is the kind of T-shirt you wear. ___

B PAIR WORK **Student A: Go to page 157. Student B: Go to page 159. Follow the instructions.**

C **Imagine you are going hiking somewhere in the mountains. What two pieces of information would you like to ask for? What information would you give someone going hiking somewhere near you? Use expressions from exercise 3A.**

4 PRONUNCIATION: Saying /w/ and /v/

A 1.16 **Listen to the** /w/ **sound in these words and then repeat the words.**

weather	wear	waterproof	worst	would
quick	quite	swim	language	

B 1.17 **Listen and circle the word you hear twice. Then check and repeat the words.**

1 wet vet
2 vine wine
3 worse verse
4 vest west

C **Underline the** /w/ **and** /v/ **sounds in the questions below. Then work in pairs and ask one another the questions.**

1 What's the worst weather you've experienced?
2 What would you wear if you were going hiking in winter?
3 Have you ever been worried about your safety?
4 What makes people do very dangerous or weird sports?

5 SPEAKING

A **Think of a free-time activity you enjoy. Imagine you're going to give some advice to someone who'd like to take up the activity. What important information could you provide?**

B PAIR WORK **Give the advice to a partner. Answer your partner's questions. Then change roles.**

What sort of equipment **would you recommend buying**?

Well, **first and foremost**, you need …

2.4 EXTREME LIVING

LESSON OBJECTIVE

- write a description of an area

1 READING

A Look at the picture. What do you think would be the most difficult thing about living in this place? Read the article. Did Noah Harris mention your idea?

COLDER THAN COLD

by Piper Reid

Noah Harris is usually behind the camera, filming documentaries in unusual places. But last month, he took some time out to talk about his most recent – and most extreme – trip. He spent a month at a research center in one of the coldest places on Earth, Antarctica.

First and foremost, I have to ask the question everyone wants to know. How cold was it?

It was absolutely freezing! Where I was, the average temperature was –5°C in January, the warmest month, and –28°C in August, one of the coldest months. I was there in October, and it was about –15°C during the day.

How about the climate in general? What was the weather like, besides cold?

They say Antarctica is the driest, windiest, and brightest continent. It's dry because it's a desert, and surprisingly, it doesn't snow a lot. The area only gets 60 to 80 millimeters of snow a year, but the wind blows up to 185 kilometers per hour. It's full of snow and ice, and everything turns white. But many days there are blue skies and sunshine. It can actually be more difficult to see when the sun is bright.

I am also wondering about the temperature indoors. Where does everyone stay? Is it warm?

I stayed at one of New Zealand's research centers, and all of the buildings are heated. It's one of the 37 centers in Antarctica open all year. In fact, 4,000 people live in Antarctica in the summer months, but only about 1,000 stay for the winter. Where I visited, up to 85 people are at the research center in the warmer months. Fewer people are there when it's colder – about 25. When it's less crowded, everyone has their own bedroom, but when more people are there, it's four to a room.

I am curious about living so close to the same few people in such limited space. What is it like? Does everyone get along?

I was only there for a month – imagine a year of living and working with the same 20 people every single minute of every single day! But everyone really got along well, and they all seem very happy. They have to have good attitudes to survive, but they also love what they do. They're doing some of the most incredible land and ocean exploration in the world.

How was the food? Always an important question!

Eating was the least difficult part of my stay. The chef was totally amazing. People often wanted her to cook meals from New Zealand rather than having international dishes. When you live in an extreme environment, it's nice to have the comforts of home sometimes.

You didn't mention eating local food. What about the fish?

It's against the law to kill any animals in Antarctica. It's also illegal to bring plant life there, so they don't grow food at the research center. All of the food comes by boat or plane. You can't "eat local" in Antarctica!

Final question: What is the most extreme part of living in Antarctica, the biggest challenge?

The scientists often go on trips far from the center to study plant and animal life. Sometimes they camp for up to 100 days! I went on a three-day research trip with a team. After staying in a tent and having no running water or indoor bathroom, the research center seemed like a five-star hotel when I got back!

B PAIR WORK What are Noah's main points about the weather in Antarctica? The people? The food? What do you think about his experience? Could you live there for a month?

C **UNDERSTAND NUMERICAL WORDS AND PHRASES** Look at the meanings of some expressions with numbers. Find examples in the article. Then think of other things to describe with the expressions.

about = approximately, could be a few more or a few less

average = usual

to = shows a range, the number can fall anywhere in that range

up to = no more than

D **THINK CRITICALLY** In what kind of text would you expect to see a lot of numbers? What kind of information do they provide?

2 WRITING

A **Read the description of a town in Canada. What are the town's attractions?**

Drumheller in Alberta, Canada

Drumheller is a town of about 8,000 people in southern Alberta. It's 138 kilometers northeast of Calgary and is located in a desert-like environment. The highest rainfall it gets is about 60 millimeters in June. Temperatures can be extreme. The record highest was 40.6°C, and the lowest was –43.9°C, but the normal range is –18° to 26°C.

Drumheller seems like the least likely place to visit, but almost 500,000 tourists arrive every year. This is because it's the Dinosaur Capital of the World. The Royal Tyrrell Museum has one of the world's largest collections of dinosaur fossils, including more than 200 complete skeletons.

For nature lovers, however, the landscape is even more attractive than the dinosaurs. Parts of it look as strange and dry as the moon's surface, but many species of wildlife live there. The hoodoos are the most fascinating things to see. They're natural towers of rock, up to 6 meters high, with "caps" on the top. People love taking selfies with them.

GLOSSARY

fossil (*n*) part of an animal or plant from thousands of year ago, preserved in rock

B **USE NUMERICAL WORDS AND PHRASES** Complete the phrases with numbers from the description in exercise 2A. Which ones are about distance (*D*), height (*H*), quantities (*Q*), or temperatures (*T*)?

1 a town of about ________ people
2 ________ kilometers northeast of Calgary
3 the record highest temperature was ________
4 the normal temperature range is ________ to ________
5 almost ________ tourists
6 more than ________ complete skeletons
7 up to ________ meters high

WRITE IT

FIND IT

C **PLAN** You are going to write a description of an area. With your partner, talk about an area with an interesting environment or features you know. Describe what makes it interesting. You can check online for ideas. Then look at the description in exercise 2A. Do you need to divide your description into paragraphs? What kind of information could you start and end your description with?

D **Write your description of the area you discussed in exercise 2C. Use comparative and superlative structures and numerical words and phrases.**

REGISTER CHECK

Make an adjective with a noun + *-like* to show that something is similar to something else.

*It's 138 kilometers northeast of Calgary and is located in a **desert-like** environment.*

*The ground is very dry and **rock-like**.*

This is more common in less formal texts, like personal writing, magazines, and web pages.

E **PAIR WORK** Read your partner's description. Have you visited the area? Would you like to?

2.5

TIME TO SPEAK
Going wild

LESSON OBJECTIVE
- plan an outdoor experience

A **PREPARE** With a partner, talk about natural places you've been to and any outdoor activities you've done. Discuss how they made you feel.

B Imagine you and your partner work for the Wild Ideas travel agency. You're planning a vacation for your class. What kinds of outdoor vacations might they like? Come up with several different ideas and compare them. Use the questions below to help you.

Home | News | About | Contact Us

Questions we ask

Where do you want to go? Mountains? Ocean? …

What do you want to see? Landscapes? Wildlife? …

What do you want to do? Hiking? Biking? Kayaking? …

Where do you want to sleep? In a hotel? In a tent? …

How long do you want to stay? A day? A week? …

For many people, outdoor vacations are way too wild. They're too tough, too long, and too far away. At ***Wild Ideas***, we're changing that by listening to our customers. They tell us how wild they want to go, and we design a suitable experience for them.

C Work with another pair and share your ideas. Ask for and give each other advice on how to improve your ideas, and note down any useful advice.

FIND IT

D **DECIDE** With your partner, use the advice from part C to help you choose your best idea and improve it. Include interesting facts with numbers. You can look online if you want.

E **PRESENT** Tell the class about your plan. Use superlatives to make it sound attractive. The class compares plans, considers the points below, and votes for the best one. Why is it the best plan?

has most interesting facts
sounds like the most fun
is not too wild or difficult
is something all would enjoy
your own ideas

To check your progress, go to page 153.

USEFUL PHRASES

PREPARE

I've been to …
I've been … before.
I've gone … in the past.
I went … once.
It felt absolutely …
It made me feel extremely …
It was the … of my life.
The environment was …

PRESENT

One of the most exciting ideas was …
Another great option was …
But that's not all!
Overall, …

THE WAY I AM

3

UNIT OBJECTIVES

- talk about personality types
- talk about things you love or hate
- make and respond to requests
- write a personal statement for a job application
- interview for a full-time position

START SPEAKING

A Imagine you were on this ride. Which person's expression would yours be most like? What would you say when you got off the ride?

B What does this picture tell us about the personalities of the people? Do you think their faces reveal their true feelings?

C What situations can you think of that reveal what people are really like? For ideas, watch Wendy's video.

EXPERT SPEAKER

Do you agree with Wendy's ideas?

3.1 POWER IN QUIET

LESSON OBJECTIVE
- talk about personality types

1 LANGUAGE IN CONTEXT

A PAIR WORK **Look at the picture. Which person are you most like? Would you describe yourself as an outgoing person? Why or why not?**

B 1.18 **Read and listen to part of a radio show. What are the three personality types mentioned?**

1.18 Audio script

Welcome to *Book Ends*. It's Saturday morning, when we discuss my choice of the week. Today, it's Susan Cain's book titled *Quiet: The Power of Introverts in a World That Can't Stop Talking*, as well as ideas on her website called Quiet Revolution. Cain, whose work explores the character of introverts, feels that American society often prefers extroverts. Her goal is to show that there is power in quiet. She says, "I prefer listening to talking, reading to **socializing**, and cozy chats to group settings. I like to think before I **speak (softly)**." She feels you don't have to **be an extrovert** to be heard.

We often talk about extroverts and introverts, but what do we really mean by these words? An extrovert is someone who easily **attracts attention**, **enjoys the company of** others, and can **be the life of the party**. Some think that extroverts like to **show off**, whereas an introvert is someone who **is reserved**, may find it difficult to **speak up** and express opinions, and often **feels left out** in social situations. These are the two stereotypes accepted by most people, but there's a third personality type, which Quiet Revolution explores: an ambivert. This is a person who sometimes needs quiet and gets energy from it and at other times works best **interacting with people**. I'd never heard of an ambivert before but immediately realized I am one! Which means part of me **is an introvert**. And suddenly, the book got a whole lot more interesting.

GLOSSARY
stereotype (*n*) a set idea that people have about what someone or something is like

C 1.18 THINK CRITICALLY **Listen and read again. What is the aim of Susan Cain's work? Why do you think she started this project? Do you think it will be helpful to people?**

2 VOCABULARY: Describing personality

FIND IT

A 1.19 **Look at the expressions in bold in the script in exercise 1B. Which describe introvert behavior? Which describe extrovert behavior? Can any of the expressions describe both? Define each expression using other words. Use a dictionary or your phone to help you. Listen and check your work.**

B **Now go to page 142. Do the vocabulary exercises for 3.1.**

C PAIR WORK THINK CRITICALLY **In what jobs or other areas of life do you think it's helpful to be an introvert? An extrovert? Explain why.**

3 GRAMMAR: Relative pronouns; reduced relative clauses

A **Read the sentences in the grammar box. Circle the correct options to complete the rules.**

Relative clauses

It's Saturday morning, **when we discuss my choice of the week.**

Cain, **whose work explores the character of introverts**, feels that American society often prefers extroverts.

An extrovert is someone **who easily attracts attention.**

These are the two stereotypes **accepted by most people.** (= that are accepted).

! **Use *which* with times, dates, and days when the word defined by the relative clause is a subject or object, not a time adverbial.**

She loves ***Fridays, which*** *is the worst day of the week for me.*

1 The relative pronoun can be **the subject** / **the subject or the object** of a relative clause.
2 Use ***when*** / ***which*** to add information about particular times, dates, and days.
3 In relative clauses, ***who*** / ***whose*** shows possession.
4 Reduced relative clauses **include** / **don't include** the relative pronoun and the verb *be*.

B **Now go to page 131. Look at the grammar chart and do the grammar exercise for 3.1.**

C **Make true sentences about yourself using relative clauses and the prompts below. Check your accuracy. Then share with a partner. Were any of your ideas similar?**

1 going to parties with a lot of people
2 the kind of people you like to be friends with
3 something you like to do in a certain type of weather
4 something you read recently
5 something to describe one of the jobs you've had

✓ ACCURACY CHECK

Use an article or possessive pronoun with a singular noun followed by reduced relative clauses with *-ed*.

Cain wrote about young introverts ~~in book~~ called Quiet Power. ✗

Cain wrote about young introverts in a/the/her book called Quiet Power. ✓

4 SPEAKING

A PAIR WORK THINK CRITICALLY **Student A: Talk about advantages of being an introvert. Student B: Talk about advantages of being an extrovert. Then try to convince your partner that you're right. Change roles and repeat. Then say which you agree with more.**

People ***who are introverts*** *often make good choices. They think about things carefully,* ***which helps them*** *make good decisions.*

People ***that are extroverts*** *often* ***speak up*** *at meetings and* ***attract*** *the boss's* ***attention****. In the office where I work, people* ***whose voices are heard*** *are promoted faster.*

3.2 THINGS AND EMOTIONS

LESSON OBJECTIVE
- talk about things you love or hate

1 LANGUAGE IN CONTEXT

A **Look at the pictures and identify the objects in them. What do you think of when you see these things? Then read the posts. What is each post about?**

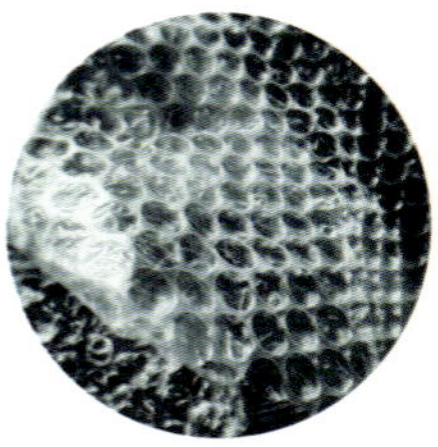

Comments Profile Sign Out

@dougj: I'm just sitting here, thinking about the strange things I love and hate. For example, most people think crows are **creepy**, but I think they're **impressive**. A crow flying slowly across the sky looks **stunning**. Some people like to stand on beaches, watching sunsets. But I watch big black birds flying by. What about you?

@dannys22: I find mushrooms **disgusting**. Not the taste. It's because they feel like rubber in my mouth. Gross!

@asans5: I love opening a jar of peanut butter and hearing that popping sound! It's more enjoyable than *eating* the peanut butter.

INSIDER ENGLISH

gross = something extremely unpleasant

Gross! *That's **gross**!*
*Mushrooms are **gross**.*

@davidortiz: Popping bubble wrap. It's *so* **satisfying**.

@happyjia: I can't stand touching wool. I find the feel of it really **irritating**. Just looking at it makes me feel **uneasy** and **tense**.

@mandymandy: This might be **bizarre**, but I think the smell of subway stations is **fabulous**. I hardly ever go on the subway these days, but as a child living in New York City, I took it a lot with my mom. Now, that smell reminds me of my childhood.

@greatj: The smell of a swimming pool reminds me of my childhood. I just love it!

@msalex5: I kind of like the smell of gasoline. It reminds me of trips with my family. Maybe we're all a little **weird**!

B **Read the posts again. What does each person like or dislike?**

C GROUP WORK **What little things in life do you love and hate?**

2 VOCABULARY: Strong feelings

A 1.20 Look at the words in the box. Cover the posts in exercise 1A on page 24 and look at the pictures. Can you remember which words were used to describe them? Which ones are used to talk about things that are good, bad, or unusual? Listen and check your work.

bizarre	creepy	disgusting	fabulous	impressive	irritating
satisfying	stunning	tense	uneasy	weird	

B **Now go to page 143. Do the vocabulary exercises for 3.2.**

C PAIR WORK **Describe something that gives you one of the feelings in exercise 2A. Your partner guesses the feeling. Take turns. For ideas, watch Wendy's video.**

EXPERT SPEAKER

Do the things that Wendy talks about make you feel the same way? Talk about other things that give you those feelings.

3 GRAMMAR: Present participles

A **Read the sentences in the grammar box. Complete the rules.**

Present participles

I'm just sitting here**, thinking** about the strange things I love and hate.
A crow **flying** slowly across the sky looks stunning.
Some people like to stand on beaches**, watching** sunsets.
… as a child **living** in New York City, I took it a lot with my mom.

1 To describe two events happening at **the same time** / **different times**, put the verb that describes the second event after a comma, and use the *-ing* form of the verb.
2 To add more information about a **noun** / **verb**, use the *-ing* form of the verb.

B **Now go to page 132. Look at the grammar chart and do the grammar exercise for 3.2.**

C **Look at the present participles in the grammar box in exercise 3A. Make new sentences true for you, using the participles to describe two events happening at the same time or to give more information about a noun.**

4 SPEAKING

A PAIR WORK **Look at the pictures. How do you feel about these things? Think what you might be doing, seeing, or experiencing when you see these things.**

I think freshly ground coffee smells ***fabulous****. It's so nice to smell it,* ***relaxing*** *on the balcony every morning.*

3.3

ASKING FOR FAVORS

LESSON OBJECTIVE
- make and respond to requests

1 LISTENING

A How do you react when your boss or teacher asks you to do something you're not confident about?

B 1.21 Listen to the conversation. Kelly is an intern at the International Student Services office of a college. What is she asked to do? What is she worried about? What does her boss, Sandra, suggest?

GLOSSARY
intern (*n*) a student, or someone who has recently finished their studies, who works for a company for a short time, sometimes without being paid, in order to get work experience

C 1.22 Listen to Mateo and his boss, David. What is Mateo asked to do? What excuses does he make? What happens in the end?

GLOSSARY
deadline (*n*) a time or day by which something must be done

D 1.21 and 22 LISTEN FOR INFERENCE Listen to both conversations again. What does Kelly say to show that she's not comfortable talking about the program? What does Mateo say to show he's not happy about giving a presentation?

E PAIR WORK THINK CRITICALLY We can often guess how people feel, even if they don't say it directly. Discuss the speakers' situations and complete the sentences together. What clues or knowledge do you use to guess how people feel?

1 Sandra probably understands that Kelly is uneasy because ______________ .
2 Hwan is probably happy to help because ______________ .
3 David wants Mateo to say yes. Therefore, David ______________ .
4 Mateo probably feels uncomfortable saying no to David because ______________ .

F Do you think Mateo acts professionally with his boss? Why or why not?

2 PRONUNCIATION: Listening for /t/ at the ends of words

A 1.23 Listen to the /t/ sounds in this sentence. Which ones are pronounced differently?

I just want the rest of the team to get a general sense of the project.

B 1.24 Underline the /t/ sounds in the conversation. Which ones could be pronounced differently? Listen and check.

A That's OK. I just want the rest of the team to get a general sense of the project.
B Um … Sorry, but I wouldn't be comfortable speaking in front of the whole team. My English isn't very good for that kind of thing.
A Your English is fine. Don't worry about it. So, will you do it?
B Yes, I can probably manage that.

C Circle the correct options to complete the sentences.

When /t/ is at the *beginning* / *end* of a word and the sound before it is /n/ or *a vowel* / *another consonant*, then the /t/ may be pronounced silently. But if that /t/ is also followed by a *vowel* / *consonant* sound, it might be pronounced more like /d/.

3 SPEAKING SKILLS

A **Look at the expressions from the conversations in exercises 1B and 1C on page 26. Write *M* (making a request), *A* (accepting a request), or *R* (refusing a request) next to each one.**

Make and respond to requests

1	Is there any chance you could … ?	___	5	Do you think it would be possible (for you) to … ?	___
2	I don't mean to be rude, but …	___	6	I don't know how much I'd be able to …	___
3	Would you be willing to … ?	___	7	Sorry, but I wouldn't be comfortable [-*ing* verb] …	___
4	I'd be happy to help out.	___	8	Yes, I can probably manage that.	___

B PAIR WORK **With your partner, take turns making and responding to requests in the two situations below. Use expressions from exercise 3A.**

1 You need help with an essay.

2 You would like your partner to work next weekend.

C PAIR WORK **Student A: Go to page 157. Student B: Go to page 159. Follow the instructions.**

4 PRONUNCIATION: Using polite intonation for requests

A 1.25 **Listen to each request said twice. Which version sounds more polite to you – the first or the second?**

1 Is there any chance you could finish the presentation today?

2 Do you think it would be possible to help me right now?

B 1.26 **Listen and circle the ending of the request that you think sounds more polite. Then repeat the polite requests.**

1 Could you please *think about it? / wait for me outside?*

2 Do you think it would be possible for you *to call me back later? / to be a little quieter?*

3 Is there any chance you could *speak to her yourself? / spell that for me?*

4 Would you be willing to *give the presentation? / check my presentation?*

C PAIR WORK **Take turns saying these requests to each other politely and agreeing to help. If you think the request is not said politely, try to explain why you feel this way. Then give your partner the chance to try again.**

Would you be willing to work on Saturday?

Do you think it would be possible to do that again?

Is there any chance you could come ten minutes earlier?

Would you be willing to share with Alex?

Do you think it would be possible to translate it into English?

5 SPEAKING

A PAIR WORK **Role play one of the situations. Decide who makes the request and who responds. The person making the request tries to convince the other to say yes. Then change roles, choose another situation, and repeat.**

1 Student A: You want help painting your apartment because you're having a party.
Student B: You don't like painting.

2 Student A: You need someone to take care of your dog for a week because you're going on vacation.
Student B: You don't like dogs.

3 Student A: You need someone to give English lessons to your child.
Student B: You've never worked with children before.

Is there any chance you could take care of my dog for a week, starting this Friday?

Your dog? Um … I don't mean to be rude, but I'm kind of uncomfortable with dogs.

3.4 THE RIGHT JOB FOR ME

LESSON OBJECTIVE

- write a personal statement for a job application

1 READING

A **Would you like to work with animals? What kind of work would you like to do? What kinds of zoo jobs do you think involve working with animals? Which don't involve working with animals? Read the text. Were any of the jobs you thought of mentioned?**

www.wellsbrookzoo/jobs.mzorg

WELLS BROOK ZOO

Job Search • View All Jobs • Internships • Volunteer Opportunities

Are you good with people and penguins? Then the Wells Brook Zoo needs you.

CURRENT JOB OPENINGS

JOB TITLE: Sales Assistant

Position Summary: Sales assistants work in the Wells Brook Zoo gift shop, called Zoovenirs, helping customers with sales.

Responsibilities: You will greet customers as they enter Zoovenirs and answer any questions they may have about the products. You will arrange merchandise, maintaining an organized appearance in the store. You will also be expected to handle cash and credit card sales.

Skills Needed: Experience with customer service and handling cash is preferred. You must have good communication skills and be able to work independently.

JOB TITLE: Zookeeper Assistant

Position Summary: Zookeeper assistants help the zookeepers take care of the animals.

Responsibilities: You will feed a variety of animals, including penguins, birds, and turtles, and will keep animal areas clean and safe. You will enter information into a database about animal behavior and health.

You will also give tours and educational information to school groups visiting the zoo.

Skills Needed: Experience working with animals and speaking in front of people is preferred.

JOB TITLE: Face Painter

Position Summary: Face painters work in areas throughout the zoo, painting animal designs on customers.

Responsibilities: You will paint animals on customers' faces and hands, using a variety of Wells Brook Zoo's preset designs. You will greet customers as they walk by and will take cash and make change if required.

Skills Needed: You must be patient and be able to interact well with children. Previous art training is required, and face painting experience is preferred. You must be comfortable working outside.

JOB TITLE: Assistant Cook

Position Summary: Assistant cooks work in the Wells Brook Zoo cafeteria, helping the cook prepare food.

Responsibilities: You will follow instructions from the head cook as you prepare and cook preset menu items. You will clean kitchen equipment and cookware. You may sometimes have to cook and serve food at food stands located throughout the zoo.

Skills Needed: You must be able to follow instructions but also work independently when necessary. Food service experience is strongly preferred.

Email a personal statement and résumé to wellsbrookzoo.job@mz.org.

GLOSSARY

database (*n*) information stored in a computer system in an organized way so that it can be searched in different ways

cookware (*n*) items such as pans, bowls, knives, spoons, etc., used in cooking

B PAIR WORK IDENTIFY AUDIENCE Read again. Who is the audience for the text? What do you think are the most important responsibilities and skills they need to do and have for each job?

C GROUP WORK Which job would you like to have the most? Which job would you be the best at? Give reasons.

D THINK CRITICALLY Which aspects of each job are good for introverts? Extroverts? Ambiverts?

2 WRITING

A Read Jonathan's personal statement for the zookeeper assistant job at the Wells Brook Zoo. What are his (1) qualifications, (2) experience, and (3) goals? How good of a candidate do you think he is?

Jonathan Mendoza | 123 Park Road, Langley, VA 22101 • 575-555-6201 • jmendoza1992@xyz.com

Personal Statement

I am a recent college graduate with a BS in Animal Science and Management. I have a lifelong interest in animals and birds. Summer jobs as an assistant animal keeper at Rosco Wildlife Center gave me practical experience in observing animals for signs of bad health, preparing their food and sleeping areas, cleaning and repairing their living areas, and educating the public about the inhabitants of the zoo. Interacting with children visiting the zoo was particularly rewarding. I am able to work year-round and on weekends and am excited about helping maintain the excellent standards of animal care at the Wells Brook Zoo. My goals are to expand my knowledge and experience in order to become a full-time zookeeper and to provide the animals with the best environment so that they can enjoy their life in the zoo.

REGISTER CHECK

In order to is often used in more formal writing. *To* is often used in less formal writing.

Formal

My goal is to expand my experience ***in order to*** *become a zookeeper.*

Less formal

My goal is to get more experience ***to*** *become a zookeeper.*

FIND IT

B PAIR WORK These are useful words for personal statements: *lifelong interest, expand, maintain, standards.* Find them in the text and discuss what they mean. You can look online for help.

C COMPOSE AND EVALUATE A PERSONAL STATEMENT Read the guide to writing and evaluating personal statements. How well does Jonathan's statement follow this advice?

IS YOUR PERSONAL STATEMENT …

CONCISE?	Keep it short. Avoid unnecessary words that add no meaning. Avoid overusing the word "I." Vary the sentence structure. Put the information in one paragraph.
RELEVANT?	Write about who you are and what you can do. Emphasize only skills and talents relevant to the job. Avoid common expressions such as "good at working on a team" or "a dedicated and enthusiastic worker." Say how you can contribute to the organization. Briefly mention your career goals.
ACCURATE?	Check your punctuation (avoid exclamation points), spelling, and grammar.

WRITE IT

D PLAN You are going to write a personal statement. Work with a partner. Choose one of the other job listings from exercise 1A on page 28. Discuss the skills, experience, qualifications, and goals to include and things to avoid. Then, looking at Jonathan's statement, say how you are going to structure yours.

E Write your personal statement. Then look at the guide in exercise 2C. Have you followed all the tips? Make any changes if necessary.

F PAIR WORK THINK CRITICALLY Read your partner's personal statement. Which job did they apply for? What are the strongest points in their statement?

3.5 TIME TO SPEAK
Getting the job

LESSON OBJECTIVE
- interview for a full-time position

A **DISCUSS** **In many jobs, it's helpful to be good at the things below. In your opinion, what personal qualities do you need in order to do each of them well?**

meet deadlines   work on a team   make decisions   give your opinion at meetings

B **Work with a partner. Read the text from a company's website. Then imagine you work for this company in human resources. It's your job to interview interns who may have the qualities to become full-time employees. Decide together what to ask in the interviews. Design two or three questions to find out about the things in part A. See the examples below.**

MEET DEADLINES
What's the main reason for missing deadlines, and how would you avoid it?

WORK ON A TEAM
How would you handle working with a person you didn't like?

MAKE DECISIONS
What steps would you take before making an important decision?

GIVE YOUR OPINION AT MEETINGS
If you disagreed with everyone else in a meeting, would you speak up?

Our company has a high percentage of "home-grown" employees. These are people who joined us as interns, showed that they were valuable to the company, and were hired for full-time positions.

C **PREPARE** **Work with a different partner. Test your questions from part B. Imagine your partner is an intern and interview them. Change roles and repeat. How well did your questions reveal whether you and your partner have the qualities to work at the company? If necessary, revise your questions to improve them.**

D **PRESENT** **Tell the class about your questions and why you chose them. The class compares all the questions and chooses the best four. What were the best answers you heard to the four questions?**

To check your progress, go to page 153.

USEFUL PHRASES

PREPARE

This question revealed that …

Our question about … shows someone who … would be a good employee.

We thought this question would … , but it didn't.

We could improve this question by …

REVIEW 1 (UNITS 1–3)

1 VOCABULARY

A **Complete the paragraph with the correct words.**

accept	adapt	company	complex	cope	extrovert
frightened	left	resist	socialize	time-consuming	waste

My family moved to Tokyo, Japan, when I was 17 because of my father's job. I couldn't speak any Japanese, so I was [1] ______ at first. And Tokyo was so huge and crowded. I had no idea how to [2] ______ with so many changes. I felt [3] ______ out of everything, even though I'm a(n) [4] ______. But then I made some friends and started to [5] ______ again. I also started learning Japanese, which was [6] ______ and [7] ______, but learning a language is never a(n) [8] ______ of time. Anyway, the whole experience taught me that if we don't [9] ______ change, but instead [10] ______ and welcome it, we'll probably [11] ______ to new situations much better. And for those who enjoy the [12] ______ of people, it helps to try to make friends right away.

B PAIR WORK **Imagine a friend is moving to a different country and is nervous about it. Give them some advice. Complete the sentences with your own ideas.**

1 It's important to tackle ______.
2 Don't underestimate your ability to ______.
3 Try not to be irritated when ______.
4 Remember: It's never a waste of time to ______.
5 It's tricky to ______, but I'm sure you'll be fine.

2 GRAMMAR

A **Complete the conversation with the correct form of the verbs in parentheses ( ). Use comparative and superlative forms when necessary. Use *would* and *used to* when possible. Sometimes there is more than one correct answer.**

A When I was a kid, I [1] ______ (hate) vegetables. I [2] ______ (not, eat) them but [3] ______ (push) them to the side of my plate. I [4] ______ (always, cause) trouble at meal times.

B Well, luckily our tastes in things [5] ______ (tend, change) as we get older. In school, I [6] ______ (play) soccer and basketball, but I [7] ______ (never, play) any sports now. My friends say I'm [8] ______ (less, active) person they know!

A I'm the opposite. I'm [9] ______ (athletic) now than I was before. And what about spending habits? As a child, I [10] ______ (spend) all my money on comics and candy. Now, two of my [11] ______ (big) expenses are electronics and my car.

B For me, a car [12] ______ (not, useful, enough, spend) money on. It's [13] ______ (important, see) friends than [14] ______ (drive) a car.

B PAIR WORK **Discuss how your tastes and habits have changed since you were a child.**

3 VOCABULARY

A **Circle the correct options.**

Some people believe that instead of exploring space or the ocean, we should explore our own backyards. By "backyards," they mean our own local area. They say there are many interesting [1]*species / animal life* in our local [2]*surface / environment*, including rare, [3]*endangered / adaptable* ones, that we can discover. So in your area, there might be a field, a park, a [4]*sea life / pond*, or a forest where you can [5]*launch / come across* various birds, insects, and small animals. It's fascinating to [6]*explore / observe* these creatures in their natural [7]*satellite / habitat*. Backyard [8]*exploration / origin* can also help teach children why it's important to [9]*preserve / use up* animal and plant [10]*life / creature*. It creates a healthy and more pleasant environment for us all. We must learn to live with the other [11]*resources / forms of life* around us. The [12]*investigation / resources* of our own backyards makes us appreciate our world.

B PAIR WORK **Complete the statements with your own ideas. Then compare ideas with another pair.**

1 I think the idea of exploring our own backyards ________________ because ________________.

2 I find zoos ________________ because the habitat in many of them is ________________.

3 It's ________________ to monitor animal and plant species because ________________.

4 Learning about Earth's resources and forms of life is ________________ than learning about space because ________________.

5 The most important thing we can do in our lives is ________________. The reason is ________________.

4 GRAMMAR

A **Complete the sentences with the correct words.**

considered	found	living	selling	that/which
when	where	which	who	whose

1 In your city, are there any activities ____________ encourage people to explore their environment?
2 Describe the area ____________ you live.
3 As a person ____________ in an urban environment, how do you keep in touch with nature?
4 Do you know any people ____________ jobs involve working in nature or with animals?
5 Name someone ____________ has helped protect or preserve animal life or natural areas.
6 Name three places ____________ to be the most natural and untouched areas in your country.
7 Describe a time ____________ you celebrated an occasion outdoors.
8 What are some ways in ____________ we can bring nature into our homes?
9 Of all the natural resources ____________ in your country, which are the most valuable?
10 Are there any stores ____________ green, nature-friendly products near you?

B PAIR WORK **Take turns responding to the sentences in exercise 4A. Give as much information as you can.**

UNIT OBJECTIVES

- talk about your support team in life
- make decisions
- discuss advantages and disadvantages
- write a summary
- plan a fund-raising event

COMBINED EFFORT

4

START SPEAKING

A What are the people doing? Have you or someone you know had a similar experience?

B What are the benefits of teamwork in this situation? What impact is it having on what the people are doing and how they're feeling?

C In your opinion, what are the biggest advantages or challenges of teamwork? Discuss your views. For ideas, watch Lucia's video.

EXPERT SPEAKER

Are any of Lucia's ideas different from yours? Do you agree with them?

4.1 IT TAKES A TEAM

LESSON OBJECTIVE
- talk about your support team in life

1 LANGUAGE IN CONTEXT

A PAIR WORK **Think of people who are important to you. What roles do they have in your life? Then read about eight important kinds of people in our lives. According to the article, which one knows the most about you?**

A TEAM FOR LIFE

We all need help sometimes. Most of us have developed a network of "helpers" who play such important roles in our lives that it would be hard to manage without them. Do you recognize any of these people in your life?

The Listener
quietly **keeps an eye on** you and is willing to listen whenever you want to talk.

The Reporter
photographs everything your group does and posts it online. This person helps **build a** good **relationship** in the group by sharing whatever you do together.

The Teacher
is the one you **turn to** for help, who **assists** you by giving advice about big life decisions. Because of their experience, they can even **steer you away from** trouble.

The Fixer
demonstrates an amazing ability to solve problems. They can suggest practical and creative solutions to problems with technology, the home, your studies, and even relationships.

The Long-Timer
has known you for so long that you've **built** total **trust**. This person knows about your background, experiences, and views. They only need to look at you to know what you're thinking.

The Organizer
knows your schedule, wants to **oversee** arrangements, and **acts as** a kind of boss. This helpful person enjoys planning trips, making reservations, buying tickets, and much more.

The Memorizer
is good at remembering important information. They **take on** the responsibility of reminding you of everything, including what you said and did in the past!

The Joker
is always cheerful and makes you laugh. This person **enables you to** see the funny side of life and **contributes** a lot to your happiness.

B **Read again. Summarize the main way in which each person is helpful.**

2 VOCABULARY: Professional relationships

FIND IT

A 1.27 **Look at the words from the article in exercise 1A in the box. Then describe each one using other words. Use a dictionary or your phone to help you. Listen and check your work.**

act as	assist	build a relationship	build trust
contribute	demonstrate	enable (sb) to	keep an eye on
oversee	steer (sb) away from	take on	turn to

B **Now go to page 143. Do the vocabulary exercises for 4.1.**

C PAIR WORK THINK CRITICALLY **Think of a situation for each of the personality types described in the article in exercise 1A in which they would be most helpful. Can you think of any situations where they would do more harm than good? Explain your answers.**

3 GRAMMAR: Adding emphasis: *so … that, such … that, even, only*

A **Read the sentences in the grammar box. Complete the rules with the words in the box.**

Adding emphasis: *so … that, such … that, even, only*

… who play **such important roles** in our lives **that** it would be hard to manage without them.
They can **even** steer you away from trouble.
The Long Timer has known you for **so long that** you've built total trust.
They **only** need to look at you to know what you're thinking.

even only so such

1 You can use *so* (*that*) and *such* (*that*) to emphasize the result of something. Use ______ + adjective or adverb (*that*). Use ______ (*an/an*) + (adjective) noun (*that*).

2 ______ can add emphasis or signal that something is surprising. ______ means "no one else" or "nothing else."

B **Now go to page 132. Look at the grammar chart and do the grammar exercise for 4.1.**

C **Complete the sentences with *so*, *such*, *even*, or *only* and your own ideas. Sometimes more than one answer is possible. Then check your accuracy.**

1 Some people have ______ busy lives that …
2 ______ quiet people sometimes want …
3 It's not good to take on ______ much responsibility that …
4 ______ people who know a lot need …
5 Friendship is ______ important that …

ACCURACY CHECK

Remember to use a pronoun or a noun after *so* + adjective + *that*.

He's so funny ~~that makes~~ everyone laugh. ✗
He's so funny that he makes everyone laugh. ✓

D GROUP WORK **Compare your sentences from exercise 3C. Whose ideas do you agree with the most?**

4 SPEAKING

A PAIR WORK **Have you ever had to coordinate a group of people? Discuss what the situation was and how it went. How did you feel about being the decision-maker? For ideas, watch Lucia's video.**

EXPERT SPEAKER

Was your experience similar to Lucia's?

I once had to **act as** a guide to a big group of friends who wanted to see my town. It proved to be **such a difficult** task to keep everyone happy **that** I'd think twice before doing it again! I did enjoy being the person they **turned to** for help, though.

4.2 DESTRUCTIVE TEAMS

LESSON OBJECTIVE
- make decisions

1 LANGUAGE IN CONTEXT

A **How do you feel when someone criticizes your ideas? Do you think negative comments are useful?**

B 1.28 **Read and listen to an interview with management consultant Zack Sanchez from a podcast called *Better Teamwork*. What are red teams? Sum them up in one sentence.**

The red team

1.28 Audio script

Host Every business school graduate knows that good teams are **constructive**, right? Well, Zack Sanchez is here to present another idea: a ***destructive*** team, or a red team. Zack, welcome to the show.

Zack Thanks for having me.

Host So, a red team. What is that exactly?

Zack Well, first, imagine you're part of a group that's starting a big project. Everyone's excited and congratulating themselves on how great it's going to be. Well, that kind of enthusiasm can actually be dangerous. When everyone is super positive, they often can't see the negative **aspects** of a plan.

Host I see. So that's why you need a red team?

Zack Exactly. A red team is two or three people from the group whose job is to play the bad guy – look for **weaknesses** and **draw attention to** possible negative **consequences**. A red team doesn't **weigh the pros and cons**, balancing **strengths** and weaknesses. That's a job for others to do. A red team honestly **assesses** a project and **points out** problem areas.

Host And teams are open to this? I mean, teams are used to supporting one another, not criticizing each other. I've been on a red team myself, and it wasn't much fun.

Zack That's why a red team's criticisms should not be **unreasonable**. You've seen for yourself that they need to be **valid** points that have been **thought through** carefully. The other team can't do that by itself.

Host And that's when destructive becomes constructive.

C 1.28 **Read and listen again. What does it mean to "play the bad guy"? How does this relate to red teams?**

2 VOCABULARY: Assessing ideas

A 1.29 **Look at the words from the podcast in the box. Which are verbs / verb phrases? Which are adjectives? Which are nouns? Listen and check your work.**

aspect	assess	consequence	constructive	destructive
draw attention to	point out	strength	think through	unreasonable
valid	weakness	weigh the pros and cons		

B **Now go to page 144. Do the vocabulary exercises for 4.2.**

C PAIR WORK THINK CRITICALLY **Discuss the pros and cons of red teams. Overall, do you think they're a good idea? Would you be a good red team member? Why or why not?**

3 GRAMMAR: Reflexive pronouns; pronouns with *other/another*

A **Read the sentences in the grammar boxes. Circle the correct options to complete the rules.**

Reflexive pronouns

Everyone's excited and congratulating **themselves** on how great it's going to be.
I've been on a red team **myself**, and it wasn't much fun.
You've seen for **yourself** that they need to be valid points.
The other team can't do that **by itself**.

1 You can use reflexive pronouns when the subject and object of a sentence are **different** / **the same**.
2 You **can** / **can't** use reflexive pronouns to emphasize that an action is performed by the subject.
3 *By* + a reflexive pronoun means **alone, without help** / **with other people**.

Pronouns with *other/another*

Zack Sanchez is here to present **another** idea. **The other** team can't do that by itself.
That's a job for **others** to do.
Teams are used to supporting **one another**, not criticizing **each other**.

4 ***Another*** / ***The other*** is the second half of a pair. ***Another*** / ***The other*** means "one more."
5 *Others* shows there **is one more** / **are several more** of something.
6 The meaning of *each other* and *one another* is **the same** / **different**.

B **Now go to page 133. Look at the grammar chart and do the grammar exercise for 4.2.**

C **Complete the questions with words from the grammar boxes in exercise 3A. Then ask and answer them with a partner.**

1 What sports can people play by ____________ ? Do you play any sports by ____________ ?
2 What do you and your friends do to enjoy ____________ ?
3 Who in your family helps you the most? How do the ____________ help you?
4 How can neighbors help each ____________ ? In what ways can they annoy one ____________ ?

D PAIR WORK **Talk about an experience working on a team. What did the team members do together, and what did they do by themselves? How did they help each other?**

4 SPEAKING

A PAIR WORK THINK CRITICALLY **How do people make group decisions? How effective is this process? What are the challenges?**

In project groups, I find some people want to **draw attention to themselves** and don't listen to others.

And some people just **point out** the **weaknesses** of other people's ideas but don't have any ideas **themselves**.

4.3 TWO PEOPLE, ONE JOB

LESSON OBJECTIVE
- discuss advantages and disadvantages

1 LISTENING

INSIDER ENGLISH

be/get stuck with = be left to deal with something you don't want

A **What do you think job sharing is? Have you, or has anyone you know, experienced it?**

B 1.30 **Listen to Rafael and Shelby talk with Heather, their college professor. What advantages and disadvantages of job sharing do they mention?**

C 1.30 LISTEN FOR ATTITUDE **Listen again. Which attitude does each speaker have? Circle one answer for each speaker.**

Rafael:	a positive	b negative	c curious
Shelby:	a kind	b sensible	c unreasonable
Heather:	a helpful	b jealous	c unpleasant

D PAIR WORK THINK CRITICALLY **Do you think job sharing is a good idea for employees, bosses, and companies? Why or why not?**

2 PRONUNCIATION: Listening for consonant–vowel linking between words

A 1.31 **Listen to this word group. Which words are linked together, and why?**

It's an interesting idea worth considering.

B 1.32 **Listen. Underline the examples of consonant–vowel linking from exercise 1B.**

1 So you're interested in job sharing?
2 I'm interested in finding out more about it.
3 … the advantage of doing the parts of a job you're best at …
4 … that's what I read in an article …

C **Circle the correct options to complete the sentence.**

When one word finishes in a consonant sound and the next word starts with a *consonant / vowel* sound, the two words are usually linked together when they are in *the same word group / different word groups*.

3 SPEAKING SKILLS

A 1.30 **Look at the expressions from the conversation in exercise 1B on page 38. Are they used to discuss advantages (A) or to discuss disadvantages (D)? Write *A* or *D*. Which words, do you think, might have linked sounds in these sentences? Listen to the conversation again to check.**

Discuss advantages and disadvantages

1 The main benefit is (that) … ___
2 A/Another plus is (that) … ___
3 The downside is (that) … ___
4 One/The tricky issue is (that) … ___
5 It gives the company/us/you/me the advantage of [-*ing* verb] … ___
6 I'd be / I'm concerned (that) … ___
7 The upside is (that) … ___
8 One/Another potential problem is (that) … ___

B PAIR WORK **Student A: Go to page 157. Student B: Go to page 159. Follow the instructions.**

4 PRONUNCIATION: Using stress in compounds

A 1.33 **Look at these pairs of words. Which word in each pair is stressed? Why?**

college student young children

B 1.34 **Draw the stress pattern at the top of each column. Then listen and add the phrases to the correct columns.**

noun + noun	adjective + noun
college student	*young children*

C PAIR WORK **Think of some more examples of compounds like these, and use them to make a short story. Give your story to another pair to read out loud. Listen and give them feedback on how they pronounce the compounds.**

5 SPEAKING

A PAIR WORK THINK CRITICALLY **Choose a job below or your own idea. Discuss the advantages and disadvantages of job sharing for that job. One person points out the advantages and the other the disadvantages. Then choose another job, change roles, and repeat.**

accountant	chef	dentist
graphic designer	mechanic	receptionist
teacher	truck driver	

It's a good idea for chefs to job share. **The main benefit is** having more personal time for creative projects. And **a plus is** that there are two people to think of ideas for the menu.

I don't know. **One potential problem** is that it can be difficult to agree on the ideas.

4.4 THE ME TEAM

LESSON OBJECTIVE
- write a summary

1 READING

A PAIR WORK **Do you prefer working alone or as part of a team? Why?**

B UNDERSTAND AUTHOR'S ATTITUDE **Read the article. Then circle the word in each pair that describes the author's writing.**

1 a curious b critical
2 a objective b subjective
3 a optimistic b pessimistic

HOME NEWS BLOG SIGN IN

Teamwork makes the dream work?

I'm not so sure.

Bev Shannon
The work-at-home office blogger

We all enjoy being part of a group – there's no better work than teamwork, right? Actually, I disagree. Teamwork can be tough. In fact, it was so difficult that I left my office job and started working from home on my own. It's a much better fit for me, and it has made me think about why teamwork can make our jobs harder rather than easier.

Personalities can make teamwork difficult. There's a famous saying, *There's no "I" in TEAM*, meaning I have to do what's best for the team, not what's best for me. But there's often someone on the team that puts their needs first: "**I** want to do it this way. **My** way is best." The team often goes along with this person, whose ideas might not be the best, just the loudest. Teamwork can be difficult for an introvert, like me. It's hard to speak up if there's a dominant voice in the group. And then there's that team member who likes to argue – and not in a constructive way – who just wants to say "no" because the others said "yes." And, my least favorite, the people pleaser – someone who is such a nice person that they feel they can't be honest. They don't want to hurt anyone's feelings, so they say "yes" to every idea. Just one difficult personality can make teamwork tough. Combine several challenging personality types, and it's even tougher.

Lack of time together can also make teamwork challenging. For example, I was once on a team where we never had enough time to meet as a group. Team member A was at a conference, B had to meet with a customer, C had an important phone call to make, and so on. To successfully work as a team, you need time together – and lots of it.

A final reason teamwork is difficult is because there's often no training on how to work on a team. You can't just put people in a room and expect them to work well with each other. You need to build trust with your team members. Think of football players: They aren't just given a ball and told to play. They practice, and they train. They also have different positions, know who does what, and how they affect one another. It helps to have clear roles on company teams, too, with the right people in them. It's not such a good idea to give the role of a leader to the ME, ME, ME person.

Teams can be tough, but working alone has its challenges, too. When my computer doesn't work, I don't have an IT person to turn to. When I have a great idea, I don't have anyone to share it with to see if it *really is a great idea*. Don't get me wrong – I still like my team of one and enjoy making all of the important decisions myself. But now I realize what was wrong with the teamwork I did in the past and how good teamwork could be if done correctly. And that's useful information – because one day I might want to turn my ME TEAM into a WE TEAM.

C **Read again. What three main reasons does the author give to support her opinion about teamwork? What's her last thought about teamwork?**

D PAIR WORK **What examples does the author give to support each of her three main reasons? Which do you think are the strongest?**

E GROUP WORK THINK CRITICALLY **Think about your answer to exercise C on page 33. Has your opinion changed at all after reading this text? If so, how? Why? What's your attitude toward teamwork?**

2 WRITING

A **Read the summary of an article called "The Power of the Team." Based on the summary, what is the main argument of the article?**

In his article "The Power of the Team," Max Jackson states that no one can achieve as much alone as they can on a team. Teamwork is essential to success in personal, educational, and professional situations. The most basic team is the family, which assists and cares for each member in order to make sure the entire family is secure. At school or college, teachers encourage their students to work together in order to produce superior projects or presentations. At work, teamwork is so important that without it, any company would fail. Even healthy competition between teams can build trust and improve relationships within the company. The secret of good teamwork is that each member should contribute their individual skills, talents, and ideas, but never forget that they are working as part of a team toward a common goal.

B **SUMMARIZE MAIN POINTS A summary is a short version of a longer text. Read about how to write a summary. Then answer these questions about the summary in exercise 2A.**

1 What three situations does the writer mention?
2 What are the main points for each situation?
3 Does the last sentence sum up the main points?

REGISTER CHECK

The verb *state* is often used in more formal writing. *Say* is often used in less formal writing.

Summary writing

- Keep your summary short (about ¼ of a page in length). Use one paragraph.
- Use your own words. Don't rewrite the original text.
- Mention the title and author of the text. State the main topic.
- Briefly describe the author's main points.
- After each main point, include the most relevant details or examples.
- Don't add your own opinions. The summary should be based on information from the article.

WRITE IT

C **PLAN You're going to write a summary of the article "Teamwork makes the dream work? I'm not so sure." in exercise 1A on page 40. With your partner, look again at the main points and reasons you discussed in exercises 1B and 1C on page 40. Try summarizing them briefly in your own words. Then look at the summary writing tips in exercise 2B and plan the structure of your summary.**

D **Write your summary of the article.**

E **PAIR WORK THINK CRITICALLY Read each other's summaries. What are the strong points of your partner's summary? How do you think you could improve your own summary?**

4.5 TIME TO SPEAK
The big event

LESSON OBJECTIVE
- plan a fund-raising event

A **AGREE** **Imagine you want to organize a local event to raise money for a cause in your community. Work in a group and choose one of the causes below or think of one of your own.**

research at a local hospital   an after-school youth program   improvements to the fire station
new equipment and uniforms for a local sports team   a music program for the local high school

B **DISCUSS** **In your group, look at the events below for raising money for the cause you chose in part A. Think of more events. Discuss the advantages and disadvantages of each event. Consider the type of people who would support the cause you chose.**

an art show   a barbecue   a concert   a fancy dress party   a marathon   a sports event

C **DECIDE** **Choose an event or a combination of events. To help you decide, consider any skills, experience, equipment, or contacts you have that could be useful.**

D **Think about the jobs your team will need to do before, during, and after the event. Agree on who will be responsible for each job.**

E **PRESENT** **Tell the class about your event. Explain why it will be popular and why the people on your team have the ability to make it successful. The class chooses the best event.**

To check your progress, go to page 154.

USEFUL PHRASES

AGREE
We could try …
Why don't we … ?
That might (not) be the best option …
That could work.

DISCUSS
The main benefit is …
Another plus / potential problem is …
The downside/upside is …
I'd be concerned that …

UNIT OBJECTIVES

- discuss how new technology can help people
- discuss the future of communication
- consider and contrast ideas
- write an online comment with examples
- plan a community improvement project

THE HUMAN FACTOR

5

START SPEAKING

A **What is happening in the picture? Do you think robots could be better at this activity than humans? Explain your answer.**

B **Discuss some examples of tasks and situations that a robot might handle better than a human. Say why.**

C **In your opinion, what things will always be done by humans and never by robots? Why? Discuss some examples. For ideas, watch Carolina's video.**

EXPERT SPEAKER

Do you agree with Carolina's predictions?

5.1 IMITATING REALITY

LESSON OBJECTIVE
- discuss how new technology can help people

1 LANGUAGE IN CONTEXT

A **Look at the picture. How does the man feel? How do you feel about flying?**

B **Read the article about a man's experience with virtual reality. How many times did he use VR therapy? How successful was his experience in the end?**

CAN VR THERAPY CURE ME?

I'm scared of flying. Not just a little. Whenever I get on a plane, **I'm scared to death**. I've cried on planes. As an adult. More than once. The fear **isn't rational**, but it is not something **I'm in control of** either. I read about a virtual reality treatment that has helped people like me, so I decided to try it.

STEP 1: GET A REAL THERAPIST
If you want to **try this therapy**, you'll need a therapist. That part's real, not virtual! During my sessions, however, we spent a lot of the time in the virtual world. And even then, the therapist was always in control of the software.

STEP 2: PANIC
The first time I put on a VR headset, I was surprised by my body's reaction. When you're in a VR environment, your mind can't tell what's real or not real. Within minutes, I **was panicking**. The therapist taught me how to **regain control** by using **a breathing technique**.

STEP 3: REPEAT
At my first session, my **anxiety level** was extremely high. There was still a lot of fear the second time, but now I **was more conscious of** what was happening. With careful breathing, I **calmed down**. By my third session, I felt almost relaxed.

STEP 4: FLY
Engine noise rising, speed increasing, ground disappearing – and all without the usual fear. I still felt nervous – a real plane is definitely more intense than a VR plane, but I really **had overcome my fear**. VR therapy had worked! I may even take flying lessons if the therapy continues to work so well. Nah!

Adapted from an article by Luke Johnson on the Wareable website

C **Read again. What feelings did the man experience before, during, and after the therapy?**

2 VOCABULARY: Dealing with emotions

FIND IT

A **Look at the expressions in the box. Then describe each one using other words. Use a dictionary or your phone to help you. Then look at how they are used in the article in exercise 1B.**

anxiety level	be conscious of	be in control of
be rational	be scared to death	breathing technique
calm down	cure (an illness)	overcome my fear
panic (about sth)	regain control	try a therapy

! *sth* = something

B 1.35 **Look at the expressions in the box again. Which are verb phrases? Which are noun phrases? Listen and check your work.**

C **Now go to page 144. Do the vocabulary exercises for 5.1.**

D PAIR WORK THINK CRITICALLY **What other strong fears do people have? What advice would you give on how to overcome these fears? Say why.**

3 GRAMMAR: Real conditionals

A Read the sentences in the grammar box. Which rule is about the *if* clause? Which is about the main clause? Complete the rules.

Real conditionals

Whenever I **get** on a plane, I'**m** scared to death.

When you'**re** in a VR environment, your mind **can't tell** what's real or not real.

I **may** even **take** flying lessons **if** the therapy **continues** to work so well.

1 When something is a general fact or a routine, you can replace *if* with *when* and *whenever* in the ___________ .

2 You can use modals to describe possible future situations and their results in the ___________ .

B Now go to page 133. Look at the grammar chart and do the grammar exercise for 5.1.

C Write sentences with real conditionals from exercise 3A using the ideas below. Check your accuracy. Then compare with a partner. How similar are your ideas? Ask questions to find out more.

ask for help · decide to try something new · feel uneasy · see a spider · want to attract attention

ACCURACY CHECK

Whenever is one word.

I feel scared ~~when ever~~ I'm in a tall building. ✗

I feel scared whenever I'm in a tall building. ✓

4 SPEAKING

A GROUP WORK THINK CRITICALLY **How can VR be useful in medicine? In sports? For shopping? In training/education? Discuss in your group. For ideas, watch Carolina's video.**

EXPERT SPEAKER

How similar are Carolina's views to yours?

If someone **wants** to learn how to drive, they **can try** a VR training program first.

Yeah, I think their **anxiety** level **won't be** so high **if** they **practice** with an app.

5.2 THE END OF THE OFFICE?

LESSON OBJECTIVE

- discuss the future of communication

1 LANGUAGE IN CONTEXT

A PAIR WORK **In your lifetime, what have been the biggest changes in how we communicate?**

B 1.36 **Read and listen to Ramon and Jack discussing communication in a college debate. Do they change their attitudes in the end?**

1.36 Audio script

Helena The topic for this month's debate is the office of the future. We've asked millennials Ramon and Jack if they'd rent traditional office space for a future company or go virtual.

Ramon Right. Well, millennials will soon be the largest group of workers. We communicate virtually day and night and **have no desire to** work in an office 9 to 5. Millennials will **be eager to** work for a virtual company as long as the technology is good.

Jack OK, that may be true, but only if we're talking about future workers. Many current employees, older than us, **aren't prepared to** work like that. Even if the tech is amazing, face time is important.

Ramon But how important? Companies can save hundreds of thousands of dollars a year in rent if they go virtual.

Jack Well, I'**m not against** saving money, and I'**d be more than happy to** use videoconferencing for most meetings. But if you'**re passionate about** an idea and **are dying to** share it, you want to do it in person. You can't really connect with your team unless you're all in a room together.

Ramon *All* communication will be virtual eventually, so we shouldn't **be reluctant to** lead the way. It could be the next big thing, providing companies invest more in technology.

GLOSSARY

millennial (*n*) a person who was born in the 1980s, 1990s, or early 2000s

face time (*n*) time spent talking to people directly, not virtually

C 1.36 **Read and listen again. What does Ramon think about the office of the future? What does Jack think? What reasons do they give? Who do you agree with?**

2 VOCABULARY: Willingness and unwillingness

FIND IT

A 1.37 **Look at the expressions in the box. Which ones were used in the script in exercise 1B? Use your phone to find examples online of the expressions that are not in the script, or make your own sentences. Which expressions mean you want to do something, and which mean you don't want to do something? Listen and check your work.**

be against	be anxious to	be dying to	be eager to
be more than happy to	be passionate about	be prepared to	be reluctant to
be unwilling to	have no desire to	have no intention of	hesitate to

B **Now go to page 145. Do the vocabulary exercises for 5.2.**

C PAIR WORK **Discuss how your friends and family communicate in different situations. When are they eager to talk face-to-face? What ways of communication are they reluctant to use?**

3 GRAMMAR: Conditionals: alternatives to *if*

A **Read the sentences in the grammar box. Circle the correct options to complete the rules.**

Conditionals: alternatives to *if*

Millennials will be eager to work for a virtual company **as long as** the technology is good.
That may be true, but **only if** we're talking about future workers.
It could be the next big thing, **providing** companies invest more in technology.
Even if the tech is amazing, face time is important.
You can't really connect with your team **unless** you're all in a room together.

! ***Providing* and *as long as* are more common in writing.**

1 Use *as/so long as*, *only if*, and *providing/provided* to show that the result **will** / **won't** happen when a specific condition becomes true.
2 Use *even if* when you believe the result **will** / **won't** change. *Even if* means "whether or not."
3 Use *unless* to describe a possible **positive** / **negative** condition in the present or future. It has a similar meaning to "except if" or "if … not."

B **Now go to page 134. Look at the grammar chart and do the grammar exercise for 5.2.**

C PAIR WORK **Complete the sentences with your own ideas. Then compare and discuss your ideas with a partner.**

1 Even if virtual reality improves a lot, ______________________ .
2 I wouldn't want to ______________________ unless I was paid a lot of money.
3 I'm prepared to work long hours, providing that ______________________ .
4 As long as ______________________ , I feel comfortable with people.
5 I'm more than happy to work in an office, but only if ______________________ .

4 SPEAKING

A GROUP WORK THINK CRITICALLY **How, and under what conditions, can changes in technology affect the way we communicate with these people?**

bank staff | coaches / gym staff | doctors/therapists | government employees | teachers

*I think we'll have more doctor's appointments by video call, **providing** our privacy is protected.*

*Yeah, but **only if** people are prepared to accept that. Some people **are unwilling to** share private information virtually.*

5.3 STOP BLAMING GAMING

LESSON OBJECTIVE

- consider and contrast ideas

1 LISTENING

GLOSSARY

isolation (*n*) being alone, especially when this makes you feel unhappy

A 1.38 **Talk about some good and bad things people say about video games. Then listen to a TV debate about video gaming. How many of your ideas do the speakers mention?**

B 1.38 **Listen again. What does Parker think is a problem? Why does Nadia think gaming is a social activity?**

C 1.38 LISTEN FOR SPEAKER'S DEGREE OF CERTAINTY **Listen again. Is the speaker certain or uncertain about their ideas? Listen to the language around these ideas and check (✓) the ones that sound confident.**

1 ☐ **Parker**: If you can't control your gaming, it's a problem.

2 ☐ **Host:** Young people spend 20 hours a week gaming.

3 ☐ **Parker:** A lot of people spend too many hours gaming.

4 ☐ **Nadia**: We would hear about major problems with gaming if there were any.

5 ☐ **Nadia:** Gaming doesn't cause isolation. It's a social activity.

D PAIR WORK THINK CRITICALLY **Whose views on video games seem the most believable? Why? Which view do you agree with?**

2 PRONUNCIATION: Listening for lower pitch information

A 1.39 **Listen to this sentence. How are the underlined phrases connected to the noun phrases before them? What do you notice about how they are pronounced?**

With me to discuss this is Nadia Rivera, <u>a video game developer</u>, and Parker Wendell, <u>from the group Game On – Game Off</u>, which offers advice about gaming.

B 1.40 **Listen to the sentence and then to a version of it with extra information added in parentheses. Repeat the original sentence and then the new version.**

And it's fantastic for the brain. It improves thinking speed, the ability to concentrate, and problem-solving skills.

And it's fantastic for the brain. It improves thinking speed (information processing), the ability to concentrate (how long we can concentrate for), and problem-solving skills (like critical thinking).

C **Circle the correct options to complete the sentence.**

When extra information is added next to a noun phrase, for example to define, explain, or give more details about the noun phrase, this extra information is usually pronounced *as part of the same / with a different* tone in a *lower / higher* key.

3 SPEAKING SKILLS

A **Look at the expressions from the TV program in exercise 1A on page 48. Which ones show the speaker is certain, uncertain, or giving a contrasting idea? Complete the chart.**

At the same time, …	I don't have a clue …	I guarantee (that) …
It's a well-known fact (that) …	On the contrary, …	That said, …
Who knows …	You can bet (that) …	

Certain	Uncertain	Giving a contrasting idea

B **Find the best place in the sentences below to add one of the expressions from exercise 3A. Use a different expression in each sentence. Then tell a partner if you agree with the statements. Say why or why not.**

1 Most children like playing video games.
2 Video games are not relaxing. They're stressful.
3 VR games are the future, but there will soon be something even better.
4 … what crazy video games creators will come up with ten years from now.
5 Many games help develop useful skills and should be encouraged. We have to be careful about the time we spend playing them.

C PAIR WORK **Student A: Go to page 157. Student B: Go to page 160. Follow the instructions.**

4 PRONUNCIATION: Saying front vowels /ɪ/, /e/, and /æ/

A 1.41 **Listen. Then repeat the words and focus on the underlined vowels.**

/ɪ/	video	figures	listen	industry	billion
/e/	ten	pleasure	bet	said	friends
/æ/	average	ask	fantastic	exact	actually

B **Circle the correct options to complete the sentences.**

The tip of the tongue is nearer to the *front* / *back* of the mouth for these vowels. The jaw moves *down* / *up* as you go from /ɪ/ to /e/ to /æ/.

C 1.42 **Listen and circle the words you hear.**

1	bit	bet	bat	4	sit	set	sat
2	slipped	slept	slapped	5	rip	rep	wrap
3	tin	ten	tan	6	hid	head	had

D PAIR WORK **Take turns saying one of the words from exercise 4C. Your partner should repeat the word you said.**

5 SPEAKING

A PAIR WORK THINK CRITICALLY **What are the different ways that video games can benefit people of all ages?**

> **It's a well-known fact that** some video games can improve concentration and reaction speed. **At the same time,** we have to be conscious of the amount of time spent gaming …

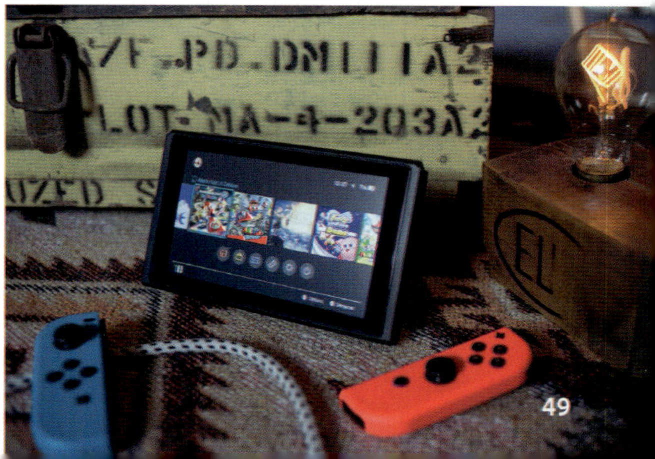

5.4 WHAT LANGUAGE BARRIER?

LESSON OBJECTIVE

- write an online comment with examples

1 READING

A **Have you ever used a translation app? Did you find it useful? Read the article. According to Lance, how can people be helped by translation apps? What can't they do?**

Sign up   Log in

THE TRAVELER'S TAKE

By Lance Levine

Do translation apps break down barriers or put up new ones?

A few years ago, while I was on a cycling trip in Brazil, I fell off my bike. I was a little banged up, but the front wheel of my bike was damaged badly. It looked like I was in for a difficult day. I needed tools to fix the bike, and I only had an air pump and some glue. I had seen a house a few minutes before, so I picked up my bike and started walking.

My Portuguese consisted of "please" and "thank you," so the language barrier was an issue. I had no idea how to explain what happened or ask for help or a ride to town. Then I remembered my translation app! What a relief. I spent about 20 minutes on the side of the road tapping out the story and creating requests for different things. I knew it wouldn't be perfect, but at least it would tell people the basics. I approached the house, app in hand, and knocked on the door.

Before I could press PLAY on my carefully constructed greeting, the elderly woman who answered the door was on the job. One look at me, my damaged bicycle, my dirty knees and torn shirt, and that translation app was about as useful as air conditioning on a motorcycle.

In five minutes' time, I was sitting on the patio with my leg on a stool, clean and bandaged. Maria (the elderly woman), her husband Gustavo, two of their kids, seven of their grandchildren, and a constantly changing group of neighbors had appeared from nowhere, and my tragedy was quickly becoming a party. Gustavo and a neighbor were enjoying a heated debate about the best way to repair the wheel on my bicycle. The kids were exploring the contents of my backpack piece by piece and finding each hilariously funny. And the smell of food started to fill the air. A bike accident is usually a bad thing. But by the time Maria and her son João left me at my hotel that night, with a full stomach and a shiny, clean, fully repaired bicycle, I felt like the luckiest man in the world.

We're so independent these days. The internet and smartphones make information and services so easy to access. Translation apps, too, have their place and are very useful. I think from now on, though, I'm going to use that app for work or maybe in stores when I travel and need something specific. When it comes to people, I'll take the risk.

I won't catch story details, and I'll misunderstand instructions now and again. I'll definitely have trouble with jokes, but humor usually doesn't translate, even if your app gives you all the right words. I'll get surprises, maybe some bad ones but mostly good ones. I'll get to act things out and look ridiculous doing it, and I'll get to solve the puzzle of what someone else is trying to tell me. I'll get gestures, laughter, attention, and the kindness of strangers.

Language barrier? What language barrier?

GLOSSARY

barrier (*n*) something that prevents communication, action, or progress
gesture (*n*) a movement you make with your hand, arm, or head to express your meaning

B UNDERSTAND PROBLEMS AND SOLUTIONS **Read again. After his crash, what problems did Lance expect to have? What happened instead?**

C **What's Lance's opinion of translation apps?**

D PAIR WORK THINK CRITICALLY **What's your opinion of translation apps? Do they make it harder to show our feelings, or do they enable us to have conversations we never thought possible?**

INSIDER ENGLISH

Be in for* means *be about to experience something unpleasant.

2 WRITING

A **Read Julieta's comment in response to Lance's article in exercise 1A on page 50. What's her opinion of translation apps? How many situations does she describe to support her opinion?**

COMMENTS

Julieta M.
New York

I think translation apps are great, but I use them more for writing than speaking. My company does business with an Italian company. We usually communicate in English, but sometimes they send me information in Italian. My app translates them just fine. I also exchange emails with a Chilean friend. Her English is only beginner level, so I use my app to send her messages in Spanish and to translate her messages. OK, we could try English, but I think she'd gradually stop writing. As long as I use my app, everything's fine.

As for speaking, when I was in Tokyo once, I got lost on my way to a meeting. I just stood there on the street, helpless. Finally, I stopped a man and used my app to ask, "Excuse me. Where's the Panorama Building?" He looked surprised, so I played it again. Then he laughed and pointed at the building right behind me. Well, at least I didn't have far to walk! So yes, I'm a big fan of these apps.

2 7 1

REGISTER CHECK

We use different organizing and connecting expressions in informal and formal texts. Look at these formal examples. Find informal examples in Julieta's comment.

Formal

__That said__, we could try English.

__With regards to__ speaking, when I was in Tokyo once …

__Therefore__, I'm a big fan of these apps.

B **STATE OPINION AND GIVE EXAMPLES** **Read about one way to organize an opinion comment. Then check Julieta's comment in exercise 2A. Does it have all these features?**

1 **Make an opening statement.** Give your opinion of translation apps: for, against, or mixed feelings.

2 **Support your opinion with examples. For each example, …**
- **give some background**. Give a short explanation about the situation at the beginning.
- **describe what happened**. You can include direct speech if you want.
- **add a comment**. You can comment after each example, e.g., *My app translates them just fine.*

3 **Make a closing statement**. Give your opinion again but in different words.

WRITE IT

C **PLAN** **You are going to write a comment in response to Lance's article. With a partner, discuss your opinion and give examples. The examples can be about your own or other's experiences. Then plan your opening statement, background information, description of what happened, and your closing statement.**

D **Write your comment.**

E **PAIR WORK** **Exchange your comments with a different partner. Do you have the same opinion about translation apps? What do you think about the examples your partner gave?**

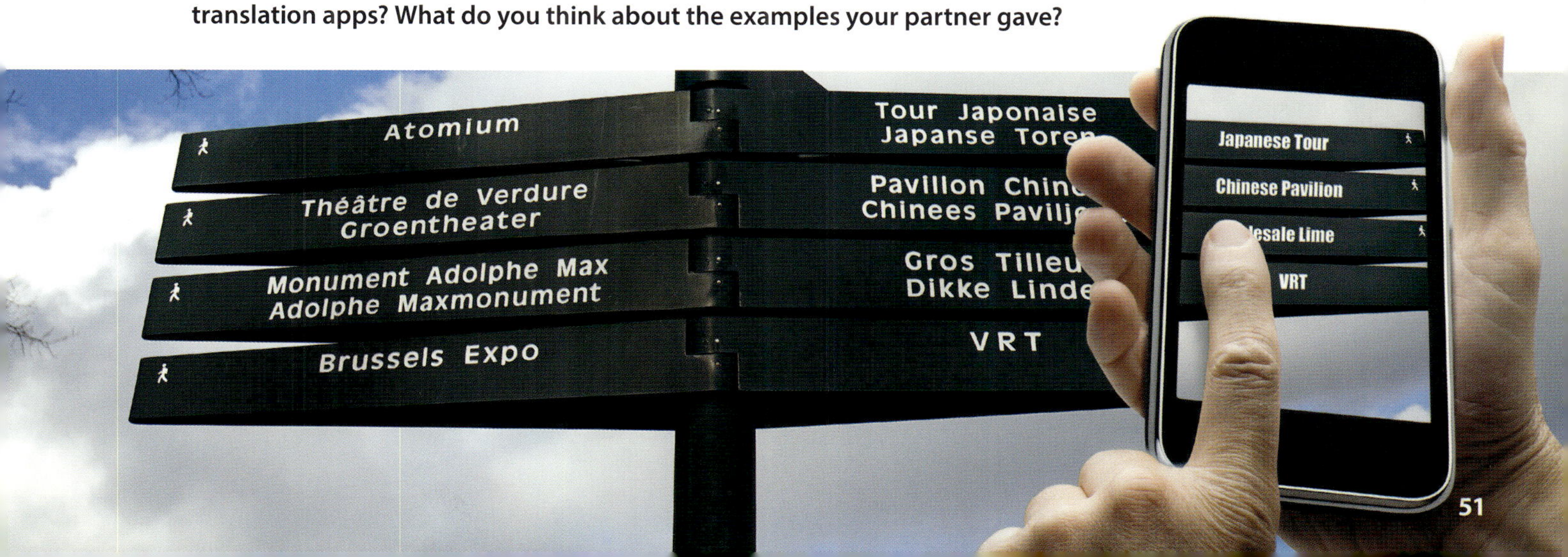

5.5 TIME TO SPEAK
Community improvement campaign

LESSON OBJECTIVE

- plan a community improvement project

FIND IT

A Talk about a community project or event you know about. What was its purpose? Did it involve working with technology? How successful was it? Tell a partner. You can look online for ideas if you need to.

B **DECIDE** Work with a group and choose something to improve in your community. Use one of the ideas below or your own idea. Discuss how people will benefit from the project.

clean up and improve a public space
plan social events or activities for elderly people
create after-school programs for teens
start a community garden

C **DISCUSS** With your group, talk about the resources you'll need. How can you use technology in your project? What other materials or tools will you need? What roles will people have? Think of ways to do the project as cheaply as possible and how to encourage others to help.

D **PREPARE** Come up with a plan for your project. Decide how you'll get the resources you talked about in part C.

E **PRESENT** Present your plan to the class. Agree on which plan will benefit the community the most. Which project, other than your own, would you most like to work on?

To check your progress, go to page 154.

USEFUL PHRASES

DECIDE

Now that's a good idea.
On second thought, …
That said, …
Good point.
I see what you mean.

DISCUSS

It's a well-known fact that …
At the same time, we need …
You can bet that …
As long as … , we can …
That will work providing (that) …
If … , we'll …
Who will be in control of …

UNIT OBJECTIVES

- describe unexpected fame
- talk about unexpected situations
- make assumptions
- write an interesting story
- tell a story

EXPECT THE UNEXPECTED

6

START SPEAKING

A What is the situation in the picture? Do you think the people expected this situation? How are they reacting? How would you react?

B Think of some unexpected situations, like winning a lottery or meeting a well-known person. Discuss how you would react in these situations.

C Describe a time when something totally unexpected happened to you or someone you know. How did you, or the person you know, react? For ideas, watch Bojan's video.

EXPERT SPEAKER

How would you handle the situation Bojan describes?

6.1 GOING VIRAL

LESSON OBJECTIVE
- describe unexpected fame

1 LANGUAGE IN CONTEXT

Kyle MacDonald

A **Look at these pictures. What are they? How do you think they are connected to Kyle MacDonald? Then read the article and check your guesses.**

FROM PAPERCLIP TO A HOUSE

What **makes a story entertaining** enough to go viral? In Kyle MacDonald's case, it was a simple red paperclip. He exchanged it online, and then kept trading for better things until he reached his final goal – his own house.

The 26-year-old from Vancouver had been trading things online for a year before he finally got offered a two-story, three-bedroom, 1920s farmhouse in Kipling, Canada, and **made the headlines**. The 14 trades that he made included a fish pen; a stove; an "instant party kit"; a snowmobile; a vacation to Yahk; a moving van; a recording contract; a year's free rent in Phoenix, Arizona; and a part in the movie *Donna on Demand*.

When Kyle was growing up in the suburbs of Vancouver, he watched children go door to door trying to trade their toys for something more valuable. He was sure as long as he tried hard enough, he would get what he wanted. And sure enough, an opportunity presented itself.

Not many people **had heard of** the small town of Kipling before the story **caught people's attention**. The mayor, Pat Jackson, was trying to promote tourism and decided to make the offer of the house to **get publicity** and **raise awareness of** the town as a friendly, welcoming place. His offer included not just the house, but the key to the town and the opportunity to be mayor for one day.

Since the trade Mr. MacDonald has **made an appearance** on a TV show, given interviews to newspapers, and set up a popular website. The red paperclip was definitely his ticket to fame.

Adapted from an article on the Mail Online website

GLOSSARY
trade (*n/v*) exchange one thing for another

B **Read again. How did Kyle achieve his goal? Who is the other person in the story? What role did he play?**

FIND IT

C PAIR WORK **Can you think of another example when an ordinary person became accidentally famous? Tell your partner. You can check online if you need to.**

2 VOCABULARY: Talking about fame

A 1.43 PAIR WORK **Look at the expressions in the box and discuss their meaning. Then listen and check the definitions. Which of them were used in the article? Can you use any of the expressions to talk about the story you told in exercise 1C?**

catch sb's attention	do a/the broadcast	get hits	get publicity
have a good/bad reputation	have (never) heard of sth	make an appearance	make sth entertaining
make headlines	praise sb	raise awareness (of sth)	seek fame

B **Now go to page 145. Do the vocabulary exercises for 6.1.**

C PAIR WORK **Why do people seek fame? What are the pros and cons?**

D PAIR WORK **Imagine that your name appeared in the news headlines. What would your reaction be? Tell your partner. For ideas, watch Bojan's video.**

EXPERT SPEAKER

Is Bojan's reaction similar to yours?

3 GRAMMAR: Narrative tenses

A Read the sentences in the grammar box. Complete the rules with the correct tenses below.

Narrative tenses

The 26-year-old from Vancouver **had been trading** things online for a year before he finally **got offered** a two-story, three-bedroom, 1920s farmhouse.

Not many people **had heard** of the small town of Kipling before the story **caught** people's attention.

The mayor, Pat Jackson, **was trying** to promote tourism and **decided** to make the offer of the house.

past continuous
past perfect (*had* + past participle)
past perfect continuous (*had* + *been* + verb + *-ing*)
simple past

1 Use the ________ for an ongoing action or situation that continued up to an event or situation in the past.

2 Use the ________ to describe a completed event that happened before another event in the past.

3 Use the ________ for the main completed events or situations in a story. Use the ________ for background activities happening at the same time as the main event.

B Now go to page 134. Look at the grammar chart and do the grammar exercise for 6.1.

C PAIR WORK **Read the beginning and end of a story. With a partner, take turns making sentences to complete the story. Use a variety of narrative tenses.**

Matt wanted his marriage proposal to be special, but he never expected it to make headlines …

… This was a truly happy ending.

Matt wanted his marriage proposal to be special, but he never expected it to **make headlines**. He **had been planning** the speech for months …

… and **chose** what he thought was the perfect ring …

4 SPEAKING

A PAIR WORK Student A: Go to page 158. Student B: Go to page 160. Follow the instructions.

6.2 NOT AGAIN!

LESSON OBJECTIVE

- talk about unexpected situations

1 LANGUAGE IN CONTEXT

A GROUP WORK **Think of a time when something did not go according to plan for you. What happened? Were you disappointed? Why? What would have made the situation better?**

B 1.44 **Read and listen to the podcast. What was disappointing about each situation? What do you understand by "managing expectations"?**

1.44 Audio script

Mike Accidents happen. Things outside our control can go wrong. So how can we make sure we keep our promises?

Tessa And keep people around us happy?

Mike Exactly. Managing expectations might be the key. It may be that explaining things clearly, promising less, and delivering more is all it takes. Let me give you an example of when that didn't happen for me. I was waiting for a flight. The airline **confirmed** that it was on time. A few minutes later, they said it was late. No surprises there. They **estimated** it would be delayed by about 30 minutes. Then they **announced** there could be an even longer wait. And on it went. Each time, they said we wouldn't have to wait much longer … Four hours later we took off. Unbelievably frustrating.

Tessa Yeah, I totally get it. I have this friend who's always late. She'll **swear** she'll be there at a certain time, and she'll always keep me waiting for ages and doesn't even call or anything. The last time we had plans, I told her I **had doubts about** her being there. She **denied** she'd ever been late and **insisted** she could make it. But guess what! No show. I wish she'd said she might be late and **proposed** a less ambitious time. I would have been so happy to see her waiting for me for a change.

C 1.44 THINK CRITICALLY **Read and listen again. For each situation, how could the speakers' expectations have been managed better? In general, what different steps can you take to manage people's expectations?**

2 VOCABULARY: Reporting verbs

A 1.45 **Look at the words and phrases in the box. How many can you find in the podcast? Which ones can you use to complete: (a) Both sentences below? (b) Only sentence 1? (c) Only sentence 2? Which verb doesn't work in either sentence? Listen and check your work. In what situations would you use each of these verbs?**

announce	argue	boast	claim	confirm	deny
estimate	have doubts about	hope to	insist	propose	swear

1 He … that the plan would work.

2 He … the plan.

B **Now go to page 146. Do the vocabulary exercises for 6.2.**

C PAIR WORK **Have you been in a situation similar to the ones described in the podcast in exercise 1B? Tell your partner what happened. Use the words in the box above.**

3 GRAMMAR: Reported speech with modal verbs

A Read the sentences in the grammar box. Complete the rules.

Reported speech with modal verbs

Direct speech	Reported speech
"It **will be** delayed by about 30 minutes."	They **estimated** (that) it **would be** delayed by about 30 minutes.
"There **could be** an even longer wait."	They **announced** (that) there **could be** an even longer wait.
"You **won't have** to wait much longer."	They **said** (that) we **wouldn't have** to wait much longer.
"I **can make** it."	She … **insisted** she **could make** it.
"I **might/may be** late."	I wish she'd **said** (that) she **might be** late.

In reported speech, change *will* to ____________ . Change *can* to ____________ and *may* to ____________ .
Other modals like *might*, *should*, and *could* don't change.

B Now go to page 135. Look at the grammar chart and do the grammar exercise for 6.2.

C 1.46 PAIR WORK **Listen to the messages and announcements and make notes. Take turns reporting them to each other. Then check your accuracy. When was the last time you heard similar messages? Do you remember what they said?**

ACCURACY CHECK

Unlike most other verbs, use an object after *tell* in reported speech.

He ~~told~~ that it wouldn't rain in June. ✗
He told me that it wouldn't rain in June. ✓
He said/swore/insisted that it wouldn't rain in June. ✓

4 SPEAKING

A PAIR WORK **Imagine you've heard some news items and you need to report them to someone who'll be affected by them. How will you deliver the news? Use the situations below and your own ideas.**

- City authority announcement: The new highway won't be ready for another two years because of costs, so your friend who commutes to work could be asked to use the longer route into the city.
- Soccer club newsletter: The star player of your friend's favorite soccer team has been injured, and the management may not be able to find a replacement in time for an important game.
- Real estate agent announcement: The construction of the apartment building where your friend bought an apartment has been delayed, they guess by about three years because the builders have discovered archaeological items on the site.

B PAIR WORK THINK CRITICALLY **Think about the news items from exercise 4A. How can officials in charge manage people's expectations in these situations using strategies you discussed in exercise 1C on page 56?**

6.3 SOMETHING IN THE WATER

LESSON OBJECTIVE

- make assumptions

1 LISTENING

A **Look at the picture. What do you think it is?**

B 1.47 **Listen to a TV reporter interviewing a couple on the beach. What did they see? How did they react?**

C 1.47 **Listen again. What do Brice and Cynthia remember differently?**

D 1.48 **What do you think happened in the end? Listen to the rest of the report and check. Was your prediction correct?**

E 1.49 UNDERSTAND MEANING FROM CONTEXT **Listen to the entire report. What do *fin*, *shaken*, and *narrow escape* mean? What other words helped you figure out the meaning?**

F PAIR WORK THINK CRITICALLY **Compare the reporter's assumptions about what happened with Brice's and Cynthia's stories. Which assumptions were totally correct, partly correct, or incorrect?**

2 PRONUNCIATION: Listening for complex verb phrases

A 1.50 **Listen and complete the sentences. Compare with a partner. Which of the missing words are stressed, and which are not stressed?**

1 You ________ ________ ________ terrified.

2 I ________ ________ pretty fast myself.

3 And if you ________ never ________ an ocean sunfish …

B 1.51 **Underline the verb phrases. Read them aloud. Then listen to how they are pronounced on the recording.**

I've never seen Brice swim so fast.

It must have been like a scene from *Jaws*.

There may have been some screaming.

It would've been cool to tell people we'd had a narrow escape.

C **Circle the correct options to complete the sentence.**

When there is a complex verb phrase, the auxiliary verbs are usually *stressed* / *unstressed* and *contractions* / *full forms* are often used.

3 SPEAKING SKILLS

A **Look at the expressions in the chart. Which ones mean "That's partly true"? Which ones mean "That's not true"? Which two words could be changed to *guess*?**

Making assumptions	Contradicting assumptions	Clarifying assumptions
You/It must have been …	Not at all.	Up to a point.
I suppose …	Not in the least.	To an extent.
I assume …	Absolutely not.	In a way.

B PAIR WORK **Imagine your partner was in the water when the sunfish appeared. You're a reporter. Interview your partner, making assumptions about how they felt. Your partner reacts. Use the expressions in exercise 3A. Take turns.**

4 PRONUNCIATION: Saying short and long vowels

A 1.52 **Listen to the recording. Can you hear the difference between the first and second word? Repeat the words and focus on the underlined vowels.**

/ɪ/ list /i/ least

/ʊ/ full /u/ fool

B 1.53 **Listen and circle the first kind of vowels and underline the second kind of vowels.**

Sue could see a shark in the sea, so the first thing she did, after screaming, was to reach for her new phone to film it. Sue's phone was deep in her beach bag, and by the time she had found it, sadly, the shark had swum farther away.

C **Practice saying the sentences in exercise 4B, paying attention to the short and long vowels.**

5 SPEAKING

A PAIR WORK **Choose a situation in the box or your own idea. Student A starts by saying one sentence about the event. Student B asks questions, making assumptions about how Student A felt. Student A reacts. Then Student B chooses a different event, and Student A asks questions.**

bus broke down	saw an unusual animal	got lost on a hike or in a city	went to an interesting party

A few weeks ago, I went to an underwater wedding.

I **assume** you were wearing a diving suit.

B GROUP WORK **Tell your group what your partner in exercise 5A said about the event. Whose story was the most interesting?**

6.4 GETTING IT WRONG

LESSON OBJECTIVE
- write an interesting story

1 READING

A PAIR WORK **Have you ever made an embarrassing mistake? What happened?**

B **Read the posts. Which one is about the wrong gift? The wrong place? The wrong time? Summarize what went wrong in each story in one sentence.**

INSIDER ENGLISH

***it hit* + object pronoun = just realized something**

*Then **it hit me**.*

*Suddenly, **it hit her**.*

1

Serena B
102 posts

My dumbest mistake was just recently. My best friend's wedding was in Salt Lake City. My husband and I, who live in Los Angeles, decided to make a long weekend of it. I planned it all out very carefully: Drive to Las Vegas on Friday (six hours) and then drive to Salt Lake City (four hours) the next morning. We'd drive the whole ten hours back on Sunday. And the plan worked! We got to Vegas right on schedule, had a great night out, and were on the road by 10:30 the next morning. The wedding wasn't until 4:00, so we took our time and enjoyed the landscape, which is so beautiful. At 3:40 p.m. we pulled into the (very full) parking lot and went inside to get seats. The place was packed, but no one was seated, which was weird. Then, even weirder, we saw the bride and groom standing around chatting with people. I told my husband I hadn't expected to see them until after the ceremony. Then it hit me. Salt Lake City is an hour ahead of Las Vegas. It wasn't 3:45. It was 4:45, and the wedding was over. What a great job I did of planning that weekend!

Like Comment

2

Vicky S
83 posts

My grandmother lived with us when I was a kid, but sometimes she'd go stay with my uncle, who lived about four hours away. They'd all meet at a McDonald's about halfway between them, and grandma would go home with my uncle. The summer I got my license, I decided I'd be grandma's driver. Mom didn't like the idea but finally agreed. She kept repeating the directions and wanted me to write them down, but I reminded her that I could use the GPS. Nothing could possibly go wrong! That was true for about 90 minutes. There was a big detour through a strange town because of road work, but we finally got back on the highway and eventually arrived at McDonald's. When we went inside, there was no sign of my uncle, so we waited. And waited. After a while we called my uncle to check what was taking him so long, and he said he'd been waiting for us for half an hour! Guess what! The GPS had taken us to the wrong McDonald's. Grandma had commented on the different layout, but we just assumed they'd redecorated. All these restaurants and parking lots look so similar. Needless to say, that was the last time I drove grandma anywhere.

Like Comment

3

Ivan P
147 posts

I hadn't been living in Marshall long when I met my new friend Jim and his wife Dana. Since I was new in town, I was really happy when Dana invited me to Jim's birthday party. I thought it would be a good way to meet new people. She said that there would be food and even a band. She insisted that I shouldn't bring anything. But I wanted to make a good impression with a nice gift for Jim. I didn't know him well, but I remembered he said he loved baseball. So I got him a Detroit Tigers T-shirt. I thought he probably wore a large. When I got there, I saw animal decorations and realized the party was for *little Jim*, Dana and Jim's one-year-old son. I suppose little Jim liked his new large T-shirt as much as I liked listening to *The Happy Journey* kids' band all day.

Like Comment

C UNDERSTAND IRONY **How did the people realize they had made a mistake? Which sentences in the posts are ironic (the opposite of what the person means)?**

D **Who do you think got the biggest shock? Why?**

E GROUP WORK THINK CRITICALLY **What do you think the following people said and did in each story: (post 1) the people getting married, (post 2) the uncle, (post 3) Jim and Dana? Why?**

2 WRITING

A **MAKE A STORY INTERESTING One way to make a story interesting is to mix longer and shorter sentences. Look at how sentences of different length are used in the two extracts from the posts in exercise 1B on page 60.**

> I planned it all out very carefully: Drive to Las Vegas on Friday (six hours) and then drive to Salt Lake City (four hours) the next morning. We'd drive the whole ten hours back on Sunday. And the plan worked!

> The place was packed, but no one was seated, which was weird. Then, even weirder, we saw the bride and groom standing around chatting with people. I told my husband I hadn't expected to see them until after the ceremony. Then it hit me.

B **You can also follow these points to make a story interesting. Find an example of each point in the posts in exercise 1B on page 60.**

1 Use a variety of narrative verb tenses in the past.

2 Use different linking and organizing expressions: *and, but, so, then, later, a few years ago*, etc.

3 Use different kinds of sentences: conditionals (*if*), relative clauses (*who, which*), time clauses (*when, after*), *There was/were*, reported and direct speech, etc.

C **PAIR WORK Improve the sentences to make the story more interesting. Use the information in parentheses ( ) and your own ideas.**

My friend rented a red car from Cars-For-U. She called me. She said she would meet me on Thursday at the mall. She said I should find the red car and wait for her. (time clauses, linking expressions, direct speech)

I went to the mall and found a red car with a Cars-For-U sign on it. I stood next to it. I waited for a very long time. Then my friend found me. (variety of verb tenses, time clauses)

She asked what I was doing by that car. She said it was the wrong one. She pointed to another red car. It was closer to the mall. Sometimes I have the best luck! (relative clauses, direct speech)

WRITE IT

D **PLAN You're going to write a story about something unexpected that happened or about someone who made a mistake. Discuss some ideas with a partner. You can use the ideas in the box or your own ideas. The story can be true, or you can make it up. Then think about how you are going to set the scene, what dramatic effects you'll use, and what comments you'll make.**

getting on the wrong bus or train	going to the wrong event	getting caught in bad weather

E **Write your story. Make sure you use a mix of longer and shorter sentences and a variety of narrative tenses, linking expressions, and grammatical constructions described in exercise 2B.**

F **PAIR WORK Exchange stories. What are the most interesting things about your partner's story?**

REGISTER CHECK

In more specific, official contexts, use other reporting verbs, rather than *say* or *tell*.

*The couple **announced** their engagement on Thursday.*

*She **promised** she would meet me in the evening.*

6.5

TIME TO SPEAK
StorySLAM

LESSON OBJECTIVE
- tell a story

A **DISCUSS** Read the rules to a storytelling contest with the theme "The Unexpected." Then look at the pictures. How do they relate to the theme? Discuss with a group.

STORY SLAM
RULES

TELLING A STORY TONIGHT?

- It must be ON THEME.
  The story you've prepared should be related to the theme.
- It should have a strong PLOT.
  How are the characters affected?
  What do they want?
  What happens in the end?
- It must be ON TIME.
  SLAM stories should be five minutes long.

Now think of stories for each of the pictures with your group.

B **PREPARE** You're going to tell a story for the StorySLAM with the theme "The Unexpected." It can be about yourself, someone you know, or someone you've heard about. Share a few ideas with a partner. Help each other choose the best story to develop. You can use one of the ideas from part A or your own idea.

FIND IT

C **RESEARCH** How can you make a story interesting and lively? With your partner from part B, think of ways for the categories below. You can look online for help. You may want to watch some videos of storytellers. Then choose one or two of your ideas and use them to make your story more interesting.

details language tone of voice gestures

D **DECIDE** Tell your story to a group. The group considers these questions and chooses the best story: Did the storyteller follow the rules? Which story was the most interesting? Which storyteller was the liveliest?

E **PRESENT** The winners from part D tell their stories to the class. The class chooses the best story.

To check your progress, go to page 154.

USEFUL PHRASES

DISCUSS
Looking at the picture, I'd say …
It could be a story about …
Maybe what happened was …

RESEARCH
You can catch the listeners' attention by …
I suppose you can …
It's entertaining to …

This website said that …
Another website claimed that …

REVIEW 2 (UNITS 4–6)

1 VOCABULARY

A **Complete the conversation with the correct expressions. There is one expression you won't use.**

acts as	constructive	contributes	draws attention to	keep an eye on
panic	point out	regain control	steer me away from	strengths
think through	turn to	weaknesses		

A Who's the most important person in your life?

B There are so many important people in my life, for example, my parents. They [1] ______________ me and always [2] ______________ making bad decisions. That's important. But then there's my older sister. When I do make a mistake, she's the first to [3] ______________ what I did wrong. It makes me mad, but then she encourages me to [4] ______________ the situation and learn from it. And she gives me [5] ______________ advice.

A That seems rational.

B Yeah. When I have a problem, I tend to [6] ______________. She helps me calm down and [7] ______________.

A It sounds like she [8] ______________ your therapist!

B Yes, I guess she does in a way. Oh, and I can't forget my friend Dave. He [9] ______________ to my overall happiness. He always [10] ______________ my [11] ______________, which makes me feel good. I can always [12] ______________ him to make me feel better.

B PAIR WORK **Who in your life is similar to the people described in exercise 1A? What other people are important in your life? Why?**

2 GRAMMAR

A **Circle the correct options.**

HOME ABOUT NEWS BLOG CONTACT US

Have you ever heard the expression "claim to fame"? It's that thing that makes someone famous or interesting. For truly famous people, it usually involves talent. For example, Shakira's claim to fame isn't [1]*only / even* her voice. People think of her voice *and* her dance moves [2]*unless / whenever* they hear her name. For [3]*others / one another*, it's often something silly or unusual. My brother's claim to fame is doing magic tricks. He would practice in his room [4]*by himself / by herself* for hours as a child before he showed the family. [5]*Providing / Even if* he's in a good mood, he still likes to show off his tricks today. He does this [6]*such / so* often that everyone expects it now. And he does the tricks [7]*only if / even if* he knows we've all seen them before. I think it's annoying, but the two of us always annoy [8]*each other / the others.*

2 7 11

B PAIR WORK **Answer the questions. Give details.**

1 Providing you're in a good mood, what's something you often do?

2 Do you have a claim to fame? Is it something you do by yourself or with others?

3 Is there something you do even if you know people don't like it?

3 VOCABULARY

A **There is one error in each sentence. Find and replace the errors with the words in the box.**

argue	claims	happy	have	headlines	make	passionate	praises

1 I'm more than unwilling to help my friends when they need it because it makes me feel good.
2 I am no desire to try extreme sports. They scare me to death.
3 I'm not interested in celebrities who always want to be in the publicity.
4 I don't enjoy being around people who propose.
5 I don't believe it when an ad denies their product is the best. That's why I read the reviews.
6 I'm reluctant about traveling to other countries. I love experiencing other cultures.
7 One of my dreams is to do an appearance on a TV talk show or game show.
8 When someone boasts me, I feel pleased but also a little embarrassed.

B PAIR WORK **Do you agree with the sentences in exercise 3A? Why or why not?**

4 GRAMMAR

A **Circle the correct options.**

If you want to go on a cheap vacation, you [1]*should try / won't try* a virtual trip. There are many websites that offer virtual vacations you can take from your couch. For some of them, all you need is a computer and some time. One website [2]*denied / boasted* that you [3]*would feel / are feeling* like you were there – without ever leaving the house. Even if it's not as good as a real vacation, a virtual vacation [4]*could make / can't make* you feel relaxed. One VR travel company [5]*hopes to / claims that* you [6]*enjoyed / might enjoy* a VR vacation more than a real trip because you don't have to deal with travel. If you take a lot of virtual trips, you [7]*shouldn't learn / may learn* about amazing places around the world. But some people [8]*told / argue* that a VR trip [9]*would be / wouldn't be* the same as going to a new place.

B PAIR WORK **Would you try a virtual trip? Why or why not? What are the advantages and disadvantages? Discuss the questions with a partner. Then work with another pair and say how your partner answered the questions.**

UNIT OBJECTIVES

- discuss worthwhile experiences
- talk about purchases
- bargain for a purchase
- write a for-and-against essay
- negotiate a boat trip

PRIORITIES

7

START SPEAKING

A Where do you think these children are going? What are the risks? Is it worth it?

B In your opinion, what kind of things are worth taking risks for? Why?

C How do you define "worth"? Who, or what, do you value most in the world? Why? For ideas, watch Odil's video.

EXPERT SPEAKER

Are the types of things that Odil values, and his reasons for valuing them, similar to your ideas?

7.1 WORTHY HELPERS

LESSON OBJECTIVE
- discuss worthwhile experiences

1 LANGUAGE IN CONTEXT

A GROUP WORK THINK CRITICALLY **What do you understand by the term "emergency services"? What type of jobs do they include? What qualities do people need to do these jobs? Why do you think they choose to do them?**

B 2.02 **Read and listen to Sofian and Nathalie talking about their jobs. What do they do? When did they choose their future careers? Does their work make them happy?**

2.02 Audio script

Sofian It's common to dream about driving a fire truck when you're a kid. But I didn't think about being a firefighter until I was 14. I was in a traffic accident, and my foot was broken. It was a horrible situation to be in. But then the firefighters arrived, and suddenly I had people to help me and calm voices to **reassure me**. It was incredible having such an amazing team around me. At that moment, I decided I wanted to **devote my life to** that profession. And today, it's my job. Actually, it's more than just a job. I believe I'm doing something that **is worthwhile** – I'**m a good influence on** others, like those firefighters were on me. It'**s an honor** to be **making a contribution** like that. Plus, driving a fire truck is a seriously cool thing to do!

Nathalie For me, it's important to have contact with people and especially to be helpful. I don't just mean helping medically. I **take pleasure in** that side of the job, but I think I **get more satisfaction out of** the interpersonal side. It can be scary being in the hospital, and some patients have trouble coping. It'**s** really **beneficial** if they have someone to talk to. So for me, it's rewarding to spend time **reassuring patients**. When I decided as a teenager to become a nurse, I guess it was the medical side that interested me. But now I find it's the human side that I **value** the most. That's where I feel I can really **be of use** and **make a difference**.

C 2.02 **Read and listen again. What aspects of their work do Sofian and Nathalie enjoy? What would and wouldn't you like about doing the two jobs?**

2 VOCABULARY: Positive experiences

FIND IT

A 2.03 **Look at the expressions in the box. Can you guess their meaning from the way they are used in the texts in exercise 1B on page 66? Describe each one using other words. Use a dictionary or your phone to help you. Then listen and check your work.**

be a good influence on	be an honor	be beneficial	be of use
be worthwhile	devote my life to	get satisfaction out of	make a contribution
make a difference	reassure sb	take pleasure in	value sth

B **Now go to page 146. Do the vocabulary exercises for 7.1.**

C PAIR WORK **Have you ever been in a situation where you were helped by someone in a caring profession? Describe the situation. How did you feel? For ideas, watch Odil's video.**

EXPERT SPEAKER

Was your experience similar to Odil's?

3 GRAMMAR: Gerunds and infinitives after adjectives, nouns, and pronouns

A **Read the sentences in the grammar box. Complete the rules with words in the box.**

Gerunds and infinitives after adjectives, nouns, and pronouns

It's **common to dream** about driving a fire truck.
I had **people to help** me.
They have **someone to talk to**.

It can be **scary being** in the hospital.
It's rewarding to **spend time reassuring** patients.

gerunds	infinitives	gerunds or infinitives

1 You can use ____________ after adjectives.
2 After nouns or pronouns, use ____________ to show purpose.
3 It's common to use ____________ after expressions like *spend / waste time* and *have (no) fun*.

B **Now go to page 135. Look at the grammar chart and do the grammar exercise for 7.1.**

C **Circle the correct options and complete the sentences with your own ideas. Then compare your sentences with a group. Whose ideas were the most unusual?**

1 It's unusual *to see / seeing* …
2 I often waste time *to do / doing* …
3 … is an interesting subject *to study / studying*.
4 I need someone *to give / giving* me advice about …
5 I usually feel nervous *to wait / waiting* to …

4 SPEAKING

A PAIR WORK **Talk about your job or a job you'd like to have. Explain what satisfaction you (would) get out of it. Compare your thoughts with your partner's.**

> As a hairdresser, I get **a chance to meet** a lot of people. I feel that I can **make a difference** for my customers. **It's not always easy to get** things just right, but when you succeed, it's really rewarding.

7.2 BUYER'S REGRET

LESSON OBJECTIVE

- talk about purchases

1 LANGUAGE IN CONTEXT

A PAIR WORK THINK CRITICALLY **Do you read product reviews when you're deciding to buy an item online? Do they influence your purchase? What other factors influence your purchase?**

B **Read the reviews. What did each person buy, and why? Why were the people dissatisfied? What do you think Dan did next?**

HOME • ABOUT • NEWS • BLOG • CONTACT SIGN IN

Grrrrreviews | The funniest bad reviews on the internet!

Brandon S

★★★★★ **An accident**

My friend **encouraged me** to buy this expensive treadmill. He **convinced me** that it **made financial sense** because it was cheaper than paying gym fees for years. So I decided to get it. After about a month, something went wrong with the speed settings. It suddenly started going too fast, and I flew off the back of it and broke my ankle. You can imagine how much I **regret the purchase**.

Like Comment

Julie R

★★★★★ **What a waste!**

I **purchased** this bed for my cat because it's so cute. My husband said it **was not worth the money** and **urged me** not to buy it. He thought I was **being foolish** because we have a closet full of things for the cat that she doesn't use. I really thought it **had potential**, but the cat sleeps everywhere *near* the bed – even in the box it came in – but never *in* the bed! Does anyone want to buy it? The bed is great – it's my cat that's the problem.

Like Comment

Dan G

★★★★★ **A professional look?**

I bought this small electric shaver and planned to use it for business trips. It seemed like it would **be** very **practical**. I first used it at a hotel a few minutes before an important meeting. I decided to shave off my mustache and beard to look more professional. I got about half way done, and the shaver completely stopped working. I **looked ridiculous**!

Like Comment

C PAIR WORK THINK CRITICALLY **Read again. Which of these reviews would you have found most helpful? Why? In general, which are more helpful: good or bad product reviews? What kind of information do you find most useful?**

2 VOCABULARY: Making purchases

FIND IT

A 2.04 **Look at the expressions in the box. What items are they associated with in the product reviews? Which one is not in the text? What do the expressions mean? Use a dictionary or your phone to help you. Then listen and check the definitions.**

be foolish	be practical	convince sb (to do sth)	encourage sb (to do sth)
have appeal	have potential	look ridiculous	make financial sense
not be worth the money	purchase sth	regret a/the purchase	urge sb (to do sth)

B **Now go to page 147. Do the vocabulary exercises for 7.2.**

C GROUP WORK **Talk about a bad purchase you've made. What was it? Why do you regret buying it?**

3 GRAMMAR: Infinitives after verbs with and without objects

A **Read the sentences in the grammar box. Circle the correct option to answer the question.**

Infinitives after verbs with and without objects

My friend **encouraged me to buy** this expensive treadmill.
My husband … **urged me not to buy** it.
Does anyone **want to buy** it?
I … **planned to use** it for business trips.

When is the subject of the main verb and the subject of the infinitive different?

a With verbs followed directly by an infinitive, without an object

b When there's an object between the main verb and the infinitive

B **Now go to page 135. Look at the grammar chart and do the grammar exercise for 7.2.**

C **Change the sentences below so that they are true for you. Add one more sentence to each statement using the words in parentheses or your own ideas. Use infinitives in each sentence. Check your accuracy. Then share your sentences with a partner. Did you have similar ideas?**

1 My friends often offer to lend me some money. (like)
   My parents often offer to lend me some money, but I don't like to borrow from them.
2 I'd like my brother to help me choose a new phone. (advise)
3 My mother expects me to help her with her shopping. (persuade)
4 My manager agreed not to give me so much work. (promise)
5 I hate ads that encourage you to lose weight. (tell)

✓ ACCURACY CHECK

Remember to use an object or object pronoun after verbs like *encourage*, *persuade*, and *urge*.

The ad ~~encouraged to buy~~ new sunglasses. ✗
The ad encouraged me to buy new sunglasses. ✓

4 SPEAKING

A PAIR WORK **Tell your partner about things you've bought for each of these categories. Why did you buy them? Were they worthwhile purchases? Use verbs + infinitives.**

clothing | furniture | sports gear | technology | transportation

*My friend **persuaded me to buy** a scooter because it **made financial sense** at the time.*

B PAIR WORK **Choose an item you talked about in exercise 4A and write a short review. Exchange your reviews with a partner. Do you want to buy the product? Why or why not?**

7.3 A GOOD BARGAIN

LESSON OBJECTIVE
- bargain for a purchase

1 LISTENING

A **Is bargaining (= trying to get a lower price) common in your culture? What kinds of things do people bargain for?**

B 2.05 **Listen. Sergio is studying abroad for a year and wants to buy a desk at a street market for his room. What price does the seller want at first? What is their final agreement?**

C 2.05 UNDERSTAND PERSUASIVE TECHNIQUES **Listen again. Check (✓) the techniques Sergio and Megan use to get the best deal.**

1 Sergio:
- ☐ points out some problems with the desk
- ☐ is prepared to walk away
- ☐ refuses to buy the desk without the chair
- ☐ pretends he doesn't have a way to get it home

2 Megan:
- ☐ says the desk was never used
- ☐ says she'll give Sergio the chair for free
- ☐ says the desk is not too old
- ☐ says she'll deliver the desk for free

INSIDER ENGLISH

you bet = certainly, I'd be happy to

D GROUP WORK THINK CRITICALLY **Can you add any more techniques to the list above? In your country, what do buyers and sellers do to get the best price when bargaining? Discuss and then describe a bargaining experience you or someone you know had. How successful was it?**

2 PRONUNCIATION: Listening for vowel linking between words

A 2.06 **Listen to how the underlined words link.**

It's <u>only a</u> few years old. Can you <u>go any</u> lower?

B 2.07 **Underline the linked words in the sentences below and write whether there is a sound like /j/ or /w/ between them.**

How much are you asking?
How about $120?
Would you be willing to accept $125?
I'll walk around and see if …

C **Circle the correct option to complete the sentences.**

When a word ends with a /uː/ or /iː/ and the next word begins with a *consonant* / *vowel*, there is usually linking. If the first word ends in /iː/, /eɪ/, /aɪ/, or /ɔɪ/, there is a linking sound like /j/. If the first word ends in /uː/, /oʊ/, or /aʊ/, there is a linking sound like /w/.

3 SPEAKING SKILLS

A 2.05 PAIR WORK **Look at these expressions from the conversation in exercise 1B on page 70. Which ones are used for (a) accepting an offer, (b) bargaining, or (c) rejecting an offer? Write *a*, *b*, or *c* next to each one. Then say which expressions can be used by the buyer, the seller, or both. Where do you think vowel linking occurs in these expressions? Listen to the conversation again to check.**

Negotiate a price

1 So, how much are you asking for … ? ___
2 That's a little on the high side. Can you go any lower? ___
3 I'm sorry, but I can't accept that. ___
4 Would you be willing to accept … ? ___
5 Sorry, but no deal. ___
6 $… is the best I can do. ___
7 Sorry, but I don't think it's worth that much. ___
8 I'll throw … in for free. ___
9 That's my final offer. ___
10 That sounds fair enough. ___
11 I think I can accept that. ___
12 You've got a deal. ___

B PAIR WORK **Choose the role of a buyer or a seller. Role play a conversation using the prompts below and expressions from exercise 3A.**

Buyer You are interested in a product. Ask the price.
Seller Suggest a price and praise the product.
Buyer Say the price is too high and point out a fault.
Seller Reject the offer.
Buyer Offer an alternative price.
Seller Accept the offer.

4 PRONUNCIATION: Saying /ŋ/

A 2.08 **Listen and underline the /ŋ/ sounds.**

1 Is this the computer you're selling?
2 Would you be willing to accept less?
3 My uncle was angry because I went shopping.
4 There's always a danger of paying too much for something.

B 2.09 **Write the word with /ŋ/ next to the definition. Then listen to check your work and repeat the words with /ŋ/.**

1 ____________ – the muscle in your mouth
2 ____________ – fast walking
3 ____________ – it connects your foot and leg
4 ____________ – the opposite of "answering"
5 ____________ – your mother's brother
6 ____________ – the sound babies make when they are uncomfortable or unhappy

C GROUP WORK **Make your own quiz as in exercise 4B, where all the answers are words with /ŋ/. Then groups exchange quizzes and say the words, focusing on the pronunciation of /ŋ/.**

5 SPEAKING

A PAIR WORK **Student A: Go to page 158. Student B: Go to page 160. Follow the instructions.**

7.4 MONEY'S WORTH

LESSON OBJECTIVE

- write a for-and-against essay

1 READING

A PAIR WORK **What kind of things do you enjoy spending money on? Why?**

B IDENTIFY MAIN POINTS **Read the article. What are the main ideas of the sections "The Problem with Possessions" and "The Power of Experiences"?**

Why you should spend your money on experiences, not things

When you work hard every single day and there's only so much money left after your regular expenses, you have to make sure you spend it well. So spend it on what science says will make you happy.

The problem with possessions

A 20-year study by Dr. Thomas Gilovich, a psychology professor at Cornell University, reached a powerful conclusion: Don't spend your money on things. The trouble with things is that the happiness they provide goes away quickly. There are three important reasons for this:

- What seemed unusual and exciting at first quickly becomes normal.
- As soon as we get used to a new possession, we look for an even better one.
- We buy something and are thrilled with it until a friend buys a better one – and there's always someone with a better one.

The power of experiences

Gilovich and other researchers have found that experiences – as short as they may be – bring happiness that lasts longer than things. Here's why:

1 **Experiences become a part of our identity.** We are not our possessions, but we *are* the combination of everything we've seen, the things we've done, and the places we've been. Buying the newest phone isn't going to change who you are, but hiking across a mountain range from start to finish definitely will.

2 **Anticipation is important.** Gilovich also studied anticipation and found that anticipation of an experience causes excitement and enjoyment, while anticipation of getting a possession causes impatience. Experiences are enjoyable from the very first moments of planning all the way through to the memories you appreciate forever.

3 **Experiences don't last (which is a good thing).** Have you ever bought something that wasn't as beneficial as you thought it would be? Once you buy it, it's right there in your face, reminding you of your disappointment. And even if an item does meet your expectations, it's common to regret the purchase: "Sure, it's cool, but it probably wasn't worth the money." We don't do that with experiences. The fact that they last for only a short time is part of what makes them worthwhile, and that value tends to increase as time passes.

Adapted from an article by Travis Bradberry, PhD, on the Talentsmart website.

GLOSSARY

anticipation (*n*) a feeling of excitement about something that is going to happen

C IDENTIFY SUPPORTING DETAILS **Write the number of the section from the article (1–3) for each supporting detail. If the supporting detail is not in the article, write *X*.**

Experiences ...

a help us gain confidence and overcome problems. ___

b aren't compared as often as things. ___

c define and change who we are. ___

d cause more excitement than possessions. ___

e can be more expensive than possessions. ___

f add value to our lives that can last a lifetime. ___

D GROUP WORK THINK CRITICALLY **Think of more ideas <u>in favor of</u> buying experiences instead of things. Then think of ideas <u>against</u> buying experiences. Which do you agree with more?**

2 WRITING

A Read part of an essay on the value of possessions. What two arguments are given? What's the author's opinion?

How Valuable Are Our Possessions?

Recently, there have been a number of articles about the value of experiences in comparison with possessions. The writers have described various ways in which experiences are more beneficial and … . Others, however, disagree and … .

Let us consider some arguments in favor of possessions. To begin with, we can keep our possessions, unlike experiences, which only last a short time. We can share … . Valuable possessions can give us a sense of … For example, … . Another advantage is that possessions can have a sentimental value. For instance, … .

On the other hand, there are a number of arguments that challenge the value of possessions. First, although some possessions contribute to our comfort, many are unnecessary and take up a lot of space. Yet we often find it hard to part with them. A lot of people … . Another disadvantage is possessions make us competitive. For example, … . In addition, … .

Overall, I believe that possessions make a great contribution to our lives. Even though there are problems associated with them, they make our day-to-day life more enjoyable and represent a part of who we are.

B **ORGANIZE AN ESSAY** Read about how to write a for-and-against essay. Match the paragraph types in the box with their descriptions.

Against | Conclusion | For | Introduction

REGISTER CHECK

Let us is often used in formal writing. *Let's* is used in less formal writing or when speaking.

A for-and-against essay is a formal piece of writing in which you write about a topic from opposite points of view. It often has four paragraphs:

1 ________ : Present the topic but don't give your opinion about it.
2 ________ : Give two or three arguments in favor of the topic with examples or reasons.
3 ________ : Give two or three arguments against the topic with examples or reasons.
4 ________ : Give your opinion. Say why you find one side more convincing than the other.

C **PAIR WORK** Which useful expressions below does the author use in the essay in exercise 2A? With a partner think of ideas that could complete the essay.

Useful expressions

Listing: First, To begin with, Second, Finally, One/Another advantage/disadvantage is
Adding: In addition, Furthermore, as well as
Contrasting: On the other hand, However, Nevertheless, Nonetheless, Even though
Giving examples: For example, For instance, such as
Concluding: In conclusion, To sum up, Overall (*followed by* it is my opinion that), I think/believe that

WRITE IT

D **PLAN** You're going to write a for-and-against essay. Choose one of the following subjects:

a How Valuable Are Experiences?
b How Valuable Are Our Possessions?

With a partner, brainstorm some ideas for the essay. Then decide what you'll include in each paragraph from exercise 2B.

E Write your essay. Make sure you use some of the useful expressions from exercise 2C.

F **PAIR WORK** Exchange essays with a partner. Did you choose the same subject? Are your conclusions the same?

7.5

TIME TO SPEAK
Bargain boat trip

LESSON OBJECTIVE
- negotiate a boat trip

A Look at the pictures. Which boat trip would you prefer to go on? Who would you go with? Discuss your reasons with a partner.

B **DISCUSS** You and a group of friends won a boat trip and beach party. The trip and activities are free, but you have to pay for extras. In pairs, look at the information from the boat company. Discuss which activities and which extras you want in order to make the day worthwhile. How much will the extras cost?

C **DECIDE** Your group's budget is $500. Compare it with the cost of the extras from part B. Decide what you need to do to stay within your budget. You can remove or add extras. Also, plan how to bargain with the boat company. Which prices do you think are too expensive or unfair and can be negotiated?

D **PREPARE** Talk with your partner about how you could negotiate a better deal. Explain why you believe your strategy could be successful.

E **AGREE** Work with another pair. One pair is the friends and the other is the boat company. Negotiate a deal. Then change roles and repeat.

F **PRESENT** Tell the class which activities you're going to do and which extras you agreed on. The class chooses the best trip.

To check your progress, go to page 155.

Beach cruise

River cruise

City cruise

PRICE LIST

Cost for a 2-hour boat tour for 25 people + 3-hour beach stop

Beach activities (choose two):
- beach volleyball
- parasailing
- dance party with a DJ
- live concert
- surfing lessons
- snorkeling

Extras (cost for entire group)

+ sodas on the boat	$50
+ cold food on the boat	$100
+ sodas on the beach	$100
+ cold food on the beach	$200
or barbecued food on the beach	$300
+ beach chairs	$100
+ beach umbrellas	$100
+ cancellation insurance (for bad weather)	$50

USEFUL PHRASES

DISCUSS

It looks like … is a really good value …
If I have to choose between … and … ,
I'd rather … than …
Having … would make a real difference.

PREPARE

We could ask them to combine … and …
We should pay for … and see if they'll throw in … for free.
Let's see if they'd be willing to accept $… for …
That might work because …
They can't say no to …

UNIT OBJECTIVES

- talk about neatness and messiness
- talk about side projects
- suggest and show interest in ideas
- write a complaint letter
- make a podcast on ways to reduce stress

SMALL THINGS MATTER

8

START SPEAKING

A What can you tell about the person who works here? What objects were used to make the work area more practical and personalized?

B How do you make your work area more practical? How do you personalize it?

C In what other areas of your life can you use small things to make them more pleasant or personal (e.g., wallpaper on your phone)? How do these items make a difference? How do they make you feel? Tell your partner. For ideas, watch Jacqueline's video.

EXPERT SPEAKER

Are any of Jacqueline's examples similar to yours?

8.1 ANNOYING LITTLE THINGS

LESSON OBJECTIVE
- talk about neatness and messiness

1 LANGUAGE IN CONTEXT

A PAIR WORK **Think about the best thing about growing up in your family home. Tell your partner what your family does that you love and appreciate. What little things do they do that annoy you?**

B 2.10 **In an episode of a TV show called *You Should Talk!*, family members talk about living with each other. Read and listen. What annoying habits do Nicole and Paul have?**

2.10 Audio script

Host So, Nicole and Paul, who's more **disorganized**?

Paul Definitely Nicole. Like, the other night, we were supposed to meet some friends at seven, and Nicole was going to drive us. We were about to leave the house, but she couldn't find her keys – as *usual*. We normally **hang them up** on the wall by the front door.

Nicole Yeah, Paul likes to **line up** all the keys from the biggest to the smallest. He also **puts his books in alphabetical order**, and his desk **is** always **organized** with all his office stuff …

Paul OK, OK, but we're talking about you right now. Her keys were bound to be in the house somewhere, so we were forced to go room by room looking for them. Eventually she found them. They **were tangled up** with some earphones in the pocket of some jeans. Unbelievable!

Nicole You should talk! At least my jeans were in the closet – unlike your shoes!

Host Wait. A minute ago, you were saying how Paul **arranges keys and books neatly**. And now I'm hearing he **leaves his shoes all over the place**?

Nicole Yes! I mean, they**'re** not all **jumbled up**. They're sure to be neatly placed side by side on the floor, but they're everywhere!

Paul At least I don't **throw** my clothes **on** the floor, like some people I know. I **fold them** neatly and **put them in a pile** on the chair by my bed.

Nicole Yeah. Even when he doesn't **put things away**, he does it neatly!

C 2.10 PAIR WORK THINK CRITICALLY **Read and listen again. Who would you find more annoying to live with? Why do you think people get annoyed over small, silly things? What compromises do we need to make when living with other people?**

INSIDER ENGLISH

Say *You should talk* to mean "You are guilty of the same behavior you have just criticized."

2 VOCABULARY: Describing neatness and messiness

A 2.11 **Look at the expressions in bold in the text. Which do we use to talk about things that are neat, messy, or both? Copy the chart and complete it. Then listen and check your work.**

Neat	Messy	Both

B **Now go to page 147. Do the vocabulary exercises for 8.1.**

C PAIR WORK **What expressions from the box can you use to describe yourself? Which ones can you use to describe the person or people you live with? Can you give some example situations to illustrate?**

3 GRAMMAR: Modal-like expressions with *be*

A **Read the sentences in the grammar box. Match the expressions (1–4) to the descriptions (a–d).**

Modal-like expressions with *be*

We **were supposed to** meet some friends at seven.
We **were about to** leave the house, but she couldn't find her keys.
Her keys **were bound to** be in the house somewhere.
We **were forced to** go room by room looking for them.
They**'re sure to** be neatly placed side by side on the floor.

1 be supposed to ___	**a** be made to do something we don't want to
2 be about to ___	**b** be certain to do something or to happen
3 be bound to / be sure to ___	**c** be expected to happen because it was arranged
4 be forced to ___	**d** be going to do something very soon

B **Now go to page 136. Look at the grammar chart and do the grammar exercise for 8.1.**

C **Imagine you have a terrible roommate who is messy and disorganized. Make a list of complaints about him or her using modal-like expressions with *be*, the prompts, and some ideas of your own. Then compare with a partner. Whose roommate is more annoying?**

1 not wiping feet when it rains

He's sure to walk in without wiping his feet, so I'm forced to clean up the muddy floor.

2 putting away clean dishes
3 cleaning up after a party
4 throwing towels on the floor
5 losing keys to the apartment

4 SPEAKING

A PAIR WORK **Imagine the terrible roommate you described in exercise 3C is gone, and you are looking for a new one. With a partner, try to agree on some house rules for your future roommate.**

OK, first, pay your rent on time. Second, **hang up** your clothes. Don't **leave them all over the place**.

Yeah, and don't just **throw the dishes in** the sink. Wash them right away, or they**'re bound** to smell bad.

8.2 SIDE PROJECTS

LESSON OBJECTIVE

- talk about side projects

1 LANGUAGE IN CONTEXT

A **Look at the title of Max's blog. What do you think it means? Then read the blog. What's (1) a side project, (2) Kyle's side project, (3) Max's side project?**

HOME ABOUT BLOG CONTACT US

Do you have a side project? You know, the thing you do that isn't your real job but you do it because you love it? Side projects are often creative, but they're more than a hobby. My friend Kyle, for example, is a mechanic, and in his free time he repairs old bikes for a kids' charity. It's work, but not work. He does it because he **thoroughly** enjoys it. And that's the great thing about a side project. It *won't* cause you stress but *will* give you a real sense of satisfaction. And unlike a job, you can usually do things **at your own pace** and **on your own time**.

I'm a film studies student, and my side project is making a documentary about college. I'm filming it **little by little**, and eventually I'm going to edit it into an hour-long show. It'll be a surprise for my friends because I'm not showing it to them until it's done. But this side project has another purpose. In a couple of years, I'll be looking for a job, and this video is going to be a useful example of my skills as a filmmaker. If things go **smoothly**, I might start my own video production business one day. So, as I work on my video, I'll also be moving **steadily** toward that goal. But if things don't go **as expected**, at least I'll have a nice souvenir of my college years.

B **Read the blog again. What are the benefits of a side project? How will Max's side project be useful to him?**

C PAIR WORK **What side projects do you or the people you know have? Do you think they will help you to achieve your dreams?**

2 VOCABULARY: Talking about progress

FIND IT

A 2.12 PAIR WORK **Look at the expressions in the box. What do they mean? Use a dictionary, your phone, or the context in the blog to help you. Which were used in the blog post? Which ones have a similar meaning? Then listen to the definitions and check your work.**

as expected	at my own pace	effectively	efficiently
little by little	on my own time	smoothly	steadily
successfully	thoroughly	with difficulty	with ease

B **Now go to page 148. Do the vocabulary exercises for 8.2.**

C PAIR WORK THINK CRITICALLY **Compare main occupations with side projects. What are their pros and cons? What are the differences in (a) how we work on them and (b) how we feel about them?**

3 GRAMMAR: Future forms

A **Read the sentences in the grammar box. Circle the correct options to complete the rules.**

Future forms

It **won't cause** you stress but **will give** you a real sense of satisfaction.
Eventually I'**m going to edit** it.
I'**m not showing** it to them until it's done.
In a couple of years, I'**ll be looking for** a job.
This video **is going to be** a useful example of my skills as a filmmaker.
If things go smoothly, I **might start** my own video production business one day.

1 Use *be going to*, *will*, or ***don't / won't*** for predictions, expectations, or guesses about the future.
2 Use *be going to* or the **present continuous / simple present** for future plans and intentions.
3 Use *will* + *be* + verb + *-ing* for **an action in progress / a finished action** at a time in the future.
4 Use *might*, *may*, or *could* when you're **certain / uncertain** about the future.

B **Now go to page 136. Look at the grammar chart and do the grammar exercise for 8.2.**

C **Write six sentences on plans and predictions about your work, studies, or side projects. Use a different future form from exercise 3A in each sentence. Check your accuracy. Then compare with a partner. Are any of your predictions similar?**

✓ ACCURACY CHECK

Use the future continuous, not the present continuous, for an action in progress in the future.

In a couple of years, ~~I'm~~ looking for a job. ✗
In a couple of years, I'll be looking for a job. ✓

4 SPEAKING

A PAIR WORK **Choose a side project from the list below or your own idea. Think about how it will fit with your short-term and long-term plans, ambitions, or goals. Is it linked to your career in any way? Then tell each other about your side project. Ask questions to find out more. For ideas, watch Jacqueline's video.**

create an app	do a podcast	grow plants
improve your cooking skills	make jewelry or furniture	play in a band
start an English speaking group	write a blog	write a children's book

I'm studying to become a teacher, but my side project is learning to play the guitar. Right now, I'm practicing the basics **little by little**, but in several months, I'**ll be successfully playing** songs. Maybe I **could** even **be** a guitar teacher someday. It'**s going to be** fun!

EXPERT SPEAKER

Is Jacqueline's side project something you'd ever do? Why or why not?

8.3 THE LITTLE TOUCHES

LESSON OBJECTIVE

- suggest and show interest in ideas

A

B

1 LISTENING

A 2.13 PAIR WORK **Look at the pictures. What kind of event do you think the items in picture A would be good for? What can you see in picture B? Are you sure? Then listen to a podcast about event planning and check your answers.**

B 2.13 RECOGNIZE EMPHASIS **Listen again. The speakers emphasize the following words. Does the emphasis for each word (a) show a contrasting idea or (b) mean *very*?**

1 and small ___
2 awesome ___
3 complex ___
4 the birthday girl ___
5 such ___
6 really ___

C 2.13 PAIR WORK THINK CRITICALLY **Listen again. What ideas do the speakers have for "little touches"? Do you like the ideas? What kind of things, do you think, make events special and memorable? What kind of things are not worth the trouble? Why?**

2 PRONUNCIATION: Listening for emphasis

A 2.14 **Listen to the emphasis on the underlined words.**

Plan all types of events – big <u>and</u> small   That's an <u>awesome</u> idea.   Or it can be a <u>complex</u> theme like travel.

B 2.15 **Listen and <u>underline</u> the words that are emphasized.**

1 Well, the birthday girl loved it, but not everyone likes strawberries.
2 That's such a terrific idea.
3 And it really is the little things they remember.

C **Circle the correct options to complete the sentences.**

When we want to show emphasis, we put the main stress on the word we want to emphasize. We usually do this by using a *higher* / *lower* pitch on this word. The main stress *can* / *cannot* include functional words like determiners.

3 SPEAKING SKILLS

A 2.13 **Complete the expressions from the conversation in exercise 1B on page 80. Then decide if they are used to suggest an idea or to show interest in an idea. Write *S* (suggest) or *Sh* (show). Listen to the podcast again to check.**

Suggest and show interest in ideas

1 One/Another ________ you/we can do is … ___	5 I ________ everyone loved / will love that! ___
2 That's ________ a terrific / an awesome idea. ___	6 It never ________ to … ___
3 What a ________ idea! ___	7 That's always ________ considering. ___
4 … always goes ________ well. ___	8 … is a good ________ to approach it. ___

B PAIR WORK **You're planning a small summer party for your classmates. Complete the conversation with your own ideas. Then compare with another pair. Which of their ideas would you like to use?**

A Do you have any ideas for the party?

B Well, I think [1] ________________ is a good way to approach it. Actually, [2] ________________ always goes over well.

A That's [3] ________________ idea. Also, it never hurts to [4] ________________ .

B True, and another thing we can do is [5] ________________ .

A Yeah, that's always worth considering. And how about [6] ________________ ?

4 PRONUNCIATION: Saying words that show a contrast

A 2.16 **Listen to the recording. Can you hear the pitch change on one key word in each sentence? Underline these words.**

1 I bet everyone loved that!
2 Well, most people did.
3 Her birthday's not in March, it's in April.

B 2.17 **Underline the words that show a contrast. Listen and check your work. Then repeat the sentences.**

1 It wasn't her birthday, it was his.
2 I don't have any ideas, but Diego does.
3 Shall we get a present or give her some money?
4 He didn't just like it, he loved it!

C PAIR WORK **One student says a sentence. The other replies with a contrast.**

1 Let's drive to the party.
No, we'll walk.
2 We'll celebrate at home.
3 Tom will be late.
4 Wasn't she wearing the red dress?
5 The party finishes at ten.

5 SPEAKING

FIND IT

A GROUP WORK **You are planning an event together. Choose an idea in the box. Talk about the theme, music, decorations, and food you'll have. Include little touches to make the event special. You can check online for ideas.**

a birthday party for a child	a company dinner
a family reunion	a graduation party

B **Describe your plan to the class. Which is the most entertaining?**

OK, let's plan a company dinner. I think choosing an interesting theme **is a good way to approach it.**

OK, well, a beach theme **always goes over well. One thing we can do is** *give everyone sunglasses to wear.*

8.4 A SMILE GOES A LONG WAY

LESSON OBJECTIVE
- write a complaint letter

1 READING

A Have you ever made a formal complaint? What was the problem? Was your complaint effective?

B IDENTIFY WRITER'S PURPOSE Read the article. What's its purpose? What specific examples of customer problems does the writer mention? Which are valid reasons for complaints?

Do you have a problem with a product, service, or company? It might be time to make a formal complaint. Anna Tims, a writer who focuses on consumer affairs, offers a list of tips for successful complaining. The secret is getting a lot of small things right.

HOW TO COMPLAIN EFFECTIVELY

Most large companies get hundreds of complaints – some silly and some serious. No matter how important your complaint is to you, it will just be added to a pile of complaints that a stressed-out customer service worker needs to read. So to be sure it makes the biggest impact, you must know how to state your complaint effectively. Follow these steps, and you're bound to get your problems solved.

MAKE SURE YOUR COMPLAINT IS VALID
Your concern needs to be realistic. For example, if fees for ending a cell phone service contract early stop you from going to a cheaper cell phone service provider, that's too bad. You should have understood the contract. If, however, you have received poor service, you have the right to end your contract early. Or if you dropped your product and then stepped on it accidentally, it's your fault. But if a product breaks when you set it down gently, it's sure to be faulty.

FIGURE OUT WHAT YOU WANT TO ACHIEVE
Do you want a refund, a replacement, or simply an apology? If you want a refund, you have to act quickly or you might lose your right to one. If you complain by phone, make a note of who you spoke to and when, and follow up the call with a letter restating your complaint and the response you got on the phone. Do the same if you sent the complaint through the company's website, so you have a record of it.

ALWAYS ADDRESS A LETTER TO A SPECIFIC PERSON
It is best to start with the customer service manager. (If you aim too high – for example, the company president – you will be waiting while your letter is passed around until it reaches the right person.) Find out the manager's name and use their full title – Dr., Mr., Mrs., or Ms. A little thing like using someone's name can make a big impression.

INCLUDE YOUR DETAILS
Remember to include your full name, address, and any order or reference numbers near the top of the letter. If a company can't easily find you in their system, they may not respond.

KEEP COPIES
Make copies of all relevant documents – such as receipts, bank statements, order forms, and advertisements – and include them to support your complaint. If you want a new but stained couch replaced, include a photo of the damage.

CHECK YOUR SPELLING
Carelessly written letters suggest you are as sloppy as the company you are complaining about.

BE POLITE AND REASONABLE
Whether you are writing or calling, stay calm. Anger will give companies an excuse to refuse to deal with you.

NAME NAMES
If you mention the unhelpful attitude of, for example, a store manager or customer service representative, try to include their names.

SET A DEADLINE
Give the company a deadline for sending a useful response – 14 days is fair. Make a note of the date so you can increase the pressure if it is missed.

MAKE SURE YOUR COMPLAINT ARRIVES
Send all letters by certified mail or special delivery so the company can't deny receiving them. If you use email, ask the person to confirm once they get it.

Adapted from an article by Anna Tims in The Guardian

GLOSSARY
consumer affairs (*n*) a system related to protecting people who buy products and services
faulty (*adj*) not perfectly made or does not work correctly
sloppy (*adj*) not being careful or making an effort

C Read the article again. Which points apply to (1) both a complaint letter and a phone call and (2) only a complaint letter?

D PAIR WORK THINK CRITICALLY Which three points in the article do you think would be the most effective? Why? Are there any points that won't have an effect? Why not?

2 WRITING

A Read Karen's letter to the customer service manager of Markus Appliances. What's the problem? Why is she not happy with the sales manager's response? What does she want?

Reply · Forward

To: Mr. Edwards
From: Karen Rebecca Mason
Subject: RE: Faulty SUPERWASH Washing Machine, model number RGM205

Dear Mr. Edwards,

I am writing to complain about the above washing machine, which I bought during your Summer Sale on July 15. I purchased it for $175.99 at the Main Street branch of Markus Appliances and include a copy of the receipt as proof of purchase.

After the machine was delivered, I tried to use it, but it wouldn't turn on. I checked the connection, which was fine, but the machine had no power. I immediately returned to the store and explained the problem to the sales manager, Rob Clark. At first, he suggested there was something wrong with the power in my house. When I insisted that the machine was faulty, he said, "Sorry, but you bought it during the half-price sale. We don't accept the return of sale items."

I find this unacceptable. First, the item is obviously faulty. Second, your company advertisement (copy included) states that you accept all returns without question. I believe that includes sale items. Third, I feel Mr. Clark should be friendlier. It's a small thing, but a smile goes a long way.

I would like your company to pick up the washing machine from my house and send me a refund of $175.99. I look forward to hearing from you within the next ten days.

Sincerely,

Karen Rebecca Mason

REGISTER CHECK

In formal written complaints, we often use expressions like *I find, I feel, I believe*, or *I think* to make statements less direct and more polite.

Direct

This is unacceptable.
Mr. Clark should be friendlier.

Less direct

***I find** this unacceptable.*
***I feel** Mr. Clark should be friendlier.*

B PAIR WORK THINK CRITICALLY **Which of the tips in the article in exercise 1A on page 82 did Karen follow?**

C AVOID RUN-ON SENTENCES AND SENTENCE FRAGMENTS **Read about two kinds of sentences to avoid in more formal writing. Look at the examples below. How could the sentences be improved? Then find good versions of each in Karen's letter in exercise 2A.**

Run-on sentences (They go on and on.)

1 I am writing to complain about the above washing machine, which I bought during your Summer Sale on July 15 for $175.99 at the Main Street branch of Markus Appliances and for which I include a copy of the receipt as proof of purchase.

Sentence fragments (Incomplete sentences)

2 Went back to the store. Explained problem to sales manager Rob Clark.
3 Unacceptable. First, obviously faulty.

WRITE IT

D PLAN **You're going to write a complaint letter. Choose an idea in the box or something you experienced yourself. With a partner, describe the problem and how you want the company to solve it. Then look at the letter in exercise 2A. What type of information should each paragraph contain in a complaint letter? How will you start and end the letter?**

a bad restaurant meal	a broken or faulty item or package
poor customer service	an item that's different from the advertisement

E **Write your complaint letter.**

F PAIR WORK **Exchange your letters of complaint. How effective is your partner's letter?**

8.5

TIME TO SPEAK
The key to less stress

LESSON OBJECTIVE

- make a podcast on ways to reduce stress

NOT STRESSED AT ALL **VERY STRESSED**

A **DISCUSS** How stressed are you? Where would you put yourself on the scale above? Would you say most of your stress is caused by one or two big things or a number of small things? In pairs, discuss examples of big and small things that can make you feel stressed. For ideas look at the pictures. Add four ideas of your own.

B Compare your ideas with other pairs. Find out common causes of stress.

C **DECIDE** Which of the causes of stress from part B can be reduced by taking simple actions? What actions can be taken? With your partner from part A, discuss the ideas in the box and your own ideas. Then choose your top three effective and simple actions.

SIMPLE ACTIONS TO REDUCE STRESS:

Delete it.	Don't read it.	Don't reply.
Make "to-do" lists.	Do it right away.	Get up earlier.
Go to bed later.	Say "No!"	Discuss the problem.

D **PREPARE** You're going to present your actions in a short podcast. Plan: (1) the introduction, (2) your actions and the reasons why you think they're simple and effective (give some examples), and (3) the conclusion. You can take notes.

E **PRESENT** Present your podcast to the class. Answer any questions about it.

F **AGREE** The class compares the podcasts and chooses two that have the best ideas and are well presented.

To check your progress, go to page 155.

USEFUL PHRASES

DECIDE

One/Another thing you could do is …
It never hurts to …
… is always worth considering.
… is a good way to approach it.

PREPARE

If you do this, you're bound to / sure to …
You're going to …
You might …
You'll be + verb + *-ing* …

UNIT OBJECTIVES

- talk about how your life might be different
- talk about mistakes
- reassure someone about a problem
- write an article giving tips
- talk about key events in your life

THINGS HAPPEN

9

START SPEAKING

A Look at the picture. What do you think the man expected to be doing that day? What happened instead? How could this situation develop?

B Think of a situation when something very unexpected completely changed your plans. What happened? Was the change for the better or worse?

C Do you believe in chance? Or are the best things that happen to us always planned? Discuss some examples. For ideas, watch Carolina's video.

EXPERT SPEAKER

Have you ever had an experience similar to Carolina's?

9.1 TURNING POINTS

LESSON OBJECTIVE
- talk about how your life might be different

X-ray technician

1 LANGUAGE IN CONTEXT

A **PAIR WORK** **What is fate? Do you believe in it?**

B **Read the online posts. What is each person's opinion about luck?**

Comments   Account   Sign out

Lara_Park *posted 2 days ago*
Do you believe in **fate**? My brother says there's no such thing. But I think everything happens for a reason, and there are no **coincidences**. When you look back on your life, you can see the **path** that has led to your life today. For example, I was studying finance and wanted to go into banking. Then my brother accidentally slammed the car door on my finger – ouch! The doctor sent me for an X-ray, which was SO COOL! I could see my own bones on the screen, and the X-ray tech explained everything and answered all my questions. Totally fascinating! If I could find her, I'd thank her because that was a **life-changing experience**. I dropped finance and enrolled in a radiology course. Now, I say that was fate. I mean, if my brother hadn't broken my finger, I wouldn't be an X-ray technician today. But he says it was just a **lucky break**!
(Ha! That's a good one.)
Like Comment

PracticalGal *posted 2 days ago*
I agree with your brother. People make **deliberate decisions** based on current circumstances, even if that's just a **chance encounter**. If you hadn't met that X-ray tech, you might have learned about radiology some other way. But you weren't unhappy in finance, so even if you were a banker now, you'd still be happy.
Like Comment

Jace_the_Ace *posted 2 days ago*
I think life is a combination of luck and **determination**. Sometimes, like Lara, you**'re in the right place at the right time**, but it takes hard work and skill to turn luck into a real opportunity.
Like Comment

C **Read the posts again. What events led to Lara's job?**

D **GROUP WORK** **THINK CRITICALLY** **Say whose opinion you agree with the most. Then talk about someone who played a part in any of your life-changing experiences.**

2 VOCABULARY: Luck and choice

A 2.18 **Which expressions in the box are about luck, choice, or either luck or choice? Fill in the chart. Then listen and check your work. Which of the expressions are nouns or noun phrases? Which are verb phrases? Which three were not used in the posts in exercise 1A?**

be fortunate	be in the right place at the right time	chance encounter
coincidence	deliberate decision	determination
fate	life-changing experience	lucky break
(not) believe my luck	path	wind up

About luck	About choice	About luck and choice

B **Now go to page 148. Do the vocabulary exercises for 9.1.**

C **Describe a time when you had good luck. What happened? What choices did you make in that situation?**

3 GRAMMAR: Unreal conditionals

A **Read the sentences in the grammar box. Which rules are about the *if* clause? Which are about the result clause?**

Unreal conditionals

If I **could find** her, I'**d thank** her. (I'd = I would)
If you **hadn't met** that X-ray tech, you **might have learned** about radiology some other way.
If my brother **hadn't broken** my finger, I **wouldn't be** an X-ray technician today.

1 Present and future unreal conditionals:
Use the past continuous, simple past, or *could* in the __________ clause.
Use *would*, *could*, or *might* + base form in the __________ clause.

2 Past unreal conditionals:
Use the past perfect in the __________ clause.
Use *would*, *could*, *may*, or *might* with *have* + past participle in the __________ clause.

3 Past unreal conditionals can also have an imaginary present result:
Use *would* + base form of a verb in the __________ clause.

B **Now go to page 137. Look at the grammar chart and do the grammar exercise for 9.1.**

C **Complete the sentences and check your accuracy. Then share your ideas with a partner. Ask questions to find out more.**

1 If I had more time, I ______________________ .
2 If I could work anywhere, I ______________________ .
3 I ______________________ if I didn't ______________________ .
4 If I hadn't ______________________ , I wouldn't ______________________ .
5 If I hadn't ______________________ , I might have ______________________ .
6 I couldn't have ______________________ if I hadn't ______________________ .

ACCURACY CHECK

In past unreal conditionals, the auxiliary *have* goes in the result clause only, not in the *if* clause.

If I hadn't ~~have~~ met the doctor, I might not have become an X-ray technician. ✗
If I hadn't met the doctor, I might not have become an X-ray technician. ✓

4 SPEAKING

A GROUP WORK **Think about how your life might be different now in the following situations.**

you were born in another country	you had gone to another school
you hadn't met someone you know	you could learn without studying
you didn't have your present job	you had fewer/more siblings

If I **hadn't convinced** my boss to enter the design competition, we **wouldn't have won** first prize – this amazing project that I am now leading. I'm also really **fortunate** that I have such great coworkers. I **might not enjoy** my job so much if I **weren't working** with such fantastic people.

9.2 WHY DID I DO IT?

LESSON OBJECTIVE
- talk about mistakes

1 LANGUAGE IN CONTEXT

A 2.19 **Look at the picture. What do you think the man regrets? What other kinds of small things do people often regret? Read and listen to a group of friends talking about small regrets. How many regrets do they talk about?**

2.19 Audio script

Anne	I was just wondering what kind of things you regret doing. Not big things, like, "I wish I wasn't studying psychology. I wish I could study art instead!" Just little, silly things.
Ruby	Oh, I have a good one! Someone once told me that it's better to wash your hair with regular soap, rather than shampoo. So I tried that …
Sonia	Uh-oh, that **was a bad move**.
Ruby	I know! If only you'd been there to stop me. I couldn't get the flakes out of my hair whatever I did. And of course I had an interview to go to that day. It **was such a silly mistake**.
Sonia	That **was unfortunate**. Well, I **found myself in an awkward situation** the other day: I was on a date – a first date – and I was trying so hard to be interesting that I was talking and talking and **not watching what I was doing**. I went to take a bite of my spaghetti and spilled it all down my white top. Ordering spaghetti with tomato sauce **was such a dumb thing to do**!
David	Well, sometimes you have to **learn things the hard way**. I recently washed my new sweater in hot water, and now it's way too small. It **was completely my own fault**: The label said to use cold. **I was in too much of a hurry**, as usual. If only I had a three-year-old brother, it would fit him perfectly!
Paulo	I once ripped my pants on a dance floor!
Anne	Awkward!
Paulo	Yeah, I was on the floor, doing a breakdance move, when *rip*! But I **saw the funny side of it**. And so did everyone else!
Anne	I bet they did!
Paulo	I'**m totally incompetent at** dancing. I don't even have a sense of rhythm. I don't know what I was thinking. I could have **kicked myself**.
Anne	Well, you could have, but you might have ripped your pants even more.

B 2.19 **Read and listen again. What were the friends' regrets? Who do you think made the biggest mistake?**

C PAIR WORK THINK CRITICALLY **Discuss the best way to deal with small regrets: laugh, forget them, try again, etc.**

INSIDER ENGLISH

Use *I bet* to express agreement and show interest in what someone says.

A I was really scared.

*B **I bet**! OR I bet you were!*

A She's so happy.

*B **I bet**! OR **I bet** she is!*

2 VOCABULARY: Commenting on mistakes

FIND IT

A 2.20 **Look at the expressions from the text in exercise 1A on page 88 in the box. Discuss what each one means. Use a dictionary or your phone to help you. Then listen and check your work.**

be a bad move	be a dumb thing to do	be a silly mistake
be incompetent (at)	be in too much of a hurry	be unfortunate
be your own fault	find yourself in an awkward situation	kick yourself
learn sth the hard way	not watch what you're doing	see the funny side of sth

B **Now go to page 149. Do the vocabulary exercises for 9.2.**

C PAIR WORK **Describe and comment on mistakes people often make involving these things.**

cleaning | clothes | computers/phones | cooking | reservations/tickets | work

3 GRAMMAR: Wishes and regrets

A **Read the sentences in the grammar box. Circle the correct options to complete the rules.**

Wishes and regrets

I wish (that) I wasn't studying psychology.

If only you**'d been** there to stop me!

I wish I could study art instead.

If only I had a three-year-old brother.

1 *I wish* (*that*) and *if only* have **a different / the same** meaning.

2 For wishes and regrets about the present, use *I wish* (*that*) or *if only* followed by the simple past, ***can*** / ***could***, or the past continuous.

3 For wishes and regrets about the past, use *I wish* (*that*) or *if only* followed by a verb in the **present perfect / past perfect**.

B **Now go to page 137. Look at the grammar chart and do the grammar exercise for 9.2.**

C **Use *if only* to describe regrets about the problems below. Then tell a partner about similar experiences of your own using *I wish* (*that*).**

1 I broke it.
If only I hadn't broken it. I wish I hadn't broken my favorite mug last week.

2 I can't find it.

3 I forgot to do it.

4 I have to go there.

5 I don't have time to do it.

6 I didn't answer it.

4 SPEAKING

A PAIR WORK **Are there any little things you've done, or haven't done, in the last few days that you regret (e.g., when shopping for clothes or groceries, decorating your home, going on vacation)? For ideas, watch Carolina's video.**

Some things you **learn the hard way**. The other day I bought lots of groceries, but what I hadn't noticed was that the bag had a hole in it. **If only I'd checked** it more carefully ...

EXPERT SPEAKER

Are your regrets similar to Carolina's?

9.3 MY MISTAKE

LESSON OBJECTIVE

- reassure someone about a problem

1 LISTENING

A 2.21 **Look at the picture. What do you think the woman just did? Then listen to a call-in radio show, where she asks for advice. What did she do? How many people call in to give her advice?**

B 2.21 **Listen again. What are the main pieces of advice the callers give to Sandy?**

C 2.21 IDENTIFY FEELINGS **Listen again. Circle the word that best describes each person's feeling.**

1 **Host**	a neutral	b confused	c annoyed
2 **Marta**	a sad	b bored	c amused
3 **Jon**	a angry	b annoyed	c surprised
4 **Ramon**	a bored	b sad	c positive
5 **Amanda**	a amused	b calm	c annoyed

D PAIR WORK **What advice would you give to Sandy, and why? How have you handled an awkward situation in the past?**

2 PRONUNCIATION: Listening for different word groups

A 2.22 **Listen to how this is divided into word groups.**

Think before you write something // think again before you send it // and check who it's going to // before pushing "Send."

B 2.23 **Listen and separate the word groups with //.**

1 Last week I wrote a personal email to a friend a very personal email but by accident I sent it to a senior manager at my company.

2 It happened to me too but with a friend not a coworker I just pretended my brother had gotten into my email and sent it as a joke.

3 That's digital communication we write and send stuff quickly and then we can't "unsend" it so we have to live with our mistakes.

C **Which statement is true about word groups?**

1 A word group has two main stresses, and there is no pause before the next word group.

2 A word group has one main stress, and it is often separated by a small pause from the next word group.

3 SPEAKING SKILLS

A 2.21 **Match the sentence halves to make expressions of reassurance from the radio show in exercise 1A on page 90. Listen to the radio show again to check.**

Give reassurance

1	You're not the only one ___	a	it goes.
2	We all make ___	b	that bad.
3	That's the way ___	c	turn out all right.
4	What are you ___	d	who's done that.
5	It's no use ___	e	is perfect.
6	It's not ___	f	mistakes.
7	It could have ___	g	worrying about?
8	It'll ___	h	been worse.
9	No one ___	i	crying over spilled milk.

B PAIR WORK THINK CRITICALLY **Which expressions in exercise 3A are not appropriate for more formal relationships? Why? Are there any expressions in your own language like the ones in exercise 3A?**

C **Student A: Go to page 158. Student B: Go to page 160. Follow the instructions.**

4 PRONUNCIATION: Using intonation in conditional sentences

A 2.24 **Circle the intonation pattern in this conditional sentence.**

If you'd sent the email, it could have been worse.

a If you'd sent the email ↗ // it could have been worse ↘
b If you'd sent the email ↘ // it could have been worse ↘
c If you'd sent the email ↘ // it could have been worse ↗

B 2.25 **Underline the word group that has a falling intonation in the conditional sentences below. Listen and check, and repeat the sentences. Then finish the sentences in a different way and read them out to a partner, focusing on the intonation.**

1	If she'd listened to me	this would never have happened // we'd be in a better situation now
2	If I had thought about it more	I might have said no // I may have agreed
3	If you hadn't helped me	no one would have // I would've failed
4	If they'd told me yesterday	things might be better // I could have gotten ready

5 SPEAKING

A PAIR WORK **Think of a problem someone might have. Imagine you're going to talk to that person. Plan what you'll say to reassure them. Then plan how to act out your conversation.**

B GROUP WORK **Act out your situation for another pair. Afterward, say if you agree with the advice given. Were the expressions of reassurance appropriate?**

I need your advice. I borrowed a suit from my friend for a party, but I lost the jacket somewhere. I don't know what to say to him – or what to do. It was an expensive suit.

What are you worrying about? We all make mistakes. Just tell him the truth, give the pants back, and offer to help him buy a new jacket.

9.4 GOOD CONVERSATIONS

LESSON OBJECTIVE
- write an article giving tips

1 READING

A PAIR WORK MAKE PREDICTIONS **Read the title of the article. Why do you think the writer calls it a "happiness experiment"? Then read the article. Was your prediction correct? Was he happy at the end?**

HOW TO MAKE SMALL TALK WITH STRANGERS: MY 21-DAY HAPPINESS EXPERIMENT

By John Corcoran

Recently I read that people who talk to strangers are happier than those who keep quiet. I decided to test that theory with an experiment. The rules were simple: For 21 days, I would look for opportunities to talk to strangers. Here are some experiences I had.

FRIDAY, MAY 9

While visiting my hometown for a wedding, I had a chance encounter with a man in the hotel café. We started talking, and I found he had just moved there from Chicago. I told him about the community, the schools, and neighborhoods where he was thinking of buying a home.

How I Felt: The conversation made me feel useful and valuable. The man's daughter was about to enter my old high school, and he seemed relieved to hear it was a good school.

MONDAY, MAY 12

While driving home, I stopped for lunch. A man was wearing a T-shirt that said "Coastal Maine Botanical Gardens." I considered commenting on it, as we have vacationed in coastal Maine, but I didn't say anything.

How I Felt: I regret that I didn't speak up. I am curious if the gardens are close to our summer vacation spot. Sure, I can Google it, but I would have liked to chat with him about the area.

TUESDAY, MAY 20

Three men were at our house to cut our trees. I watched as they climbed the trees like monkeys and went straight to the top. I asked one of them if they fall out of trees frequently. He said, "Almost never." One said, "I've been climbing trees for 27 years," and said he fell out of a tree once and broke his knee.

How I Felt: It's not every day I talk to someone whose job is climbing trees, and it was interesting learning about how they do it.

THURSDAY, MAY 29

Today, I had to take the ferry to my office. I decided to try talking with other commuters and sat at a table. Although I exchanged a few comments, I had no meaningful conversations. At one point, I chatted with a woman, but eventually the conversation died, and she returned to reading her book.

How I Felt: I wish I'd had more conversations, but digital devices often got in the way. The important lesson I learned is to begin a conversation before people put on headphones or start reading.

FRIDAY, MAY 30

I went to a neighborhood party with my wife and our baby. The baby was a great conversation starter.

How I Felt: It's almost too easy to start talking with people when you have a baby because strangers come up and chat. I enjoyed the opportunity to meet more people.

Overall, I felt great about most of my interactions with strangers. Almost every one left me feeling a little happier. However, I will report a few disappointments: I am pretty outgoing, but I often missed an opportunity to talk because I was unsure of what to say. Second, sometimes I wanted to chat, but nearly everyone was on a digital device. I felt like speaking to them would have been interrupting. Third, I would love to report that I made new lifelong friends and found new clients. Unfortunately, that didn't happen.

MY FINAL ADVICE Just go out and try talking with strangers. It is likely that you will improve your own day and make the person you talk to happier as well.

Adapted from an article by John Corcoran on the Art of Manliness website

B **Read again. Which experiences was the writer happy about? What regrets does he have? Would you try the same experiment? Why or why not?**

C IDENTIFY IMPLICATIONS **Match the main things the writer learned from the experiences he had (1–5) with the correct dates (a–e).**

1 Talk about things you have in common. ___
2 Start conversations right away. ___
3 Share useful information. ___
4 Have something with you that attracts attention. ___
5 Talk to people who are different from you. ___

a Thursday, May 29
b Friday, May 30
c Friday, May 9
d Monday, May 12
e Tuesday, May 20

D PAIR WORK THINK CRITICALLY **What is "small talk"? What are good topics for "small talk" with strangers? Are there any topics it's best to avoid? Why?**

2 WRITING

A **Read the article about small talk. Summarize the tips it gives. Can you think of more tips on how to be a good listener?**

SMALL TALK: HOW TO BE A GOOD LISTENER

DON'T INTERRUPT

When someone else is talking, don't interrupt them. It's sometimes OK to ask a question in the middle of someone's point, for example, if you don't understand what they mean. But in general, it's best to let someone finish their point before making a comment or asking a question.

SHOW INTEREST

While you're listening to someone else, don't think about what you'll say next. Instead, show interest in their points by asking questions about the topic they're talking about. Don't change the topic or start talking about yourself.

LISTEN WITH YOUR EYES

Watch a speaker's body language, such as eye contact, hand gestures, and posture. Do they seem excited, angry, or worried? This can help you understand their feelings. Then you can ask questions, make a comment, or give advice in an appropriate way.

THINK BEFORE YOU RESPOND

Think about what you're going to say before you speak. Sometimes your opinion is helpful. Other times, it's best just to tell someone you understand or reassure them instead of telling them what you think.

REGISTER CHECK

Describe the situation using *when* or *while* before the imperative to soften the advice you give. Compare:

Strong, direct

Don't interrupt when someone else is talking.

Softer, less direct

When someone else is talking, don't interrupt them.

B PARALLEL STRUCTURES **When listing items, try to use parallel structures. This means the items have the same grammatical pattern. Look at the sentences. Why are the underlined parts not parallel? Correct them with words from the article in exercise 2A.**

1 **Adjectives:** Do they seem excited, angry, or <u>are worried</u>?

2 **Noun phrases:** Watch a speaker's body language, such as eye movement, hand gestures, and <u>how they stand.</u>

3 **Verb phrases:** Then you can ask questions, make a comment, or <u>you should give advice</u> in an appropriate way.

WRITE IT

FIND IT

C PLAN **Think of tips for an article entitled "Small Talk: How to Be a Good Talker." Discuss the categories in the box. You can check online for more ideas. Then think about the title and structure of your article. Which tips will you include? What headings will you use for each tip? What advice/explanations will you include under each heading?**

audience (who is listening)	body language (eye contact, hand gestures, posture)
content (topic)	delivery (how you speak: attitude, volume)
language (words you use)	

D **Write the article you planned. Remember to use parallel structures in lists.**

E PAIR WORK THINK CRITICALLY **Exchange your articles. What's the best tip in your partner's article?**

9.5 TIME TO SPEAK
Class reunion

LESSON OBJECTIVE
- talk about key events in your life

Gaby Arnold
School of Management
BS Finance

Mark Bevilaqua
School of Nursing
BS Nursing

Mia Asner
Arts & Sciences
BA Sociology

Rodney Dacosta
Arts & Sciences
BS Mathematics

A Would you like to go to a class reunion at a school you went to years ago? How would you feel about meeting people you haven't seen for a long time? What would you talk about? Discuss with a partner.

B **PREPARE** Imagine you're going to a class reunion. Work alone to plan what you're going to talk about. Use the topics in the box. Think of important and interesting things you've done or experienced since you were a child.

education	free time	homes	regrets
relationships	sports	travel	work

C **DISCUSS** Share your news and memories with at least three people in the class and listen to what they say. As you listen, make positive comments about good things you hear and reassuring comments about not-so-good things. Encourage people to tell you more about surprising things they did.

D **PRESENT** Tell the class about the most interesting or surprising thing you heard from someone. Each time, the class asks that person to say more about it.

E **DECIDE** The class chooses the most interesting things people did or experienced.

To check your progress, go to page 155.

USEFUL PHRASES

DISCUSS

You were really fortunate!
It sounds like you were in the right place at the right time.
You're not the only one who …
That's the way it goes.
Was it luck or a deliberate decision?

PRESENT

You'll never guess what …
Not only that, but …
Apparently, …
Isn't that amazing?
Are you ready for this?

REVIEW 3 (UNITS 7–9)

1 VOCABULARY

A **Complete the product review with the correct forms of the expressions in the box.**

arrange	bad move	be jumbled up	be organized
be practical	be worth the money	convince	learn the hard way
purchase	regret	throw in	urge

HOME ABOUT NEWS BLOG CONTACT US

I needed to [1] ________________ a new backpack before I started college. I didn't want something with just a single space inside it because I don't think bags like that [2] ________________ when you have a lot of different things to carry. You [3] ________________ your stuff and close the zipper, and then when you open it, everything [4] ________________ inside, and it takes ages to find things. I hate that. I like my stuff to [5] ________________. So when I saw this model, it looked perfect. The many different pockets inside immediately [6] ________________ me that it was ideal. I figured I could [7] ________________ my stuff neatly in them. So I bought the backpack and did just that. Unfortunately, it was a [8] ________________ because it turned out there's no way to close the pockets. So the first day I used my new backpack, I [9] ________________ that stuff falls out of the pockets and ends up in the bottom of the bag. I paid extra for the bag with pockets, expecting it to [10] ________________. It wasn't. Needless to say, I now [11] ________________ the purchase. I [12] ________________ you not to buy this backpack.

5 12 3

B PAIR WORK **Tell a partner about something you bought that you were disappointed with. Use some of the phrases from exercise 1A to describe your experience.**

2 GRAMMAR

A **Use the correct forms of the verbs (*to* + verb or verb + *-ing*) in parentheses ( ) to complete the sentences.**

1 I think it's a fascinating subject ________ (read) about.
2 A lot of people don't think it's possible ________ (do) that, but I do.
3 I was dying to have something ________ (eat).
4 It's so easy to waste a lot of time ________ (do) that.
5 Because of the problem, I was forced ________ (start) the whole thing again.
6 I knew I was bound ________ (have) problems with it.
7 That's where I planned ________ (go), but in the end, it wasn't possible.
8 I get bored quickly ________ (play) that game.
9 I have trouble ________ (understand) that subject.
10 If you ask me, it's sure ________ (happen) soon.

B PAIR WORK **Think of examples of your own opinions and experiences that match the sentences in exercise 2A. Tell a partner about them.**

3 VOCABULARY

A **Complete the sentences with the words in the box.**

break	difference	ease	encounter	expected
lesson	life	life-changing	pleasure	time

1 To be successful, you need a lucky ___________ .
2 Generally speaking, if you take ___________ in doing something, you'll do it well.
3 Mistakes are the best way to learn because they always teach you a(n) ___________ you won't forget.
4 It's often the small things, not the big things, that make a(n) ___________ .
5 If you want to learn a new skill, you should do it on your own ___________ .
6 You can expect to change careers at some point – not to devote your ___________ to one occupation.
7 Planning things in detail isn't very helpful, since things hardly ever go as ___________ .
8 If someone is doing something with ___________ , it usually means they're good at it.
9 Learning to speak a second language is a(n) ___________ experience for several reasons.
10 The best way to meet your future husband or wife is through a chance ___________ .

B PAIR WORK **Say whether you agree, partly agree, or disagree with the sentences in exercise 3A. Say why and give examples to help explain your views.**

4 GRAMMAR

A **Circle the correct options.**

1 One day, I'm *learning / going to learn* to ride a motorcycle.
2 I'm sure next week *might be / will be* fairly relaxing.
3 According to my schedule, *I'm having / I'd have* my next English lesson tomorrow.
4 Tonight, I *might / would* do some work at home or maybe just get some rest.
5 This time next year, *I'll study / I'll be studying* in college.
6 If I *moved / would move* to Europe, I would live in Spain.
7 If I *could / would* have a free plane ticket to anywhere in the world, I'd go to South Korea.
8 Out of all foreign languages, I wish I *can / could* speak Korean.

B PAIR WORK **Say which sentences from exercise 4A are true for you, or change them so they are true for you.**

10 PEOPLE, PROFILES

UNIT OBJECTIVES

- talk about people's characteristics
- talk about customer research
- give your impressions
- write a professional profile
- develop a plan to improve a company website

START SPEAKING

A **When you look at the picture, what do you think of the person? Would it be a good choice for a profile picture? What kind of profile would it be appropriate for?**

B **Talk about a profile picture you have for social media, work/college, or on an ID card. What impression does it give about the kind of person you are? Is it a true impression?**

C **What kind of things do people change about their appearance when they want to make a specific impression in these situations: an extended family gathering, going on a date, a job interview, making new friends? For ideas, watch Lucia's video.**

EXPERT SPEAKER

Do you agree with Lucia? Can you think of more examples?

10.1 ARE WE UNIQUE?

LESSON OBJECTIVE
- talk about people's characteristics

1 LANGUAGE IN CONTEXT

A **PAIR WORK** **Look at the picture. How do you think the people are connected?**

B **Read the article. How did the author try to find her doppelgänger? Would you want to meet your doppelgänger?**

Doppelgängers are people who look alike but aren't related to each other.

Home About Blog Contact Us

Maxine Frith

Can you find your doppelgänger in a day?

by Maxine Frith

Doppelgänger means "double walker," that is, someone walking around this planet that looks just like you. It is said that we are each likely to have at least seven **look-alikes** somewhere in the world. I wondered about the possibility of discovering a few of mine.

I posted a message and picture on Facebook, Twitter, and Instagram, but it didn't result in finding anyone with my **likeness**. Next, I used the "I Look Like You" website, which uses facial recognition software to compare your image with millions of others. The site matched me with a **female** named Kathryn Laskaris. She wasn't a perfect **match**, but we have a similar **look**.

Next, I tried some doppelgänger-matching apps. I was matched with a 20-something **male** and a baby. Finally, I uploaded my photo into a Google Images search and then clicked to search for something "visually similar." Within seconds, my doppelgänger appeared: Michal Ben-Josef Hirsch. I stared at her, noticing our **similarities** – she has the same **features** as me, the same hair, and the same smile. She's also smart and successful – everything I could hope for in a twin stranger.

I was really interested in learning more. Psychologist Amima Memon explains, "It may seem bizarre that people become obsessed with finding strangers who look exactly like them, but … research shows that … we like people who look like us … ."

I haven't succeeded in learning more about Michal. I suppose I'll just have to be happy with me.

Adapted from an article by Maxine Frith in The Telegraph

C **Read the article again. What matches did the author get? How were they similar to her?**

D **GROUP WORK** **THINK CRITICALLY** **How would you feel about your doppelgänger contacting you?**

2 VOCABULARY: Describing characteristics

FIND IT

A 2.26 **What do the nouns in the box mean? Use a dictionary or your phone to help you. Then listen and check. Can you remember which eight were used in the text? Which three words can also be adjectives?**

build	characteristic	feature	female	gender	individual
likeness	look	look-alike	male	match	similarity

B **Now go to page 149. Do the vocabulary exercises for 10.1.**

C **PAIR WORK** **Describe yourself and some of your typical characteristics using the words in exercise 2A.**

3 GRAMMAR: Gerunds after prepositions

A Read the sentences in the grammar box. Circle the correct options to complete the rules.

Gerunds after prepositions

I wondered about **the possibility of discovering** a few of mine.
I **was** really **interested in learning** more.
I haven't **succeeded in learning** more about Michal.

1 You can use a gerund (verb + *-ing*) **before** / **after** some phrases with a noun + *of.*
2 You can use the verb ***be*** / ***have*** + an adjective + a preposition + a gerund.
3 You can use a gerund as **an object** / **a subject** after a verb + preposition.

B **Now go to page 138. Look at the grammar chart and do the grammar exercise for 10.1.**

C PAIR WORK **What are different ways of meeting new people? Make questions with a gerund and your own ideas. Use the prompts below to help you. Check your accuracy. Then ask another pair the questions.**

1 places for / ways of meeting new people
Have you ever thought of meeting people online?
2 things you would most care about / be interested in
3 things you could plan on doing
4 things you might be concerned about / risks

✓ ACCURACY CHECK

Be sure to use the correct form after a verb + preposition.

It didn't result in ~~find~~ anyone with my likeness. ✗
It didn't result in ~~to find~~ anyone with my likeness. ✗
It didn't result in finding anyone with my likeness. ✓

4 SPEAKING

A GROUP WORK **Do you like to be similar to your friends or different? Discuss using the topics below and your own ideas. Do most people in your group like to be similar or different?**

clothes	education	experiences	goals	hairstyle
hobbies/interests	humor	music	personality	

I often wear trendy clothes. I like the ***idea of looking*** *like my favorite celebrities.*

I ***wouldn't dream of dressing*** *like other people. I like to be an* ***individual*** *and have my own* ***look****.*

10.2 YOU, THE CUSTOMER

LESSON OBJECTIVE
- talk about customer research

1 LANGUAGE IN CONTEXT

A 2.27 **What kinds of information do you think companies collect about their customers, and why? Discuss with a partner. Then read and listen to a radio interview with Lina, a marketing executive. Were your ideas correct?**

2.27 Audio script

Host We all know that companies collect a lot of information about us as customers. Why do they do it?

Lina Well, basically it allows them to **identify** your needs and understand what kinds of things you might want to buy.

Host So, what kind of information do they collect?

Lina Well, it can be things like gender, family situation, age, profession, um … financial situation, interests. It could also include likes, goals, … fears. This is the kind of information companies can get from social media, **surveys**, and from past purchases you made.

Host OK. And how is this information used?

Lina Well, let's say a store is **analyzing** a list of customers' purchases for a month. This list lets the store **calculate** how much the customer spent. And the store can also **examine** the types of purchases to see what they reveal. So let's say this person spent $280 on lipstick, expensive sunglasses, baby clothes, two different products to prevent insects from biting, a video game, two tablet cases, and three books: about leadership, negotiating, and Italian cooking. Now, what does an **analysis** of that information **demonstrate**? It allows the store to figure out a lot about this person and helps the store *guess* other things. And that **assessment** enables the store to predict how much this person might spend per month and what other products they might want to buy.

B 2.27 **Read and listen again. How do companies get information about their customers? Why is it useful?**

C PAIR WORK **How do you feel about companies collecting different kinds of information about you? For ideas, watch Lucia's video.**

EXPERT SPEAKER

Do you agree with Lucia? How, do you think, does Lucia's job inform her answer?

2 VOCABULARY: Describing research

FIND IT

A 2.28 PAIR WORK **Look at the words in the box. Discuss their meanings. Use a dictionary or your phone to help you. Which are verbs? Nouns? Then listen and check the parts of speech. Were verbs or nouns used out of each pair in the interview in exercise 1A?**

analyze/analysis	assess/assessment	calculate/calculation	demonstrate/demonstration
examine/examination	identify/identification	survey/survey	

B **Now go to page 150. Do the vocabulary exercises for 10.2.**

C PAIR WORK THINK CRITICALLY **Look again at the customer's purchases in exercise 1A. What can you figure out, or guess, about this person? Think about: family situation, age, profession, financial situation, interests, likes, goals, and fears. Then compare your ideas with others in the class.**

*We can **identify** the person's interests. They bought lipstick and expensive sunglasses so that **demonstrates** that they care about their appearance.*

3 GRAMMAR: Causative verbs

A **Read the sentences in the grammar box. Complete the rules with the options in the box. There is one option you do not need to use. Which verbs do we use to talk about things we do not want to happen?**

Causative verbs

It **allows them to identify** your needs.
… two different products to **prevent insects from biting** …

base form of the verb	gerund	infinitive

1 After *allow, cause, enable*: Use an object + ________ .
2 After *keep, prevent, protect, stop*: Use an object + *from* + ________ .

! **We use *let, make,* and *have* + base form of the verb when something or someone causes something to happen.**
This list ***lets*** *the store calculate how much the customer spent.*

B **Now go to page 138. Look at the grammar chart and do the grammar exercise for 10.2.**

C **Complete the sentences about shopping habits with your own ideas. Then compare with a partner. Ask questions to find out more.**

1 Shopping for new things makes me ________ .
2 Having a mall nearby helps me ________ .
3 Credit cards allow me ________ .
4 Nothing can stop me ________ .
5 Online shopping enables me ________ .
6 Having a budget prevents me ________ .

4 SPEAKING

A **A new department store is opening near you. Write down some customer information about yourself. Explain what you want and need there. Use these headings:**

1 Description (of me) 2 What I want/need to buy 3 What facilities I want/need to use

List three to five things under each heading.

B PAIR WORK **Analyze your partner's profile. Then give your assessment of products and services that would be of interest to your partner. Say why.**

10.3 A CAREFUL CHOICE

LESSON OBJECTIVE

- give your impressions

1 LISTENING

A PAIR WORK Imagine you need to order a cake for a party. What kind of things would you need to consider to make a good choice?

B 2.29 Listen to two friends deciding which company to order a cake from. Why do they want a cake? How many companies do they consider? How do they feel at the end?

C 2.29 LISTEN FOR CONTRASTING IDEAS Listen again. List the strong points and weak points of each cake company and its products. Then predict which cake company you think they'll choose. Which one would you choose?

D 2.30 Listen to the rest of the conversation. Which cake company did they choose, and why?

E PAIR WORK THINK CRITICALLY How can you tell if a company and its products are good when you're shopping online? For example, what can web design, photos, reviews, and the range of products for sale reveal?

2 PRONUNCIATION: Quoting from a text

A 2.31 Listen to the speaker reading aloud from the cake website. Which parts are direct quotations? Add quotation marks " " around these parts. How are these pronounced differently?

The company profile says cakes for all occasions, designs for all themes and budgets, and skilled, professional cake decorating. That all sounds good.

It also says free personal advice – that's nice.

B 2.32 Look at the quoted section in the extract below. How would this be pronounced differently? Listen and check.

Madrona Cakes … "freshly baked, a variety of flavors, reasonable prices." And they also make cakes low in sugar, cakes with no egg, and dairy-free cakes.

C PAIR WORK Look back at the article on page 98. Choose a short extract to quote to your partner, like in exercises A and B above. Prepare your whole sentence (including the direct quotation from the article). Then say it to your partner. Can your partner identify which words came directly from the text?

3 SPEAKING SKILLS

FIND IT

A PAIR WORK **Look at the expressions from the conversation in exercises 1B and 1C on page 102. Discuss the meaning of the underlined words. Use a dictionary or your phone to help you.**

Give your impressions

1 I have a funny feeling (that) …
2 I get the impression (that) …
3 From what I can see, …
4 I have a hunch (that) …
5 Judging by the description, …
6 My gut feeling is (that) …
7 What strikes me (about …) is (that) …
8 As far as I can tell, …

B PAIR WORK **Imagine you are in the following situations. Give your impressions.**

1 You are standing in front of a new restaurant. You can see inside, and you can see the menu on the window. One of you thinks it looks good (clean, comfortable, good food). The other does not (crowded, noisy, not enough food choices).

Hmm, from what I can see, this restaurant looks …

INSIDER ENGLISH

lose track of time = forget when something is due or supposed to happen, often because of being busy with other things

2 You have to turn in a research and writing assignment on ancient pyramids. You lost track of time, and it's due tomorrow. One of you thinks you can finish in time (easy to find information, can divide the work, can stay up late). The other does not (takes time to research, no time to work together, have other homework).

About our essay, I have a funny feeling that I won't be able to … because …

4 PRONUNCIATION: Recognizing /eɪ/, /aɪ/, /ɔɪ/

A 2.33 **Underline the /eɪ/, /aɪ/, and /ɔɪ/ sounds. Listen and check your work. Then repeat.**

1 What strikes me about this place is the choice of cakes.
2 I have a funny feeling that I may enjoy it.
3 Try one of our nice and tasty pies – you won't be disappointed!

B 2.34 **Circle the word that has a different diphthong.**

1	straight	climb	fail
2	voice	joy	ache
3	weight	cycle	height
4	break	crayon	finally
5	design	choice	voyage

C PAIR WORK **Write down six of the words from exercise 4B. Take turns reading aloud one of the words from exercise 4B, saying the diphthong carefully. If you hear the word on your list from your partner, cross it out. The first student to cross out six words is the winner.**

5 SPEAKING

A PAIR WORK **You want to join a gym. Look at the online profiles of three gyms on page 158. Discuss the gyms, giving your impressions of each. Decide which one you'd each like to join and why. Then check with another pair and see if they had similar impressions and chose the same ones.**

*Well, **judging by** the description, gym 3 is modern and pretty large.*

*I agree, and **as far as I can tell**, it has good facilities. For example, …*

10.4 A PROFESSIONAL PROFILE

LESSON OBJECTIVE
- write a professional profile

1 READING

A **Is it a good idea to have a profile on a social networking site for professionals? Why or why not? Read the article. Why does the author have a profile? Why does she decide she needs to improve it?**

I recently graduated from college and am looking for a job. I joined a social network for professionals and wrote a fantastic profile for my page. I was sure that the first employer who read it would want to hire me.

KINSLEY GORDON *last updated six months ago*

Contact me at 646-555-4302 or by email.

I am an individual with a unique personality, and I work very well with others. I recently graduated from New York University from the Gallatin School of Individualized Study. I put together my own program combining several areas of study. I hope to work for an English–Japanese bilingual company in the marketing department. In college, I had an internship at VTL-Wire, a large tech company. I also wrote poetry for a community magazine. Right now, I'm doing part-time freelance work, but I want to work full-time. Please contact me to find out how my skills could best work for your company.

No employers were responding, so I started reading articles about how to write a good profile. Mack Gelber, in his article called "8 Ways to Make Your Social Media Profile an Employer Magnet," had some really good advice. Here are some of his main points:

1 Have a complete and relevant profile

Make sure your profile contains your complete employment history and education, as well as any skills related to your job. Try to think through the eyes of an employer – no one wants to see a half-written profile.

2 Highlight skills and achievements that help employers

In your career history, be careful about the information you include. We don't need to know about how you organized the office softball team. Instead, try talking about specific goals you've met, and support your information with numbers. For example: "Sold $X while cutting costs by Y%."

3 Update your profile frequently

It's important to stay active on all social media sites. Start a new job? Post an update. Get a promotion? Update your title.

4 Keep your connections career-focused

Getting requests to connect from old roommates and people you don't remember from high school is only to be expected on social media, but you want to make sure the majority of the people you're connected to have similar career goals. This gives employers the impression that you're serious about your career.

5 Provide a clear link to your email address

Say an employer sees your profile and wants to get in touch with you about a potential job opportunity. Can they find your email address in a few seconds? Make sure it's linked somewhere that's clear and easy to see.

6 Have a professional-looking headshot

A good headshot is key to having a strong profile. That's not to say you need to wear formal office clothing (business casual is fine), but it pays to look engaged and put together.

Adapted from an article by Mack Gelber on the Monster website

B TAKE NOTES **Read again. Take notes about each of the six points. Summarize each one with a phrase or two. Then share your notes with a partner. Were your ideas the same?**

C THINK CRITICALLY **According to Gelber's points, what problems does Kinsley's profile have? What do you think she could do to improve it?**

2 WRITING

A **THINK CRITICALLY Read Kinsley's new profile. What improvements did she make from her profile in exercise 1A on page 104?**

KINSLEY GORDON

last updated yesterday

Marketing and more

I'm a recent graduate of New York University from the Gallatin School of Individualized Study who is dedicated to doing my best. I work very well on my own and with others. In order to focus on a marketing career, my field of study combined business, Japanese, and creative writing. I hope to work for an English–Japanese bilingual company in the marketing department. In college, I had an internship at VTL-Wire, a large tech company. My responsibilities included making online product demonstrations in English and Japanese, analyzing the comments people made on the demonstrations, and reporting people's impressions of the products to the company. I'm tech-savvy and learn new programs quickly. Although I'm currently doing part-time freelance work helping people design their websites, my ultimate goal is to work for a company full-time. I realize the benefits of starting small, especially at a company where there's the possibility of career progression. Please contact me to find out how my skills could best work for your company.

646-555-4302 • www.kinsleysays.com • kgordon@mailme.net • CONNECTIONS 225

REGISTER CHECK

Contractions are not normally used in formal writing. However, it's OK to use contractions on social media, like professional job sites.

Résumé, cover letter, etc.
I am *tech-savvy and learn new programs quickly.*

Social media site/profile
I'm *tech-savvy and learn new programs quickly.*

GLOSSARY

progression (*n*) when someone goes up to the next level or stage

B **USE PROFESSIONAL LANGUAGE Read about three things to avoid when using professional language. Look at the examples, and then find good versions of each in Kinsley's profile in exercise 2A.**

1. Don't use slang (= very informal language).
   not: I'm uber-excited to work for a company 24/7.
2. Avoid words like *kind of*, *probably*, and *maybe*. Use language that makes you sound confident.
   not: I'm kind of tech-savvy and probably can learn new programs pretty fast.
3. Don't be negative. Be positive and polite.
   not: I'm not sure I have the experience you're looking for, but contact me to see if my skills might work for your company.

WRITE IT

C **PLAN You're going to create a professional profile on a social networking site. Tell your partner about the education, skills, and characteristics you have that make you a good candidate for future jobs. Then look at the profile in exercise 2A. What kind of information do you need to include at the beginning and end? How long should your profile be?**

D **Write your professional profile. Be sure to use professional language.**

E **PAIR WORK Exchange profiles. Does your partner use professional language? Can you suggest any improvements?**

10.5 TIME TO SPEAK
Attracting talent

LESSON OBJECTIVE
- develop a plan to improve a company website

Tech company

Hospital

Restaurant

Engineering company

A **PREPARE** In pairs, imagine you are experts who give advice to companies on how to make the career section of their website as attractive as possible to first-time employees. Choose a type of company from the pictures above or use your own idea.

B **DISCUSS** In pairs, brainstorm answers to this question: What do most first-time employees think about when choosing a company to work for? For example:

career progression	kinds of jobs available	products the company makes
training opportunities	workplace environment	

C Compare your ideas with other pairs. Which areas do people think are most important?

D **DECIDE** In your original pairs, consider all the ideas you have. Decide which three areas are the most important to first-time employees of the company you chose in part A. Then decide how to present these areas on the company website in order to attract these employees. Use some of these options and your own ideas: photos, videos, interviews, reviews.

E **PRESENT** Tell the class what type of company you chose, present your ideas, and explain why first-time employees will like them.

F **AGREE** After the presentations, decide as a class which ideas will be most attractive to first-time employees. Then discuss which company you would like to work for.

To check your progress, go to page 156.

USEFUL PHRASES

DISCUSS

I get the impression that …
Judging by the people I know, …
Judging by what I've heard, …
As far as I can tell, …
My assessment is (that) …

PRESENT

This will allow first-time employees to …
This will help them …
This will enable them to …

UNIT OBJECTIVES

- talk about fake goods
- talk about untrue information
- express belief and disbelief
- write a persuasive essay
- share tips on solutions

REALLY?

11

START SPEAKING

A Do you think this picture is real or fake? Why do you think so?

B Can you think of some examples of fake photos you've seen? How easy or difficult is it to see that the photos are fakes?

C When and why do some people choose to edit their photos? List the reasons. What kind of changes might they make to their photos? How do you feel about this? Answer the questions. For ideas, watch Bojan's video.

EXPERT SPEAKER

Do you agree with Bojan's opinion? Can you think of any other examples?

11.1 FAKE!

LESSON OBJECTIVE
- talk about fake goods

1 LANGUAGE IN CONTEXT

A **Look at the picture of fake goods being destroyed. Do you think it's a waste? Read the newspaper article. What fake goods does the journalist mention?**

THE HIGH PRICE OF CHEAP FAKES

By Emilia Flores

*Watches, purses, sneakers, jeans – **fake** consumer goods have become so common that the problems they cause are being forgotten.*

Hundreds of **counterfeit** soccer jerseys were recently discovered by the U.S. government while they were being shipped to Texas ahead of the World Cup. **Illegal** copies of clothes like these are often **imperfect** and even dangerous since they're not always made of safe materials, such as **fireproof** fabrics. Buying other kinds of counterfeit goods can be risky, too. Fake cosmetics often contain banned chemicals. Counterfeit electrical goods are often **second-rate** and can cause fires. And nobody is going to be helped by fake medicine; in fact, it can be **deadly**.

But not all fakes are so **inferior**. It's possible to buy copies of expensive watches, purses, and other top-quality products that look almost **genuine**. And when **sophisticated** counterfeits are offered cheaply, many people are willing to buy them, even though they know the items aren't **authentic** or **legal**. When the **original** products are being sold for over $1,000, it's easy to say that cheap copies are fair, since many of us couldn't afford to buy the real thing. But when we make this excuse, we forget that somebody's creative ideas have been stolen. We also fail to consider that the workers who produce fakes are normally paid very little and are often forced to work in dangerous conditions.

Unless we open our eyes to these realities, it's unlikely that counterfeiting will be stopped.

B **Read the article again. According to the journalist, what problems do fake goods cause?**

C PAIR WORK THINK CRITICALLY **Which do you think is the most serious of these problems? Why? To what extent do you agree with the journalist's opinion?**

2 VOCABULARY: Describing consumer goods

FIND IT

A 2.35 PAIR WORK **Look at the words from the article in exercise 1A in the box. Discuss their meaning. Use a dictionary or your phone to help you. Then listen and check your work.**

authentic	counterfeit	deadly	fake	fireproof
genuine	illegal	imperfect	inferior	legal
original	second-rate	sophisticated		

B **Now go to page 150. Do the vocabulary exercises for 11.1.**

C PAIR WORK **Have you ever seen or bought fake goods? What were they like? How can customers tell the difference between counterfeit and authentic goods?**

3 GRAMMAR: Passive forms

A **Read the sentences in the grammar box. Circle the correct options to complete the rules. Then add the correct passive form (a–f) to complete the rules (3–8).**

> **Passive forms**
>
> Counterfeit soccer jerseys **were** recently **discovered** by the U.S. government while they **were being shipped** to Texas.
>
> They**'re** not always **made** of safe materials.
>
> Nobody **is going to be helped** by fake medicine.
>
> It's unlikely that counterfeiting **will be stopped**.
>
> The original products **are being sold** for over $1,000.
>
> We forget that somebody's creative ideas **have been stolen**.

We use passive forms when we don't know, or it's not important, who [1]**did** / **received** the action. The person or thing [2]**doing** / **receiving** the action is more important, so it becomes the subject of the sentence.

a	simple past	**3**	The ___ passive: *am/is/are* + past participle.
b	past continuous	**4**	The ___ passive: *was/were* + past participle.
c	simple present	**5**	The ___ passive: *has/have been* + past participle.
d	future	**6**	The ___ passive: *will* + *be* + past participle or *am/is/are going to* + *be* + past participle.
e	present continuous	**7**	The ___ passive: *am/is/are* + *being* + past participle.
f	present perfect	**8**	The ___ passive: *was/were* + *being* + past participle.

B **Now go to page 138. Look at the grammar chart and do the grammar exercise for 11.1.**

C PAIR WORK **Make sentences about counterfeit goods using these words, passive forms, and your own ideas. Check your accuracy. Then compare with another pair.**

1 Fake sunglasses / sell / in my city

______

2 In the future, / fake products / sell

______

3 Not long ago, / buy / by teenagers

______

4 Discover / by the police / recently

______

> ✓ **ACCURACY CHECK**
>
> **Don't forget to use the auxiliary *be* in continuous tenses: correct form of *be* + *being* + past participle.**
>
> *Counterfeit soccer jerseys were discovered while they ~~were shipping~~ to Texas.* ✗
>
> *Counterfeit soccer jerseys were discovered while they were being shipped to Texas.* ✓

4 SPEAKING

A GROUP WORK **Where are counterfeit goods usually sold? Why do people buy them? Discuss using the ideas below. Then compare your answers with the class.**

Fake goods: accessories, clothes, cosmetics, electronic goods, shoes, etc.

Illegal copies: books, computer games, DVDs/Blu-rays, music, software, etc.

> Fake brand-name watches **have been sold** in our city's markets for years. These days, they**'re** sometimes **found** in stores, too. They're usually second-rate, but people buy them because ...

11.2 INTERNET TALES

LESSON OBJECTIVE
- talk about untrue information

1 VOCABULARY: Degrees of truth

FIND IT

A 2.36 PAIR WORK **Look at the words in the box. Describe them in other words. Use a dictionary or your phone to help you. Which are adjectives? Nouns or noun phrases? Then listen and check the parts of speech.**

accurate	biased	controversial	dishonest	exaggerated
false	hoax	inaccurate	misinformation	misleading
rumor	suspicious	trustworthy	urban legend	white lie

B **Now go to page 151. Do the vocabulary exercises for 11.2.**

2 LANGUAGE IN CONTEXT

A 2.37 **Read and listen to a radio show about five possibly fake stories. What are they about? Then answer the host's last question with a partner.**

2.37 Audio script

Host Today's topic is **rumors**, **urban legends**, and other fake stuff on the internet. When I was ten, I told my parents the moon landing was filmed in a TV studio. They said that was a lie, but I replied, "No, it's true. I read it on the internet!" I didn't expect to be laughed at, but I was. I learned, as we all do, that you can't always trust the web. So, I asked my listeners for internet stories that might be **false**. Listen to a few. Here's Raúl from Doral, Florida.

Raúl I read that hundreds of deadly snakes escaped from a truck that crashed in our town. But I never heard anything more, so I guess the information was **exaggerated** or **inaccurate**. This kind of **misinformation** has to be stopped because in the end, all news becomes **suspicious**.

Host Nina from Denver, Colorado, said this.

Nina Recently I saw a photo of a purple watermelon on Snapchat. It was probably a **hoax**. People say **misleading** photos shouldn't be posted, but they usually don't do any harm.

Host Let's listen to Gabe from Portland, Oregon.

Gabe I read online that there are more trees on Earth than stars in the galaxy. That can't be **accurate**! All online articles need to be checked. But where do you check? Online?

Host And Britt called in, all the way from Windsor in Canada.

Britt A video of a human-looking robot walking down a street went viral. A few people thought robots were taking over the world! If you look closely, the video seems to be made on a computer. I don't think it's from a **trustworthy** site.

Host So, are these stories true or not? I'll tell you after the break.

GLOSSARY
the galaxy (*n*) a very large group of stars that contains our sun and the planets that go around it

B 2.37 **Read and listen again. Which speakers explain why they think the information is false? What are their reasons?**

C 2.38 **Listen to the end of the program. Were the stories true or not?**

D GROUP WORK THINK CRITICALLY **Do you think the internet spreads more truth or lies? Why? For ideas, watch Bojan's video. Can you think of some recent examples?**

EXPERT SPEAKER

Do you agree with Bojan? What do you think of his solution?

3 GRAMMAR: Passives with modals and modal-like expressions; passive infinitives

A **Read the sentences in the grammar box. Complete the rules about the passive with *be* or *to be*.**

Passives with modals and modal-like expressions
Misleading photos **shouldn't be posted**.
This kind of misinformation **has to be stopped**.
All online articles **need to be checked**.

Passive infinitives
I **didn't expect to be laughed at**.
The video **seems to be made** on a computer.

1 After modals, like *should* and *could*, use ________ + a past participle.
2 After modal-like expressions, like *have to*, *need to*, and *had better*, use ________ + a past participle.
3 After verbs like *expect*, *seem*, and *want*, use ________ + a past participle.

! In the passive, the main verb is always in its past participle form, never the base form. So, for passives after modals and modal-like expressions, use *be* + past participle, not the base form. *Something* ***has to be done*** *to stop fake stories from spreading.*

B **Now go to page 139. Look at the grammar chart and do the grammar exercise for 11.2.**

C **Complete the sentences with the correct passive form of the verbs in parentheses ( ) and your own ideas. Then compare with a partner. Do you agree with your partner's ideas?**

1 If we … , we are ________ (not be likely / believe) by anyone.
2 I think controversial issues ________ (shouldn't / discuss) during …
3 Friends ________ (must / inform) when our social media photos are …
4 I ________ (hope / tell) the truth when I …
5 We ________ (could / trick) by reading … , so be careful.
6 I only ________ (want / tell) white lies if …

4 SPEAKING

FIND IT

A PAIR WORK **What stories have you heard or read online that weren't true? You can look online for stories if you want. Did people believe them? Why? Did you believe them at first?**

I read that alligators live in the sewers in New York City. I think people believed the story because it gave a lot of ***accurate*** *information about alligators. But the article had a lot of grammar mistakes and* ***seemed to be written*** *by a teenager, so I thought it was a* ***hoax*** *right away.*

B GROUP WORK **Share two of your stories with another pair. Do you think stories like this need to be stopped? Why or why not?**

Urban legends*, like alligators in the sewers,* ***shouldn't be spread*** *because they make people panic.*

11.3 BELIEVE IT OR NOT ...

LESSON OBJECTIVE

- express belief and disbelief

1 LISTENING

A **Do you often look at the night sky? What kind of things do you think of? What questions would you ask someone who's been in space?**

B 2.39 **Listen to Damon and his friends talking about the NASA Parker Solar Probe. How many of them definitely believe the probe is going to the sun?**

C 2.39 UNDERSTAND IMPORTANT DETAILS **Listen again. What arguments do the friends make for and against the story?**

D 2.40 **Listen to part of a news program about the Parker Solar Probe. What's the significance of these numbers?**

a 6 million **b** several million **c** 1,400

E THINK CRITICALLY **Who is more believable, Damon or Rose? Why? How can you normally tell if someone is telling the truth?**

2 PRONUNCIATION: Listening for intonation on exclamations and imperatives

A 2.41 **Listen to the high falling intonation on exclamations and imperatives.**

Yeah, right, Damon! ↘ Tell me another one! ↘

B 2.42 **Listen and mark the high falling intonation.**

1 The connection's worse than in outer space!
2 They're going to land at night!
3 I'm telling you, it's true!
4 Wow! That's hot!
5 That's still hot!

C **Circle the correct option to complete the sentence.**

There is a *high*/*low* / *fall*/*rise* intonation on exclamations and imperatives.

3 SPEAKING SKILLS

A **Match the correct headings from the box to each column. Write headings in the correct places. Would high falling intonation occur in any of these expressions? If so, where?**

Belief   Disbelief   Some belief

________	________	________
Yeah, right! Tell me another one. I find that hard to believe. There's no truth in it/that.	Maybe there's some truth in it. It's/That's partly true.	… , believe it or not. I'm absolutely positive (that) …

B PAIR WORK **Take turns saying these rumors and expressing belief or disbelief about them.**

1 By 2025, we'll be able to text just by thinking.
2 It won't be long before people will be settled on the moon.
3 In the next 20 years, there will be no ice in the Arctic.
4 Dinosaurs have been created in a lab somewhere, using DNA from fossils.
5 The number of people who own cars will soon decline, and car-sharing will be used instead.
6 Young people will increasingly work online from home, so they'll be able to live anywhere.

4 PRONUNCIATION: Saying /oʊ/ and /aʊ/

A 2.43 **Listen to the difference between the /oʊ/ and /aʊ/ sounds.**

/oʊ/	/aʊ/	/oʊ/	/aʊ/
no	now	tone	town
coach	couch	load	loud
known	noun		

B 2.44 **Choose a suitable word with either an /oʊ/ or /aʊ/ sound to put in the conversation. Then listen to check your work.**

A I don't believe a p__________ could g__________ s__________ far into space. H__________ a__________ you?

B It'd be difficult, but it's possible, th__________. Maybe not n__________ but in ten years or s__________.

A Come on, there's z__________ chance! I d__________ k__________ much a__________ science, but that's impossible.

B There's n__________ reason why not. When it happens, I'll say, "I t__________ you s__________!"

C PAIR WORK **Read the conversation aloud, focusing on the /oʊ/ and /aʊ/ sounds.**

5 SPEAKING

A PAIR WORK **Create a role play of two people discussing a rumor, real or imaginary, about one of the topics in the box. Express belief or disbelief about the rumor. Practice your role play and then act it out for another pair. They express belief or disbelief about the rumor, as well.**

college/workplace   food/health   places in your city or country
politics   sports/entertainment

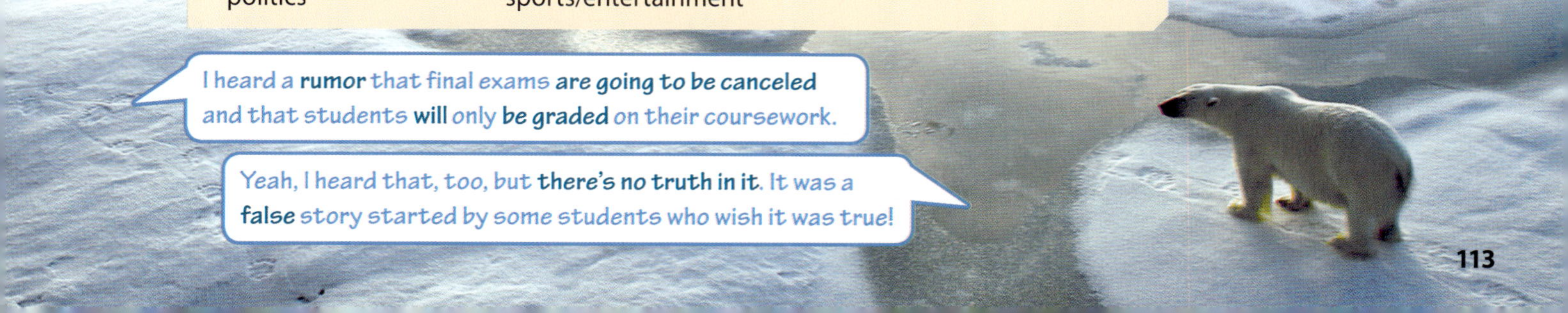

I heard a **rumor** that final exams **are going to be canceled** and that students **will** only **be graded** on their coursework.

Yeah, I heard that, too, but **there's no truth in it**. It was a **false** story started by some students who wish it was true!

11.4 CONVINCE ME

LESSON OBJECTIVE

- write a persuasive essay

1 READING

A **SUMMARIZE KEY POINTS** **Have you ever trusted a review that turned out to be fake? Read the article. Why do companies want to stop fake reviews? What can we do to figure out if reviews are fake? Summarize each of the nine tips.**

SPOT 'EM –

Fake product reviews

by Ken Evoy

Companies depend on hundreds of thousands of consumer reviews that point you to "the best of whatever." They work hard to minimize fake reviews because it's good business to prevent customer disappointment due to inaccurate information. There are honest reviews, of course, but you still need to check reviews yourself, whether you're buying a book, a hotel room, or a Ferrari. Here are some tips to help you.

1 Fight technology with technology

A good way to assess whether a review is computer-generated is to use a computer program. *Fakespot* is an online tool that helps you figure out which reviews are trustworthy and which are not. Simply paste a review's URL into Fakespot's search engine to get results. It may not always be totally accurate, but it's a good place to start.

2 Check the reviewer's profile

Most sites ask users to register before leaving a review. Click on the username to see past reviews. Most "real" people buy a wide range of products from large companies, so they'll have a wide range of reviews.

3 Compensation

Is this review paid? Did the reviewer receive the product in return for a review? If so, it's not necessarily fake – but it may be biased.

4 Review quality

Reviews that rely on individuals being paid small amounts of money to write as many as possible will be short and nonspecific. The goal is to put the item into the five-star category quickly by posting as many "excellent" reviews as possible. So the author needs to be able to copy and paste a large number in a short time. Look for phrases like "great product" or "wonderful service."

5 Lack of detail

Researchers found that some reviewers of hotel rooms did not talk about the specifics of the hotel at all. They couldn't – they had never been there. So they'd write instead about the *reason* they were there. "Spent a wonderful weekend here with the family" and "will always use this hotel for future business trips" are the kinds of things that show a hotel review might be fake.

6 Lack of experience

Similarly, if the reviewer has never had a product, the explanation of what's good and bad about it will be limited. If a review sounds more like a product manual than a real-life experience, it probably is.

7 Use of language

Some dishonest companies will provide templates for their "reviewers" to make it easier for quick copying and pasting. If you see the same or similar words and phrases in different reviews, be suspicious. Reviews with words like "best thing ever" and "worst thing ever" without any explanation are likely to be created from a template.

8 When haters start to love

A common form of fake review is for the reviewer to insist that they hated a product but were given one as a gift and they suddenly discovered it's the best thing since sliced bread. Also look for a lot of question marks and exclamation points. "Why didn't I buy this sooner??? I love it!!!!!!"

9 All or nothing

Fake reviews tend to be either one star or five stars. Make sure you check reviews at two, three, and four stars, too – real reviews tend to be more moderate.

B GROUP WORK **THINK CRITICALLY** **Why do you think people write fake reviews? Which tips from the article have you used or might you try in the future to identify fake reviews? Can you think of more tips for identifying them?**

INSIDER ENGLISH

Say *the best* or *greatest thing since sliced bread* to describe extremely useful and important things.

2 WRITING

A Read part of an essay. What's the author's position? What research and example are given?

Are product reviews useful or not?

Although many people don't trust product reviews, **I strongly believe that** they are useful. You can't trust advertisements to … However, you can trust honest reviewers to … It's very easy to read reviews before you buy to help you …

Reviews are valuable because they give you a genuine picture of … **Research shows that** 84 percent of people trust online reviewers as much as they trust their friends. This is because … **One time I** wanted to a buy a toaster, so I read several reviews on the product. I found out … This was helpful because … Mistakes can be avoided if you read reviews first.

While it's true that many reviews aren't authentic, it's easy to figure out whether they're fake or not. You can … You can also … Reviews must not be ignored because … If you read a large number of reviews for a product, it helps you … The benefits are more numerous than the problems.

In conclusion, **I feel that** reviews help us make better decisions. They give us a true idea … Many are … , and it's not difficult to … Read reviews to avoid bad purchases.

REGISTER CHECK

We often start a persuasive essay with a strong opening sentence. An effective way to do this is to give the opposite opinion first, using *Although* or *While*, and then state your own opinion.

Although *many people don't trust product reviews, I strongly believe that they are useful.*

B **USE PERSUASIVE LANGUAGE** **Read about how to write a persuasive essay. Add the bold expressions in the essay in exercise 2A to the examples of persuasive language below. Then, in pairs, think of ideas to complete the essay.**

In a persuasive essay, your aim is to convince your reader to agree with your view. It usually has three or four paragraphs:

Introduction: State your position on the topic.

Body (one or two paragraphs): Support your position with facts and examples. You can also state the opposite position and say why it is not true.

Conclusion: Restate your position and main points. Give a strong concluding statement to make your reader agree with you.

Useful persuasive language:

Give your opinion: I firmly believe that … , ______________ … , ______________ …

Give facts: According to … , ______________ …

Give personal examples: When I used/tried … , ______________ …

Give the opposite position: Although some will say that … , ______________ … , ______________ …

WRITE IT

C **PLAN** **You're going to write a persuasive essay. Work with a partner. Choose one of the options below, and discuss your ideas. Then plan the structure of your essay: What opening sentence are you going to use? What information are you going to include in each of the paragraphs listed in exercise 2B?**

Are product reviews / restaurant reviews / movie reviews / app reviews / hotel reviews useful or not?

D **Write your persuasive essay. Make sure you use some persuasive language.**

E **PAIR WORK** **Exchange essays with another partner. Do you agree with the writer's position?**

11.5 TIME TO SPEAK
Does it really work?

LESSON OBJECTIVE
- share tips on solutions

how to cure a cough
how to sleep better
how to keep mosquitos away
how to remove coffee stains
how to fix a wet phone

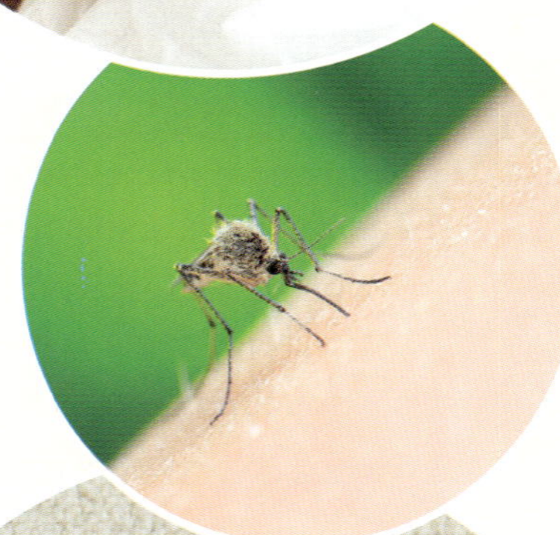

A **PREPARE** **With a partner, look at things people searched for on the internet. Discuss examples of tips the searches might find. Talk about any you have tried and say how effective they were.**

how to cure a cough	how to sleep better
how to keep mosquitos away	how to cool soda quickly
how to remove coffee stains	how to get in shape in a month
how to fix a wet phone	

FIND IT

B **RESEARCH** **With your partner, think of a few other tips you have heard of or tried. You can choose two or three topics from the ideas in part A or use your phone to check for ideas online. The tips can be effective or ineffective.**

C **DISCUSS** **In groups, share your topics and tips. The others guess which ones are effective. If you have tried any of the tips, at the end of the discussion, say how effective they were. The group chooses two of the most interesting tips: an effective one and an ineffective one.**

D **PRESENT** **In your groups from part C, present your two tips to the class without mentioning the problems they solve. The class guesses what the problems are. Then each group reveals the answers.**

E **DECIDE** **As a class, discuss whether the tips you heard are effective or not and say whether you've tried any.**

To check your progress, go to page 156.

USEFUL PHRASES

PREPARE
I've tried that before and …
… seems like a great tip.
… can't be true.
That just doesn't sound right.

DISCUSS
… , believe it or not.
I find that hard to believe.
It's partly true.
Maybe there's some truth in it.
Tell me another one!

PRESENT
According to … ,
The best way to … is …
In order to …
It turns out, if you …

UNIT OBJECTIVES

- talk about talent
- discuss how to make life better
- describe your ambitions
- write a review of a performance
- give a presentation about yourself

GOT WHAT IT TAKES?

12

START SPEAKING

A What can you see in the picture? Why do you think the person chose to learn this skill?

B What skills or characteristics do you think a person needs to have to be good at the activity in the picture?

C In your opinion, what does it take to be highly successful – whatever you choose to do in life? For ideas, watch Wendy's video.

EXPERT SPEAKER

Are any of Wendy's ideas similar to yours?

12.1 PRACTICE MAKES PERFECT

LESSON OBJECTIVE
- talk about talent

1 LANGUAGE IN CONTEXT

A PAIR WORK **Look at the picture. How long do you think it took the person to learn to do this? Talk about an activity you know about that takes a lot of practice to do well.**

B **Read the social media posts. What is the 10,000-hour rule? What talents and skills are mentioned?**

Comments Profile Sign Out

Victor Gomez
I just read about the 10,000-hour rule: You have to practice something for 10,000 hours to become truly good at it. It made me wonder if anyone is really born **gifted** or if ability just comes from being **determined** and working really hard. Thoughts?

Rhonda Peters
Jimi Hendrix was one of the greatest guitarists in history, but he never took guitar lessons. So, if he wasn't a **trained** musician, then you figure he was just exceptionally **talented**. But it's not necessarily true that his natural **musical** ability was the only factor. When he got his first guitar at age 15, he practiced for hours and hours every day. So he didn't play especially well at first. It takes practice to become a **skilled** musician, no matter what natural talent you may have.

Kyle Manson
I'm studying engineering, and some of my classes are technically advanced, but I pick up the ideas fairly easily. Others are having real difficulty, even though I'm no smarter than they are and they work as hard as I do. Design classes are where I struggle. I'm reasonably **imaginative**, but I'm definitely a **technical**, **analytical** person, not **artistic** at all. I can make a diagram of a complicated structure like a bridge without much effort, but drawing never came particularly easily to me. So we're studying the same things, but we're each better in different classes. The only **logical** explanation is natural ability. That's my (analytical) conclusion!

C **Read again. How do Rhonda and Kyle feel about practice versus being born with talent?**

2 VOCABULARY: Skill and performance

FIND IT

A 2.45 **Look at the adjectives in the box used to describe talents and skills. Which of them are used in the posts in exercise 1B? Count the syllables in the words and guess where the main stress is. Discuss their meanings. Use a dictionary or your phone to help you. Then listen and check your work.**

analytical	artistic	athletic	competent	determined	gifted	imaginative
intellectual	logical	musical	skilled	talented	technical	trained

B **Now go to page 151. Do the vocabulary exercises for 12.1.**

C PAIR WORK THINK CRITICALLY **Do you think very successful people are born gifted, or is their talent due to practice? For ideas, watch Wendy's video.**

EXPERT SPEAKER

Do you think Wendy is right? Can you think of other examples?

3 GRAMMAR: Adverbs with adjectives and adverbs

A **Read the sentences in the grammar box. Answer the questions.**

Adverbs with adjectives and adverbs

You have to practice something for 10,000 hours to become **truly good** at it.
But it's not **necessarily true**.
So he didn't play **especially well** at first.
Drawing never came **particularly easily** to me.

1 What part of speech can you use with an adjective or an adverb to provide more detail about it? ____________

2 Is it placed before or after the adjective or adverb it modifies? ____________

B **Now go to page 139. Look at the grammar chart and do the grammar exercise for 12.1.**

C **Write something about yourself that is true for each topic below. Use adverbs with adjectives or adverbs. Then work with a partner. Guess what your partner's sentence might be. Then compare your answers.**

1 Cooking: ____________
2 Technology: ____________
3 Fixing things: ____________
4 Money: ____________
5 Decision-making: ____________

4 SPEAKING

A GROUP WORK **Think about your experiences in these areas and discuss the questions. Did you ever (a) find it especially easy to become good at something because of natural talent, (b) find it particularly difficult or impossible to accomplish something even with practice, or (c) become good at something through practice even though it was difficult at first?**

art (painting, drawing, photography, etc.)
athletic activities (soccer, yoga, running, etc.)
education (math, language learning, computers, etc.)
performance (singing, playing an instrument, dancing, etc.)

I think I'm **exceptionally skilled** with technology. For example, **technical** issues with my computer are easy for me to understand and fix. But I've never been **artistically gifted**. I took an art class, but I couldn't even do a simple drawing of a bowl of fruit.

12.2 CHANGE THE WORLD

LESSON OBJECTIVE
- discuss how to make life better

1 LANGUAGE IN CONTEXT

A 2.46 **Imagine you have to give a short talk on how to make the world a better place. What would you talk about? Then read and listen to Pietro giving a talk at a conference. Circle the best title for his talk.**

a Big Ideas for a Better World

b A Better World for Everyone

c Think of Others before Yourself

2.46 Audio script

Hello! Wow, thank you for that warm welcome. It really makes me smile! I actually smile a lot these days, but that wasn't always the case. In fact, meeting me used to **be a real downer**. I know this because a good friend told me so. She said seeing me would instantly **ruin her day** because I was always complaining about something. She told me that my negative attitude **was getting her down**. Well, that was a shock, but it **did me good** because it showed me that I needed to change.

I started doing small, simple things to **raise my spirits**. Listening to a great piece of music while getting dressed. Having a cup of coffee and a cookie in the afternoon, just because. Changing my desktop wallpaper to a beautiful work of art. Sticking an inspirational quote or a great piece of advice on the fridge so it was the first thing I saw every morning.

Then I used the same idea – small, simple things – to help **brighten up** other people's lives. Just simple acts of kindness, like cooking a meal for my mom, driving my elderly neighbor to her friend's place, or offering a few words of encouragement to my younger brother for something he was doing. A little bit of kindness can really **make someone's day** and **leave a lasting impression on** them and on you.

So here's my big idea for how to change the world – think small. By all of us doing small things, we all collectively make the world a better place.

B 2.46 **Read and listen again. How does Pietro suggest making (a) yourself happy and (b) others happy? In your opinion, what's Pietro's best idea? Why?**

2 VOCABULARY: Describing emotional impact

FIND IT

A 2.47 PAIR WORK **Look at the expressions in the box. Which describe a positive impact, a negative impact, or both? Use a dictionary or your phone to help you. Then listen and check your work.**

be a (real) downer	brighten up sth	capture sb's imagination
do sb good	get sb down	leave a lasting impression on sb
make sb's day	put sb's mind at rest	raise sb's spirits
ruin sb's day	stress sb out	take sb's mind off sth

B **Now go to page 152. Do the vocabulary exercises for 12.2.**

C PAIR WORK THINK CRITICALLY **Talk about examples of people's behavior that affect you negatively and positively.**

3 GRAMMAR: Making non-count nouns countable

A **Read the sentences in the grammar box. Circle the correct options to complete the rules.**

Making non-count nouns countable

Listen to **a** great **piece of music** while getting dressed.
Have **a cup of coffee** and **a cookie** in the afternoon.
Change my desktop wallpaper to **a** beautiful **work of art**.
Stick an inspirational quote or **a** great **piece of advice** on the fridge.
A little bit of kindness can really make someone's day.

1 You can make non-count nouns countable by using expressions that describe specific **qualities or characteristics** / **quantities or amounts**.

2 **Sometimes you can** / **You can never** use the same noun (e.g., piece) with different categories of things.

B **Now go to page 140. Look at the grammar chart and do the grammar exercise for 12.2.**

C **Complete the sentences with your own ideas. Check your accuracy. Then compare ideas with a partner. Are they similar?**

1 One of my favorite pieces of ____________ is ______________________.
2 I think ______________________ is a really nice act of ____________.
3 I once got a very useful piece of ____________ from a friend. It was: ______________________.
4 I'd really like to get a bunch of ____________ together for a game of ______________________.
5 I never have enough articles of ____________ ! I need some more ______________________.
6 I sometimes go out for ______________________ to brighten up my day.

✓ ACCURACY CHECK

When making non-count nouns countable, be sure the subject and verb agree.

All of the ~~piece~~ of advice he gave were useful. ✗
All of the pieces of advice he gave were useful. ✓

4 SPEAKING

A PAIR WORK THINK CRITICALLY **Think of more small things you can do to make the world a better place for yourself and others. Explain why they're good ideas. Make a list.**

Well, one way to **make someone's day** is to give them a gift for no reason. Maybe **a box of Turkish delight** or some flowers.

Nice one! And if someone's stressed, you could suggest a day trip together to **take their mind off things** – or maybe **a game of** soccer.

B GROUP WORK **Share your ideas and reasons with another pair. Then choose the two best ideas that the other pair suggested.**

Turkish delight

12.3 MAYBE ONE DAY ...

LESSON OBJECTIVE

- describe your ambitions

1 LISTENING

A PAIR WORK **Daniel is interviewing to get into a theater program in college. What do you think the interviewer asks him about?**

B 2.48 **Listen to the interview. What does the interviewer ask about? Were your guesses in exercise 1A correct?**

C 2.48 LISTEN FOR CONTRASTING IDEAS **Listen again and match Daniel's optimistic ideas with his cautious ones.**

1 My dream scenario is to play leading roles. ___
2 There's no guarantee I'll end up in Hollywood. ___
3 I may not succeed in playing any type of character. ___
4 It may not be easy to learn new things. ___

a But there's no harm in trying.
b But I realize things might not go as planned.
c But I'm determined to be open-minded and try everything.
d But I'm confident that I'll have some level of success.

D PAIR WORK THINK CRITICALLY **How realistic do you think Daniel's ambitions are? What do you think of his attitude during the interview? Does he have the right attitude to be an actor? Explain.**

2 PRONUNCIATION: Listening for sounds that change

A 2.49 **Listen to how the /d/ sound changes in connected speech.**

Well, my dream scenario woul<u>d</u> be to play leading roles in movies. (/d/ → /b/)

Listen to examples of how other sounds change:

I think she had the bes<u>t</u> part in the film. (/t/ → /p/)

There were only seve<u>n</u> people in the theater. (/n/ → /m/)

I met o<u>ne</u> guy who ha<u>d</u> been in Hollywood. (/n/ → /ŋ/) (/d/ → /b/)

B 2.50 **Work in pairs. Mark the possible sound changes at the end of words. Listen and check.**

1 I love that part where the son meets his real father.
2 They arrived before everyone came.
3 The movie had bad reviews on most websites.
4 It was an action movie set in Greece.

C **Circle the correct options to complete the sentence.**

In connected speech, words that *start* / *end* in /t/, /d/, and /n/ can change before words *starting* / *ending* in /p/, /b/, /m/, /k/, and /g/.

3 SPEAKING SKILLS

A 2.48 **Complete the expressions from the interview in exercise 1B on page 122 with the words in the box. Then decide which ones are used to (a) describe ambitions, (b) express optimism, or (c) express caution. Write *a*, *b*, or *c* next to each one. Will any of the sounds change in these expressions in connected speech? If so, which ones? Listen again to check.**

certain confident determined guarantee harm planned reason scenario ultimate

Describe ambitions; express optimism and caution

1 My dream ________ would be to … ___
2 I realize things might not go as ________ . ___
3 There's no ________ (that) … ___
4 I'm ________ (that) … ___
5 My ________ goal is to … ___
6 There's no ________ in trying. ___
7 I can't say for ________ (that) … ___
8 I'm ________ to … ___
9 I see no ________ why I can't … ___

B PAIR WORK **Choose one of the situations below and interview your partner about their ambitions. Use expressions from exercise 3A and your own ideas. Then choose a different situation and change roles.**

attending a music school
getting an internship at a museum
attending law school
working as an English teacher
being on a reality TV show
volunteering at a hospital

4 PRONUNCIATION: Using syllable stress in words

A 2.51 **Listen to which syllable is stressed (a stressed syllable is said more loudly, longer, and at a higher pitch).**

ultimate guarantee scenario

B 2.52 **Which syllable is stressed in these words? Complete the chart. Listen, check, and repeat the words.**

character difficulties encouragement impression interviewer particular
performance photograph photography positively successful technical

● • • competent	• ● • determined	● • • • satisfying	• ● • • exceptional

C 2.53 **Complete the conversation with the word that matches the stress pattern. Listen and check your work. Practice the conversation with a partner.**

I think Maria is such a ● • • *hard-working / positive* person. She's • ● • • *amazingly / wonderfully* talented.

Max is quite • ● • *creative / competent*, too. He did this ● • • • *incredible / complicated* work so well.

5 SPEAKING

A PAIR WORK **Think of one or two of your ambitions – educational, personal, or professional. Then ask each other what you need to do to achieve the ambitions and how difficult it will be. Explain, expressing optimistic and cautious opinions.**

I'm determined to become an architect. My ultimate goal is to improve my city. I'll need a lot of training, but I'm confident I can manage it.

12.4 SUCCESS BEHIND THE SCENES

LESSON OBJECTIVE

- write a review of a performance

1 READING

A **Who helps make a concert successful in addition to the musicians? Read the article. What were Kevin's job responsibilities? What does he think was difficult about the job?**

INSIDER ENGLISH

Say *by word of mouth* or *through word of mouth* when news, gossip, or other information is spread from person to person in conversation.

BACKSTAGE PASS

I loved life on the road when I was a guitar tech. Over the years, I traveled with many different bands – some small acts and some big stars. My job included unloading the equipment, setting it up on stage, tuning guitars, and making sure everything worked – pretty much getting things ready so the musicians could perform without problems in front of a bunch of excited fans.

When I was about eight years old, I saw the Rolling Stones perform on TV. I noticed that someone handed Keith Richards a guitar between songs, and I thought I'd like to do that one day. It left a lasting impression on me, but I didn't really think about the job again until I was 25. That's when a friend asked me to travel with his band as a guitar tech. I already knew a lot about music and guitars, but on the job, I really became technically skilled over time. People hired me by word of mouth, mostly musicians from headlining acts that we were touring with. I quickly had several jobs on my résumé – but it's really more of a see-and-be-seen business. You look at the people around you and see what jobs might be coming up. And you do your job exceptionally well every day – others see you work, know your skill set, and often ask you to work for them on future shows.

I enjoyed the pressure of live performances, but life on the road wasn't always easy. You take the good with the bad. Sometimes I slept in vans and sometimes on tour buses. When I stayed in hotels, they weren't necessarily nice, but with some of the more-famous musicians, we were in beautiful hotels, like the time I stayed on the Champs-Élysées in Paris. I worked in several different cities around the world, and dealing with the unknown often made the job especially challenging. A lot of times I was working outside, and it could be very hot, really cold, or even raining. I also dealt with things like getting big trucks down tiny streets and getting huge equipment up narrow stairs or in small elevators. One time, in Malaga, Spain, the power went out in the entire city, and it messed up our schedule and computers, but the show went ahead as planned.

Any type of work in the music business is difficult. I've seen musicians on the way up, and I've seen them on the way down. It's tough to get to the top in my line of work, too, but the work is steadier once you're successful. And how do you stay at the top? Start with being on time. Then stay focused, and always remember you're not in the band. You're there to do a job – not to hang out with rock stars. I've seen a lot of techs make that mistake.

My last words of advice? I think there are three kinds of people in this world: (1) the kind that make things happen, (2) the kind that watch things happen, and (3) the kind that wonder what just happened. Be the kind of person that makes things happen. And remember, no matter what happens – the show must go on!

by Kevin Hurdman

GLOSSARY

unload (*v*) remove something from a vehicle

headlining act (*n*) the main performer or performers at an entertainment event

steadier (*adj*) happening in a more regular way than something else

B **UNDERSTAND CAUSE AND EFFECT** **Read the article again. What is/was the result of these events?**

1 Kevin got everything ready for the performance.

2 Kevin saw someone give Keith Richards a guitar on TV.

3 The power went out in Malaga before a concert.

4 You do your job exceptionally well.

C **PAIR WORK** **THINK CRITICALLY** **In what other types of jobs is it helpful to "see and be seen"? What other advice does Kevin give that can be applied to different jobs?**

2 WRITING

A **Read the concert review from an online music magazine. What did the reviewer like? Did anything go wrong?**

CONCERT REVIEW | ALEJANDRO SANZ

The Alejandro Sanz concert on Friday night was amazing. He's from Spain and tours all over the world. I was fortunate to see him in New York City at a sold-out show. He was the headlining act and sang exceptionally well. The band members were from Puerto Rico, the Dominican Republic, and the United States. The drummer was particularly good. They played mostly songs from his newest albums, but they also played some old favorites.

The show was a huge success due to the talented musicians, but it wasn't only their work that made it so special. The lighting and special effects were terrific, so the behind-the-scenes crew clearly did a great job, making sure everything ran smoothly and that there were no technical problems. And I loved the video clips on the giant screen at the back of the stage. It all helped to make the concert feel spectacular.

But the best part was when Sanz sang "Corazón Partío" and had the audience sing along. Everyone was disappointed when the show was over, and they shouted for more. As a result, Sanz performed an encore, which really made our day.

GLOSSARY

encore (*n*) an extra song or piece of music played at the end of a show because the audience shouts for it

B **SHOW REASON AND RESULT** **Look at the sentences with words that show reasons and results. Find one more expression for each sentence from the review in exercise 2A.**

The show was a huge success **because of /** [1] ____________________ the talented musicians.

They shouted for more. **Consequently / Therefore /** [2] ____________________, Sanz performed an encore, which really made our day.

REGISTER CHECK

In conversation, *so* is often used instead of more formal expressions like *as a result*, *consequently*, and *therefore*. It's used to join two sentences.

Formal writing

*They shouted for more. **As a result**, Sanz performed an encore.*

Conversation

*We shouted for more, **so** Sanz performed an encore.*

WRITE IT

C **PLAN** **You are going to write a review of a performance. With a partner, talk about a concert, play, or other performance you have seen. Discuss facts about the events and information about your experience: where and when it was; what you liked and didn't like about the performers, lighting, sound, and special effects. Then look at the concert review in exercise 2A. How will you organize the information you discussed?**

D **Write your performance review. Remember to use expressions for showing reason and result.**

E **PAIR WORK** **Read your partner's review. Would you have liked the event? Why or why not?**

12.5 TIME TO SPEAK
Me, in two minutes

LESSON OBJECTIVE
- give a presentation about yourself

A Choose three items that you always carry in your purse or bag. You can think about the apps on your phone that you never do without, if you like. Show them to your partner or group, or describe them. What do they show about you? (For example, your personality, hobbies or interests, or what you focus on each day.) Who has the most unusual items? Whose are the most revealing?

B Look at the mood board above. What objects and text can you identify? What does it tell you about the person who created the mood board? How does the person see themselves? What are their aspirations and dreams?

C **PREPARE** Now you're going to expand on how you described yourself in exercise A. Work with your partner to design a mood board for each of you. What objects and texts are on your boards? Why? To help you, look at the list of categories below and choose the ones that are relevant to you or use your own ideas.

current/past jobs, future plans/ambitions, childhood, family, friends
interests, personal ambitions, personality, challenges, skills

D Describe your mood board. What can your partner tell about you from the items you've chosen to include?

E Imagine you're going to talk about yourself for two minutes. Using your mood board, work alone to plan what you're going to say about yourself. Choose the best order to present your topics or areas of interest, and use examples to illustrate each topic.

F **DISCUSS** In groups, take turns talking about yourselves. Then say what aspects of each person's talk you liked (e.g., examples, topics, timing, body language / gestures, tone of voice). What lessons did you learn on how to talk about yourself in an interesting way?

G **AGREE** Share your ideas from part D with the class. Agree on a short list of tips on the most interesting way to talk about yourself (topics, sequence, etc.).

To check your progress, go to page 156.

USEFUL PHRASES

PREPARE
I'm determined to …
I'm fairly talented at …
I'm more analytical/artistic/…
My ultimate goal is to …

AGREE
You could try …
It might work well if you …
… could be very effective.
I've always had luck with …

REVIEW 4 (UNITS 10–12)

1 VOCABULARY

A **Complete the questions with the correct forms of the words in parentheses ( ). Sometimes, you do not need to change the word.**

1 These days, do children really need to learn to do __________ (calculate) without a calculator?
2 If you think an email is suspicious, how can you check that it's __________ (authentic)?
3 Are there many __________ (similar) between your native language and English?
4 Is there a __________ (like) between you and anyone famous?
5 Is asking people to fill out forms a good way to __________ (survey) customers?
6 In your country, are there any snakes or insects whose bites are __________ (dead)?
7 To be an __________ (art) person, do you need to be born with a natural talent?
8 Is it true that most jobs require people to be __________ (imagine) in some way?
9 If you do something that you didn't know was __________ (legal), should you be punished?
10 Is it good to change your __________ (look) completely sometimes?

B PAIR WORK **Discuss the questions in exercise 1A.**

2 GRAMMAR

A **Circle the correct option.**

1 Carrying your phone in your back pocket increases the risk *to break* / *of breaking* it.
2 When you apologize *to arrive* / *for arriving* late, you should always explain why you're late.
3 If I drink coffee in the evening, it prevents me *to sleep* / *from sleeping*.
4 People in my country learn English particularly *easy* / *easily* because it's similar to our language.
5 They should allow people *take* / *to take* phones into exams as long as they are put away.
6 Companies should let their employees *wear* / *to wear* what they want at work.
7 I've listened to my favorite piece *from* / *of* music at least 100 times.
8 Most *exceptional* / *exceptionally* gifted people discover their talent before they're 18.
9 It's always easy to find stuff online to help you *understand* / *understanding* difficult subjects.
10 I sometimes dream *to become* / *of becoming* famous.
11 I have one article *of* / *in* clothing that I wear much more often than any other.
12 Traffic jams cause me *arrive* / *to arrive* late more than any other problem.

B PAIR WORK **Do you agree or disagree with the sentences in exercise 2A? Discuss your views.**

3 VOCABULARY

A **Circle the correct options.**

HOME NEWS BLOG CONTACT US

Regular readers of this blog will know that truth – or the lack of it – is one of my most frequent topics. I'm always complaining about things being posted online about other people, which are either totally [1]*accurate / inaccurate* or which are intended to be [2]*misleading / suspicious*. There's something about it that really [3]*gets me down / raises my spirits*. It's not so much that the actual information is [4]*false / trustworthy*. It's the fact that the people who post it are often deliberately being [5]*dishonest / exaggerated*. They're happy to [6]*make / ruin* someone's day (or week, or more) and don't seem to care. This kind of behavior came to mind recently after I saw several negative stories about celebrities, all of which were based not on facts, but on [7]*rumors / white lies*. In my view, the people who write this stuff are not [8]*biased / competent* journalists, and so I struggle to understand why there are so many of them. Is it true that the public enjoys reading this stuff? And if so, why? Do people have some kind of problem with [9]*features / individuals* who are famous because they're [10]*determined / gifted*?

5 2 9

B PAIR WORK **Say whether or not you agree with the views in the blog in exercise 3A. Discuss the questions at the end.**

4 GRAMMAR

A **Complete the sentences with the correct form of *be*.**

1 All my work will ___________ finished by the end of this week.
2 All my photos ___________ stored on my phone.
3 I have some old stuff that needs ___________ thrown out.
4 Most of the English words I know ___________ learned in the classroom.
5 I always feel nervous when I'm ___________ interviewed.
6 A lot of the things I say shouldn't ___________ taken seriously.
7 I ordered something online, and it hasn't ___________ delivered yet.
8 When I ___________ delayed by traffic, I never get stressed about it.
9 Once, one of my online accounts ___________ hacked.
10 Next weekend, all my time is going ___________ spent relaxing.
11 I once saw a car that was ___________ chased by the police.
12 I expect ___________ invited to a party fairly soon.

B PAIR WORK **Say which sentences from exercise 4A are true for you. For ones that are not, say a similar sentence that is true.**

GRAMMAR REFERENCE AND PRACTICE

1.1 PRESENT HABITS (PAGE 3)

Present habits

Talk about present habits in different ways:

1 Simple present (sometimes with adverbs of frequency)
*My friend **tells** me she **resists** change because she **usually likes** things the way they are.*

2 *Tend to* + the base form of a verb
*I **tend to adapt** to new situations quickly.*

3 *Will* for events that happen often (present, not future)
*I**'ll** often **call** my parents when I want advice.*

4 Present continuous for a continuing activity that happens at the same time as another habit
*I usually listen to music when I**'m cooking**.*

5 Present continuous for noticeable/unusual (often undesirable) habits; use *always* and *constantly* for emphasis.
*I**'m always worrying** about how I'll cope with all of my work.*

A **Cross out the options that are not correct. Sometimes both options are correct.**

1 I usually forget all about the time when *I'm studying / I will study.*
2 *I'll often take / I tend to take* a shower in the morning unless I have to leave home early.
3 I *never listen / am constantly listening* when he complains about his job.
4 My friends *often tell / are always telling* me to stop working so hard.
5 How do you communicate with people when *you'll travel / you're traveling*?
6 *I'll usually think / I usually think* about a task for a few days before I start on it, unless it's urgent, of course.

1.2 PAST HABITS (PAGE 5)

Past habits

There are different ways to talk about habits, actions, and states that happened in the past but don't anymore:

1 *Used to* for past habits, repeated past actions, and states
- *used to / didn't use to* + the base form of the verb
  *We **didn't use to make** video calls, but we do now.*
- *never* + *used to* + the base form of the verb
  *They **never used to ride** their bikes to school.*
- *use to*, not *used to*, with *didn't/did* in negative statements and questions
  ***Did** you **use to take** the bus?*

2 *Would* for past habits and repeated past actions, not for past states
- *would* ('*d*) / *would not* (*wouldn't*) + the base form of verb
- Use *would* only if it is clear when the action happened. Use *used to* if the time reference is not given.
  *We **would text** each other every night.* *not ~~I would have a big cell phone~~.*

3 The simple past for past habits, repeated past actions, and past states (often with time expressions)
*I **had** a big bedroom. I **went** to bed at 6:00 **every night**.*

4 The simple past for single completed actions in the past, not *used to* or *would*
*I **watched** three shows **last night**.* *not ~~I'd watch three shows last night.~~ / ~~I used to watch three shows last night.~~*

A **Change the simple past to *would* (*not*) when possible. When not possible, use (*not*) *used to.***

When I was young, I [1]didn't have a TV in my room. My older brother [2]had one in his. I [3]was very jealous. But on the weekends, he [4]let me watch his TV. We [5]watched our favorite shows, but I usually [6]fell asleep halfway through.

2.1 COMPARATIVE STRUCTURES (PAGE 13)

Comparative structures

1 *Fewer/less* + noun to show there is less of one thing than another

- *fewer* + count nouns   *less* + non-count nouns

The new project will require ***fewer resources*** *and* ***less time****.*

2 *Rather than* to show a preference for something

- Compare nouns/pronouns
- Use verbs to compare activities (base form of the verb or verb + *-ing*)
- *To* can be used instead of *rather than* with *prefer* but not with other verbs

I prefer ocean exploration ***rather than space exploration****.*

I prefer to study the ocean ***rather than learn/learning about*** *space.*

I ***prefer*** *the ocean* ***to*** *deep space.*

I ***want to study*** *Earth* ***rather than*** *Mars.*   not ~~*I* ***want to study*** *Earth* ***to*** *Mars.*~~

3 Verb + *more/less* (as a pronoun)

I ***know less/more*** *about Venus* ***than*** *about Mars.*

4 Adjective + (*not*) *enough* + infinitive to compare the degree of actual and required ability

Technology is (***not***) ***advanced enough to send*** *people to Mars.*

5 A comparative + infinitive to compare actions

It's ***easier*** *to use a tablet* ***than*** *(to use) a laptop.*

6 For many comparative structures, you do *not* need to repeat the first subject and verb.

We're ***less likely*** *to find life on the moon* ***than*** *(we are to find life) on Mars.*

A **Complete the sentences. Use constructions from the grammar box above.**

1 We haven't been lucky ________ to see a whale in the ocean.
2 Larry prefers sea animals ________ land animals.
3 We see ________ turtles on the beach than in the ocean. There are many more of them in the ocean.
4 Scientists know ________ about Venus than about Mars. Venus hasn't been explored as much.
5 Vicky wants to work with animals ________ people.
6 It's ________ difficult to memorize dates than it is to remember names.

2.2 SUPERLATIVE STRUCTURES; UNGRADABLE ADJECTIVES (PAGE 15)

Superlative structures

1 With quantities: Phrases such as *one of, two of,* and *some of* + superlative adjective + plural noun

This country has ***some of the highest*** *mountains in the world.*

2 With *to*: Use a superlative + infinitive to show function or purpose.

May is ***the best*** *time* ***to hike*** *here.*

3 *Least* is the opposite of *most* (the comparative form is *less*).

This is surely ***the least suitable*** *environment for anything* ***to live****.*

4 With *that* clauses:

- Use a superlative + a *that* clause.
- The use of *that* is optional.

It's ***the most fascinating*** *place (****that****) I've ever visited.*

5 Ellipsis with *the*: Shows that one or more words have been left out to avoid repetition.

I have three sisters. Susana is ***the youngest*** *(sister).*

Ungradable adjectives

1 Ungradable adjectives do not have different degrees and therefore don't usually have comparative or superlative forms.

*They were **furious** and **exhausted**.*

2 With most ungradable adjectives, we can use intensifiers such as *absolutely, completely, totally,* and *utterly.*

*The green parrots of Masaya Volcano are **totally amazing**.*

3 With other ungradable adjectives – for example, *male, female, married, single* – we don't use intensifiers.

*My first dog was **male**, but the second one was **female**.*

> **!** **Gradable adjectives have degrees and can be used with adverbs, such as *very, a little,* and *really,* but not with intensifiers like *absolutely, completely,* etc.**
>
> *Those animals are **very tough**.*
>
> **Note: *Really* can be used with both gradable and ungradable adjectives.**

A **Circle the correct option.**

1 I think your cat is very *male / cute*.

2 It seems like the worst place for birds *building / to build* their nests.

3 My friends were absolutely *furious / interesting*.

4 The weather is a little *cold / freezing* right now.

5 For many of us, snakes are probably the *less / least* lovable species.

6 The lion and the elephant are two *most / of the most* popular animals at the zoo.

3.1 RELATIVE PRONOUNS; REDUCED RELATIVE CLAUSES (PAGE 23)

Relative pronouns; reduced relative clauses

1 Relative pronouns are used to introduce relative clauses.

that/which = for things, *that/who* = for people, *where* = for places, *when* = for times, *whose* = to show possession

*My sister, **whose** children I often take care of, lives next door.*

*Today is the day **when** we decide it's time for a change.*

2 Subject relative clauses can be reduced by omitting the relative pronoun and the verb *be*. You can't reduce object relative clauses.

The following relative clauses are often reduced:

- with *be* + an adjective
- with *be* + past participle
- with noun phrases

*People **who are worried** about meeting strangers often get nervous at parties.* → *People **worried** about meeting strangers often get nervous at parties.*

*The bus **that is parked** in front of the office is the one we'll take to the conference.* → *The bus **parked** in front of the office is the one we'll take to the conference.*

*Steven, **who is a quick learner**, adapts easily to new situations.* → *Steven, **a quick learner**, adapts easily to new situations.*

A **Cross out the words you can omit to reduce the relative clauses when possible. When not possible, write *X*.**

1 The company whose logo is an apple is famous around the world.

2 Vincent van Gogh, who was an introvert, painted landscapes and self-portraits.

3 The book that was published anonymously sold millions of copies.

4 Psychology, which is normally a popular subject, is not her favorite.

5 This is the restaurant where my brother works.

6 People who are interested in others are often good conversationalists.

3.2 PRESENT PARTICIPLES (PAGE 25)

Present participles

Present participle = verb + *-ing*

1 To shorten sentences that describe two events happening at the same time, use the present participle of the second verb after a comma. Do not use *and*.
*I often work **and listen** to music. → I often work, **listening** to music.*

2 In reduced relative clauses, use the present participle. Do not use the relative pronoun and the verb *be*.
*Look at all those **lemons that are growing** on that tree. → Look at all those **lemons growing** on that tree.*

A **Rewrite these sentences to shorten them or use reduced relative clauses.**

1 The mall is full of people who are shopping for the holidays.
____
2 We're standing in line and waiting to check in for our flight.
____
3 There are a lot of fans who are waiting outside the stadium.
____
4 I love to stand on top of that hill and look down at the valley.
____
5 In college, I saw a guy who was skateboarding down a hallway.
____
6 The storm will affect people who live in the South.
____

4.1 ADDING EMPHASIS: *so … that, such … that, even, only* (page 35)

Adding emphasis

1 *So* + adjective or adverb (*that*) … emphasizes the results or effects of something.
*It was **so funny (that)** I couldn't stop laughing.*

2 *Such* (*a/an*) + (adjective) noun (*that*) … also emphasizes the results or effects of something.
*She is **such a good friend (that)** everyone turns to her when they have a problem.*

3 *Even* before a word, phrase, or part of the sentence adds emphasis or signals that something is surprising.
***Even** the most confident person needs help sometimes.*
*He works long hours during the week and **even** works on Saturdays sometimes.*
*Building trust with people makes your life **even** happier.*

4 *Only* before a word, phrase, or part of the sentence adds emphasis.
- *only* = "no one else" or "nothing else" than the people, things, amount, or activity mentioned

***Only** you can steer him away from making a big mistake.*
*Quitting your job will **only** hurt your career.*

A **Complete the sentences with *so*, *such*, *even*, or *only*.**

1 It was __________ a big decision to move to Canada and start over again.
2 __________ a very intelligent person can do that job.
3 She is __________ ambitious that she has decided to work toward a PhD.
4 Everyone was on time, __________ Joseph, who is usually late for class.
5 It was time to leave, but they had __________ packed one of their suitcases.
6 He demonstrated __________ talent that they hired him immediately.

4.2 REFLEXIVE PRONOUNS; PRONOUNS WITH *OTHER/ANOTHER* (PAGE 37)

Reflexive pronouns

Use a reflexive pronoun:

1 when the subject and object of a sentence are the same
*I enjoyed **myself** at the party.*

2 directly after a noun or pronoun for greater emphasis
*The employees **themselves** decide what time they start and finish work.*

3 at the end of the clause for some emphasis
*You and your brother should be able to do the job **yourselves**.*

4 after *by* to mean "alone" or "without help"
*I can't lift this box **by myself**.*

! ***You*** **has two reflexive pronouns: *yourself* (singular) and *yourselves* (plural).**

Pronouns with *other/another*

1 *the other* = the remaining member of a pair
*One of his shoes was blue, **the other**, brown.*

2 *another* = an additional member of a group
*I'd like to hire **another** assistant.*

3 *the others* = the remaining members of a group
*Six people in my class are from this city. **The others** are from different cities.*

4 *others* (without *the*) = not the members of the group already mentioned, but different ones
*Some people drink coffee. **Others** prefer tea.*

5 *each other* and *one another* = show that each person in a group does something to the others
*During exams, students are not allowed to help **each other / one another**.*

A **Complete the sentences with the correct reflexive pronouns or pronouns with *other/another*.**

1 We knew it was going to be a tough job, but we told ____________ we could do it as a team.
2 Do you and Antonio need help moving your furniture, or can you do it ____________ ?
3 I know you already have two roommates, but is there room in your apartment for ____________ ?
4 Come on guys, work as a team! Help ____________ !
5 My job involves a lot of teamwork, so I'm used to working with ____________ .
6 I was fixing the ceiling light and almost fell. I had one foot on a chair and ____________ on the table.

5.1 REAL CONDITIONALS (PAGE 45)

Real conditionals

1 Present: *if/when/whenever* + simple present + simple present in the main clause
- to describe general facts or routines
*I **feel** nervous **if/when/whenever** I **think** about flying.*

2 Future: *if/when/whenever* + simple present + *will / be going to* in the main clause
- for possible future situations and their results
***If** you **try** the therapy, it **will make** you more confident.*
(You may or may not try the therapy. But if you do, it will make you more confident.)
***When/Whenever** you **try** the therapy, it **will make** you more confident.*
(You will try the therapy, and when you do, it will make you more confident.)

3 With modals and modal-like expressions: *if* clause + a modal in the main clause
- to show how likely or necessary the result is
***Whenever** you're worried, you **have to** try not to panic.*

A **Add the words in parentheses ( ) to the correct places in each sentence. Use a capital letter when necessary.**

1 I arrive at the airport, I call you right away. (when, will)
2 Max anxious he sees a plane. (feels, whenever)
3 That app really helps people exercise, I buy it. (if, may)
4 I face my fear of heights I go over that bridge. (have to, whenever)
5 Everyone take off their shoes they want to enter that building. (must, if)
6 We take a trip to France your French improves. (can, when)

5.2 CONDITIONALS: alternatives to *if* (page 47)

Conditionals: alternatives to *if*

You can use real conditionals with expressions other than *if*, but they have different meanings:

1 *Even if*: Stresses that the condition doesn't matter. The condition may happen, but the result will be the same.
__Even if__ video calls improve, talking in person is much nicer.

2 *Only if, providing / provided (that), as/so long as, on condition that*: Show the result or effect will happen when a specific condition becomes true. No other condition will have this result.
I'll lend you my phone, __only if__ / __provided__ / __providing__ / __as/so long as__ / __on condition that__ you promise to return it soon.

3 *Unless*: Describes a possible negative condition in the present or future = "except if" or "if … not."
We can't reach an agreement __unless__ you communicate more openly.

A **Circle the correct option.**

1 I'm willing to try virtual office meetings *providing / unless* the technology is reliable.
2 *On condition that / Even if* we meet in person, we may not be able to reach an agreement.
3 We'll leave at 3:00 *provided / even if* everyone is ready.
4 You shouldn't study late *unless / only if* it's absolutely necessary.
5 *Even if / So long as* the company makes a profit, the boss is happy.
6 He should be able to get into that college *as long as / unless* he gets unexpectedly bad grades in high school.

6.1 NARRATIVE TENSES (PAGE 55)

Narrative tenses

1 Simple past for the main completed events and situations in a story.
He __became__ famous when he __was__ only 14.

2 Past continuous (*was/were* + verb + *-ing*) for background activities in progress at the same time as the main event in the simple past.
She __translated__ what the president __was saying__.

3 Past perfect (*had* + past participle) for an event that happened before another event in the simple past.
All my friends __went__ to the concert, but __I'd forgotten__ to buy a ticket.

4 Past perfect continuous (*had* + *been* + verb + *-ing*) for an event that continued up to another event in the simple past. It shows the continuing nature of a past activity/situation leading up to a more recent past time.
- It can show a reason.
- It can give background information.

The band __had been playing__ all night, so they __were__ very tired.
I __had been dreaming__ of being famous for years, and suddenly it __happened__.

A **Complete the sentences with the verbs in parentheses ( ) in the correct tense.**

We were exhausted when we [1] ________ (reach) the town. We [2] ________ (travel) for days! There, we [3] ________ (interview) several people about what they [4] ________ (see). As we [5] ________ (travel) back, we [6] ________ (hear) that the story [7] ________ (already / go) viral.

6.2 REPORTED SPEECH WITH MODAL VERBS (PAGE 57)

Reported speech with modal verbs

1 Some modals change when the reporting verb is in the past:
will – would *can – could* *may – might*
*"**Will/Can** you **help** me?" → Jen asked me if I'**d** / I **could help** her.*

2 Some modals don't change, even if the reporting verb is in the past: *might, could, should, must*
*"What **could** they do about traffic?" → He wondered what they **could** do about traffic.*

> **!** **Only change the tense of the main verb when the reporting verb is in the past tense.**

A **Complete the sentences.**

1 "We won't study space next week." The teacher announced ______________________.
2 "Everyone should study for the test." The teacher feels ______________________.
3 "We may not have time to see a movie." Lisa explained ______________________.
4 "Could the Tigers win the baseball game?" Joe asked me ______________________.
5 "When will you finish the project?" My boss asked me ______________________.
6 "I can play the piano well." I said ______________________.

7.1 GERUNDS AND INFINITIVES AFTER ADJECTIVES, NOUNS, AND PRONOUNS (PAGE 67)

Gerunds and infinitives after adjectives, nouns, and pronouns

Infinitives (*to* + verb)

1 Adjective + infinitive
***It's boring and difficult to work** at night.*

2 Noun + infinitive – to show purpose
*It was an interesting **place to visit**.*

3 Pronoun + infinitive – to show purpose
*I need **something to eat**.*

Gerunds (verb + *-ing*)

1 Adjective + gerund
*It was **boring waiting** in line for the roller coaster. But it was **cool riding** on it.*

2 Fixed expression + gerund
e.g.: *be worth, have fun, spend/waste time*
*I **spend a lot of time traveling** for my job.*

A **Circle the correct options. More than one answer may be possible.**

I start work at 6:00 a.m. It's hard [1]*to get / getting* up so early, and I usually don't want to spend time [2]*to make / making* breakfast, but I try to have something simple [3]*to eat / eating*. At least I have no trouble [4]*to get / getting* to work, as I don't waste time [5]*to sit / sitting* in traffic jams. I think that's a big advantage [6]*to have / having*.

> **!** **Some adjectives can be followed by either gerunds or infinitives, others - only gerunds or only infinitives.**

7.2 INFINITIVES AFTER VERBS WITH AND WITHOUT OBJECTS (PAGE 69)

Infinitives after verbs with and without objects

1 Verb + infinitive Common verbs: *agree, decide, hope, manage, plan, seem, tend*
*They **agreed not to climb** the mountain without an instructor.*

2 Verb + object + infinitive Common verbs: *allow, convince, encourage, teach, tell, urge, warn*
*He **did not convince us to hire** him.* (The object performs the action of the infinitive.)

3 Verb + (object) + infinitive Common verbs: *ask, expect, need, promise, want, would like*
- No object – subject performs the action of the infinitive
- With object – object performs the action of the infinitive

***I'd like to buy** the lamp. (I'm buying it.)* ***I'd like you to buy** that lamp. (You're buying it.)*

> **!** **Use *not* before the infinitive to show the infinitive is negative. Use *not* before the main verb to show it is negative.**

A **Which of these sentences are correct without an object? Add the object in parentheses ( ) where possible.**

1 I like to shop online. (you)
2 I'd like to move closer to my dad. (my sister)
3 Jack tends to forget his friends' birthdays. (them)
4 My parents advised to save money. (me)
5 You convinced to buy a new computer. (them)
6 They expect to get good grades. (her)

8.1 MODAL-LIKE EXPRESSIONS WITH *BE* (PAGE 77)

Modal-like expressions with *be*

1 *Be bound to / Be certain to / Be sure to* for things that are definitely going to happen
*If you drop that glass, it**'s bound to** / **certain to** / **sure to** break.*

2 *Be likely/unlikely to* for things that are probably (not) going to happen
*There's a lot of traffic, so we**'re likely to** be late.*

3 *Be supposed to* for things expected to happen (because they were arranged or sb is responsible for them)
*My mom **was supposed to** pick me up at 3:30, but she didn't arrive until 4:00.*

4 *Be about to* for things that you're going to do soon or are going to happen soon
*Quick, turn on the TV. The game **is about to** start.*

5 *Be required to* for things that we are made to do (e.g., because of rules)
*Everyone who travels by plane **is required to** have a passport or some kind of photo ID.*

6 *Be forced to* for things that we are made to do, but don't want to
*I missed the last bus, so I **was forced to** walk home.*

7 *Be allowed to / Be permitted to* for things that we have permission to do
*They**'re allowed to** / **permitted to** use their phones in school, but not in class.*

A **Circle the correct option.**

1 The president just came into the room, so I think she's *about to / unlikely to* start her speech.
2 He hardly went to any classes, so he was *bound to / about to* do badly on the exam.
3 My coworker was off from work all week, so I was *sure to / forced to* do two jobs – mine and his.
4 We were *allowed to / required to* give our passport numbers when we checked into the hotel.
5 Only people who bought tickets online were *forced to / permitted to* go into the theater.
6 They're *about to / supposed to* announce the exam results in six weeks.

8.2 FUTURE FORMS (PAGE 79)

Future forms

1 Present continuous: for general future intentions and definite plans or arrangements *I**'m making** a film about college life.*
*I**'m meeting** my friends tomorrow at 6:00 p.m.*

2 *Be going to*: for general future plans and intention and predictions about the future *I**'m going to make** a film about college life.*
*It**'s going to be** a big surprise for them.*

3 *Might, may,* or *could:* when you're not sure about the future
*I **might start** my own business one day.*

4 *Will*: for predictions about the future and decisions made at the moment of speaking
*It **will be** a big surprise for them.*
*That looks difficult. I**'ll help** you with it.*

5 *Will* + *be* + verb + *-ing* (the future continuous): for an action in progress at a future time and for plans and intentions
*In a few years, I**'ll be looking** for a job.*
***Will** you **be coming** to the meeting on Thursday?*

> **!** **The future continuous and *be going to* can both express future plans and intentions. The future continuous is more formal.**

A **Complete the conversation with the verbs in parentheses ( ) in appropriate future forms.**

A I'm not sure yet, but I [1] ______ (ask) Juan for help. Do you know if he [2] ______ (come) out with us tonight?

B No. He [3] ______ (not, leave) the office yet. He's so busy these days! He [4] ______ (get) sick unless he takes it easy.

A No. I think he [5] ______ (be) fine. His vacation starts next month, so soon he [6] ______ (relax) on a beach somewhere.

9.1 UNREAL CONDITIONALS (PAGE 87)

Unreal conditionals

Present and future

if clause: *could*, simple past, or past continuous (imagined situation)

result clause: *would/could/might* + base form of a verb (predicted or possible result)

If *Josh* ***was/were studying*** *at the library, I* ***could help*** *him with his homework.*

If *we* ***got*** */* ***could get*** *tickets to the concert, we* ***wouldn't watch*** *it on TV.*

Past

if clause: past perfect (something possible that did not happen)

result clause: *would/could/may/might have* + past participle (imaginary past result that didn't happen)

I ***could have been*** *an X-ray technician* ***if*** *I* ***had studied*** *medicine.*

Or *would* + base form of a verb (imaginary present result)

I ***would have*** *a nicer apartment* ***if*** *I* ***hadn't bought*** *a new car.*

A **Complete the sentences with the correct form of the words in parentheses.**

1. If Brenda was trying out for that play, she ______ (get) a good part.
2. I would take a dance class if I ______ (not hurt) my ankle.
3. I ______ (change) jobs if I could, but I can't right now.
4. If I had gotten to the restaurant later, I ______ (not see) my cousin.
5. If I had heard the news, I ______ (be) at your house right now.
6. If they ______ (work) fewer hours, they wouldn't be so tired.

9.2 WISHES AND REGRETS (PAGE 89)

Wishes and regrets

I wish (*that*) / *If only* express a wish for something to be different or feelings of regret.

1. For wishes about general situations in the present: *I wish / If only* + simple past
   I wish / ***If only*** *I* ***knew*** *the answer to this question.*
2. For wishes about continuous situations in the present: *I wish / If only* + past continuous
   I wish / ***If only*** *I* ***was/were sitting*** *at home and not in this traffic jam.*
3. For wishes about ability or possibility in the present: *I wish / If only* + *could/couldn't*
   I wish / ***If only*** *I* ***could*** *find that book.*
4. For wishes about situations in the past: *I wish / If only* + past perfect
   I wish / ***If only*** *I* ***had bought*** *tickets in advance.*

! **After *I wish / If only*, you can use *was* (informal) or *were* (more formal) with *I*, *he*, *she*, and *it*.**

A **Complete the conversation.**

Jose Wow, it's hot on this bus! I wish it [1] ______ ten degrees cooler.

Ed If only we [2] ______ buy some cold sodas.

Jose Yeah, this water's warm. I wish I [3] ______ the bottle in the refrigerator last night.

Ed Right now, I wish I [4] ______ in a refrigerator! If only the air conditioning [5] ______ broken!

10.1 GERUNDS AFTER PREPOSITIONS (PAGE 99)

Gerunds after prepositions

1 Verb + preposition + gerund (e.g., *boast about, care about, insist on, plan on, result in, think of, worry about*)
*Josh **boasted about buying** a new car.*

2 *be* + adjective + preposition + gerund (e.g., *be afraid of, be excited about, be guilty of, be interested in*)
*We **are guilty of spending** too much time on social media.*

3 Noun + *of* + gerund (e.g., *benefits, cost, danger, fear, idea, importance, possibility, process, risk, way*)
*My **fear of flying** has stopped me from visiting you.*

A **Complete the sentences with the gerund form of the correct words.**

develop do recycle try win work

1 Mia often complains about ______________ on the weekends.
2 What are the benefits of ______________ plastic?
3 Larry isn't afraid of ______________ unusual foods.
4 The soccer team succeeded in ______________ every game this season.
5 I'm guilty of ______________ the same thing instead of trying new things.
6 You need to concentrate on ______________ your plan before you can start a business.

10.2 CAUSATIVE VERBS (PAGE 101)

Causative verbs

1	*Help/let/make/have* + object + base form of the verb	*My parents **make me save** money for my future.*
2	*Allow/cause/enable* + object + infinitive	*Surveys **enable stores to estimate** sales.*
3	*Keep/prevent/protect/stop* + object + *from* + gerund	*Her advice **kept me from losing** my job.*

A **Complete the sentences with the words in parentheses ( ) in the correct form. Add *from* when necessary.**

1 Customer feedback frequently ______________________ our products. (make, we, improve)
2 We tried to ______________________ too much money, but we failed. (prevent, he, spend)
3 Having my own home has ______________________ independent. (enable, I, be)
4 After a business trip, I usually ______________________ an extra day off. (let, my team, take)
5 My computer is broken, which has ______________________ any work done. (keep, I, get)
6 Worrying about his business ______________________ a lot of weight last year. (cause, he, lose)

11.1 PASSIVE FORMS (PAGE 109)

Passive forms

Passive and active sentences have similar meanings. But in the passive, the receiver of the action is more important than the doer and becomes the subject of the sentence. Add *by* + the agent if necessary.

1	Simple present passive: *am/is/are* + past participle	*These products **are** usually **imported**.*
2	Simple past passive: *was/were* + past participle	***Were** you **given** a refund?*
3	Present perfect passive: *has/have been* + past participle	*The order **has been canceled**.*
4	Future passive: *am/is/are going to/will* + *be* + past participle	*The goods **will be checked** before they're shipped.*
5	Present continuous passive: *am/is/are* + *being* + past participle	*Many goods **are being imported**.*
6	Past continuous passive: *was/were* + *being* + past participle	*The store **wasn't being used** until now.*

A **Rewrite the sentences in the passive form. Add *by* + the agent if it's important.**

1 We won't solve the problem of counterfeit goods easily . ______
2 A man found illegal copies of movies and games in a garage. ______
3 They're going to debate the issue of fake goods on TV. ______
4 For a long time, people were selling fake goods openly in markets. ______
5 Recently, they've changed the laws on counterfeit goods. ______
6 The government is now watching traders more carefully. ______

11.2 PASSIVES WITH MODALS AND MODAL-LIKE EXPRESSIONS; PASSIVE INFINITIVES (PAGE 111)

Passives with modals and modal-like expressions; passive infinitives

1 Passive with modals + *be* + past participle

- Common modals: *can, could, might, may, should, must*
  ***Should** the photos **be taken** in natural light?*

2 Passive with modal-like expressions + (*to*) + *be* + past participle

- Common expressions: *have to, need to, had better, be likely to, be supposed to*
  *Rumors **had better not be spread** at this school.*
  *Good journalists **don't need to be told** what to do.*

3 Passive infinitives (verb + *to be* + past participle)

- Common verbs and expressions: *ask, be likely, expect, hope, refuse, seem*
  *The problem **isn't likely to be solved** soon.*

! **For negative sentences, use *had better not* + *be* + past participle.**

A **Write sentences with passive forms.**

1 the facts / must / check / by the editor / ______ .
2 the manager / ask / show / the sales figures / ______ .
3 people / might / harm / by that false story / ______ .
4 the rumor / couldn't / control / ______ .
5 the journalists / refuse / tell / what to write / ______ .
6 that photo of me / had better / removed / from your post / ______ .

12.1 ADVERBS WITH ADJECTIVES AND ADVERBS (PAGE 119)

Adverbs with adjectives and adverbs

With adjectives

1 Use an adverb before an adjective to provide more detail about it.

- Common adverbs: *especially, exceptionally, mainly,* (*not*) *necessarily, particularly, reasonably*
  *John is **especially skilled** at painting, while his brother is **mainly good** at drawing.*

2 Use an adverb before an adjective to say what the adjective is related to.

- Common adverbs: *artistically, athletically, financially, musically, physically, scientifically, technically*
  *Sandra is **artistically talented** in many ways, but she's not **musically gifted** at all.*

With adverbs

3 Use an adverb before another adverb to provide more detail about it.

- Common adverbs: *especially, exceptionally, particularly, reasonably*
  *Some people are able to learn languages **particularly easily**. For example, my friend Paolo learned five languages **exceptionally fast**.*

! **An adverb + an adjective describes a noun.**
*The concert was **reasonably good**.*
An adverb + an adverb describes a verb.
*Sandra paints **exceptionally well** for a beginner.*

A **Circle the correct option.**

1 My accountant always gives me financially *correct* / *correctly* information.
2 Is she exceptionally *good* / *well* at music?
3 Jorge finished the test especially *quick* / *quickly*.
4 Eve learns new computer programs particularly *easy* / *easily*.
5 I like all kinds of music, but I'm mainly *interested* / *interestingly* in classical music.
6 Natasha's house is full of artistically *beautiful* / *beautifully* objects.

12.2 MAKING NON-COUNT NOUNS COUNTABLE (PAGE 121)

Making non-count nouns countable

Make non-count nouns countable with expressions describing specific quantities or amounts. For example:

1 Abstract ideas

- a little bit of (kindness/luck/space/time)
  ***A little bit of kindness** brightens up people's lives.*
- a piece of (advice/information)
  *This is **a** useful **piece of information**.*
- a word of (advice/encouragement/sympathy/wisdom)
  *He was full of **words of wisdom** and useful **pieces of advice**.*

2 Activities and sports

- a game of (basketball/chess/soccer/tennis)
  *We played **a few games of basketball** over the weekend.*

3 Food

- a box of, a bunch of, a can of, a grain of, a loaf of, a package of, a piece/slice of, a pound of, a serving of
  *I need **a bunch of parsley** and **a packet of cereal**.*

4 Liquids

- a bottle of, a cup of, a glass of, a drop of, a gallon of, a quart of
  *At the café, we ordered **two cups of coffee** and **a glass of juice**.*

5 Miscellaneous

- an act of (bravery/kindness) — *Helping me move was **an act of kindness**.*
- an article/item of (clothing) — *What is your favorite **item of clothing**?*
- a piece of (clothing/equipment/furniture/music/news) — *That's **a** fantastic **piece of equipment**!*
- a work of (art) — *This painting is my favorite **work of art**.*

!
A pound = about .45 kilograms
A gallon = about 3.8 liters
A quart = about .95 liters

A **Complete the sentences with the words in the box. Use the plural form when necessary.**

act article game serving word work

1 His ________ of encouragement really raised my spirits.
2 She gave each person a ________ of ice cream.
3 I think that being able to change yourself is a real ________ of bravery.
4 I lost three ________ of chess with my brother, and it ruined my evening.
5 I don't think we need any more ________ of art in this room.
6 How many ________ of clothing can you fit in that tiny suitcase?

VOCABULARY PRACTICE

1.1 FACING CHALLENGES (PAGE 2)

A **Circle the correct option.**

1 I usually *welcome / resist* change – unless it's dangerous, of course!
2 Many people *accept / get a grip* that they have a limit to what they can do.
3 I've never *been capable of / been frightened of* learning new things. I love it!
4 When I'm really busy at work, I can't *cope with / underestimate* other things. I'm too tired.
5 My dad used to tell me, "You need to *welcome / adapt* in order to be successful."
6 I *tackle / can't take* all this work. It's too much!
7 When I'm stressed, I tell myself to *get a grip / be a step forward* and deal with things.
8 My good friends often help me *underestimate / get through* difficult times.
9 They say it's hard to *survive / be capable of* in this city, but I'm doing fine!

B **Complete each sentence with the correct word or phrase from the box.**

accept	adapt	can't take	capable of
frightened of	step forward	tackle	underestimate

1 I'm afraid I'm not ________________ doing a sales manager's job. I don't have the skills.
2 We told the police what happened, but they wouldn't ________________ our explanation.
3 You usually ________________ well to big changes in your life.
4 Congratulations on your graduation! It's a ________________ in your life, and a big one.
5 Don't ________________ your ability to face challenges. You've always been good at dealing with new things.
6 She's moving to the country because she ________________ the pressure of city life anymore.
7 I have to ________________ some boring jobs around the house this weekend. They have to be done.
8 My mom says I was ________________ other people when I was a child. Actually, I was just shy.

1.2 DESCRIBING ANNOYING THINGS (PAGE 4)

A **Cross out the word or phrase that does not work in each sentence.**

1 This app always crashes. It *is infuriating / is awkward / drives me crazy.*
2 My little sister asks a lot of questions. It *gets on my nerves / drives me crazy / is hard to operate.*
3 This remote control is *complex / time-consuming / tricky.* I can't figure out how to record a show.
4 Old laptops *were awkward / were clumsy / lost my patience* because they were too big and never fit in a bag.
5 This door is *a waste of time / infuriating / frustrating.* It always makes a loud noise when someone opens it.

B **Complete each sentence with the correct form of the words or phrases in the box.**

be a waste of time	be hard to operate	complex
get on sb's nerves	lose patience	time-consuming

1 These drones ________________ . The remote controls aren't easy to use at all.
2 Our internet connection really ________________ . I can't stream any movies.
3 Jackie ________________ over little things – like when people ask her the same question more than once.
4 Painting our house is ________________ . We've been working for hours, and we've only done one room.
5 These directions are ________________ . I can't figure out how to put this table together.
6 Playing that game on your phone ________________ . You should be studying.

2.1 SPACE AND OCEAN EXPLORATION (PAGE 12)

A **Complete each sentence with the correct word. There is one item you won't use.**

atmosphere	come across	investigation	launched	observe
resources	satellite	species	surface	

What's Mars like? The [1] ______ of Mars is very different from the air around Earth. For example, there's very little oxygen in it. From [2] ______ images we can see that the [3] ______ of Mars is covered with rocks and red dust, so Mars is often called the Red Planet. People haven't been to Mars, but they've [4] ______ spacecraft to [5] ______ and explore it. They haven't [6] ______ any plant or animal [7] ______ on the planet, but they've found [8] ______, like water and iron.

B **Circle the correct option.**

Ocean [1]*exploration / atmosphere* is useful in many different ways. For example, scientists are making breakthroughs in medicine by [2]*launching / observing* different ocean [3]*species / investigation*. So it's important to [4]*monitor / come across* the ocean waters to [5]*preserve / use up* life there, not only for food [6]*exploration / resources*, but also because we have so much more to learn from it.

2.2 THE NATURAL WORLD (PAGE 14)

A **Circle the correct option.**

1 We climbed to the top of the *pond / volcano* to admire the view.
2 Ants and rats are excellent *sea life / survivors*.
3 How many animals are *endangered / adaptable* in your country?
4 What other *creatures / territory* can you find in this area?
5 The frog's natural *form of life / habitat* is in or around water.
6 There's a huge variety of *plant life / environment* in the Amazon rainforest.
7 Box jellyfish, which are fairly common, are one of the most *poisonous / endangered* species on Earth.
8 Dinosaur bones give us clues to their *origins / animal life*.

B **Complete each sentence with the correct word or phrase. Use each option only once.**

adaptable	animal life	forms of life	pond
survivors	sea life	territory	

1 Animals and birds try very hard to protect their ______.
2 Foxes are good ______ in both the city and the countryside.
3 There are many more ______ on Earth than we know of.
4 Unfortunately, there isn't much ______ in this forest anymore.
5 There's something swimming on the surface of the ______.
6 Ants might be small, but they are ______ creatures that can live in many environments.
7 Fish are one of the most common forms of ______.

3.1 DESCRIBING PERSONALITY (PAGE 22)

A **Match the words (1–5) with their definitions (a–e).**

1 show off ___ **a** talk and do things with other people
2 speak up ___ **b** try to get attention
3 extrovert ___ **c** someone who is shy and quiet
4 interact ___ **d** an energetic person who enjoys being with other people
5 introvert ___ **e** to speak in a louder voice so that people can hear you

B **Circle the correct option.**

My sister and I often go out together. She likes meeting new people and [1]*enjoys the company of / shows off* strangers, but I prefer to hang out with people I know. She loves to [2]*feel left out / socialize* in any environment, but I need to feel comfortable before I [3]*interact / speak up* with people. When people invite us to their homes, she's [4]*reserved / the life of the party*, and everyone loves her stories and jokes. I tend to [5]*speak softly / speak up* and often [6]*feel left out / attract attention* because I feel that no one wants to hear my stories. Sometimes, I think she [7]*shows off / interacts*, but I guess that's not really true. I'm probably just a little jealous. The truth is, I never [8]*am reserved / speak up*. If I did, everyone would probably listen to me, too. It's OK – if I find one person to talk to, I'm perfectly happy.

3.2 STRONG FEELINGS (PAGE 25)

A **Complete each sentence with the correct word. Sometimes there is more than one possible answer.**

bizarre	creepy	disgusting	fabulous	impressive	irritating
satisfying	stunning	tense	uneasy	weird	

1 My internet connection has been slow lately. It's really ________________ .
2 We saw some strange species of insects in the forest. They were like aliens – really ________________ .
3 Having worked so hard painting the apartment, it was extremely ________________ to see the results.
4 I'll never eat in that restaurant again. The food was absolutely ________________ !
5 I felt confident in the interview but not before it. Before it started, I was really ________________ and couldn't relax.
6 This landscape is ________________ ! Let's take some pictures before it gets dark.
7 I used to get scared going into that old house. It was such a(n) ________________ place.
8 We had a wonderful time on the coast. It was a(n) ________________ weekend.

B **Cross out the word that does not work in each sentence.**

1 From our hotel balcony, we could see the ocean. The view was *fabulous / uneasy / stunning*.
2 Cheryl thinks spiders are *creepy / disgusting / fabulous*, but she likes snakes.
3 I think it's *satisfying / weird / bizarre* that John can't stand the feel of plastic.
4 I always feel *tense / uneasy / irritating* when I have to speak in public.
5 Martin's new car is *tense / impressive / stunning*. I wish he'd let me drive it.
6 It was *an irritating / a tense / an impressive* situation, but we got through it.

4.1 PROFESSIONAL RELATIONSHIPS (PAGE 34)

A **Circle the correct option.**

1 I think they need to *build trust / demonstrate* before they start that project.
2 Can you tell me who *oversees / acts as* student registration?
3 I had a difficult time at first because I had no one to *take on / turn to*.
4 The adviser at my college *enabled me to / contributed* get my first job.
5 My mother *steered me away from / kept an eye on* a lot of trouble when I was a child.
6 We want you to *build a relationship / assist* the general manager as soon as you can.

B **Complete each paragraph with the correct words in the simple past.**

act as	build trust	enable me to
keep an eye on	steer me away from	take on

My cousin Frederico [1] ________________ my tutor when I was in college. He [2] ________________ the responsibility of helping me study and prepare for exams. He [3] ________________ all my work and [4] ________________ making mistakes. We [5] ________________ together, and I can honestly say that he [6] ________________ graduate with good grades.

assist	build a relationship	contribute
demonstrate	oversee	turn to

Marina quickly [7] ________________ with her students, and they [8] ________________ her whenever they needed help. She [9] ________________ them with their studies in every way and [10] ________________ all their exam preparations. She [11] ________________ useful suggestions and ideas at every staff meeting and always [12] ________________ interest and enjoyment in her job as a teacher here. I'm sorry she's leaving, but I wish her all the best for the future.

4.2 ASSESSING IDEAS (PAGE 36)

A **Circle the correct option.**

It can be hard to make decisions. It's not always easy to [1]*assess / draw* what the final [2]*aspects / consequences* might be. And even if it's possible to think [3]*out / through* everything in detail, ideas often have both good and bad [4]*aspects / strengths*. This sometimes forces us to [5]*be destructive / weigh the pros and cons*. Things get even more complicated if a decision has to be made as a team. Team members often point [6]*out / up* the problems with each other's ideas. This can cause problems. Success depends on the personal strengths and [7]*cons / weaknesses* of team members. Some people are good at expressing criticism in a positive, [8]*constructive / destructive* way. They are careful to [9]*draw / point* attention only to valid points. Others are not as careful. They can sound rude, and the results can be [10]*constructive / destructive* to team relationships.

B **Cross out the word or phrase that doesn't work in each sentence.**

1 I think he was being too critical. A lot of his points were *destructive / valid / unreasonable*.
2 We need to *assess / think through / point out* this plan and decide if it will work.
3 I'm really concerned about the *aspects / consequences / weaknesses* of his proposal.
4 Can I just *draw attention to / weigh the pros and cons / point out* a possible problem?
5 The boss was pleased with my *unreasonable / valid / constructive* suggestions.

5.1 DEALING WITH EMOTIONS (PAGE 44)

A **Circle the correct option.**

1 When planes land, I'm *scared to death / conscious of* an uneasy feeling among the passengers.
2 You need to *calm down / panic* and think clearly.
3 Do you think the therapist can *regain control / cure* my fear of spiders?
4 Right now, my *breathing technique / anxiety level* is low.
5 I was afraid to drive, but my mom helped me *be scared to death / overcome my fear*.
6 It's important to *be rational / be in control of* when faced with fear.
7 Do you think trying *therapy / an anxiety level* will help him?

B Complete each sentence with the correct word or phrase from the box.

be in control of	be rational	breathing technique	cure
panic	regained control	was scared to death	

1 After panicking for a few minutes, I ________________ and started to relax.
2 Do you want to ________________ your emotions when flying? If so, try our VR therapy.
3 The movie was so frightening. I ________________ .
4 We're trying to ________________ about the decision, but it will change our lives completely.
5 Try not to ________________ about your driving test. Breathe deeply and relax.
6 She feels much better, but the medicine didn't completely ________________ her cough.
7 You might feel more relaxed if you try this ________________ .

5.2 WILLINGNESS AND UNWILLINGNESS (PAGE 46)

A **Circle the correct options.**

1 I'm *passionate* / *eager* to learn languages, but my friend has no *desire* / *intention* of learning another language.
2 My dad is *more than happy* / *reluctant* to help me study, but he is *against* / *eager* helping me write my essays.
3 Some of us are *dying* / *hesitating* to go camping, but others are *anxious* / *passionate* to stay at home and study for their exams.
4 It's great you're *prepared* / *unwilling* to meet us at the airport. We're *reluctant* / *dying* to see you again!

B **Complete each sentence with the correct phrase.**

am prepared to	am unwilling to	are anxious to	have no intention of
hesitated to	is against	is passionate about	are reluctant to

1 I saw he was in trouble, but I ________________ help him. I didn't want to make the situation worse.
2 We ________________ meet your new friends. We can hardly wait.
3 I hate flying and ________________ getting on a plane ever again!
4 She ________________ keeping fit. She runs ten kilometers every day.
5 Sorry, but I ________________ work this weekend. I'm tired and need to rest.
6 My mother can repair anything. She ________________ buying new things if she can fix the old ones.
7 They ________________ leave their house because they're watching a soccer game on TV.
8 I ________________ accept the job if the salary is good enough.

6.1 TALKING ABOUT FAME (PAGE 54)

A **Circle the correct option.**

Jason [1]*had a good reputation* / *got hits* as a music student in college. One of his performances [2]*caught the media's attention* / *made an appearance*, and he soon [3]*heard of it* / *was getting a lot of publicity*. He never intended to [4]*seek fame* / *praise himself*, but he enjoyed the attention. After that, he [5]*raised awareness* / *made appearances* on several TV shows. I noticed he [6]*did the broadcast* / *made headlines* almost every day, so I went to one of his concerts. Jason really [7]*raised my awareness of* / *caught my attention* the power of music.

B **Cross out the expression that does not work in each sentence.**

1 The singer's videos *got a lot of publicity* / *got a lot of hits* / *made an appearance* in a short amount of time.
2 As a young artist, he *praised* / *caught everyone's attention* / *sought fame*.
3 Our band *did a broadcast* / *has heard of* / *made an appearance* online.
4 Famous people often have a need to make *headlines* / *appearances in public* / *a bad reputation*.
5 The teacher *raised awareness of* / *praised* / *made them entertaining* our creative videos.

6.2 REPORTING VERBS (PAGE 56)

FIND IT

A Match the words (1–12) with the definitions (a–l). Use a dictionary or your phone to help you.

1	announce ___	a	not be sure of something
2	argue ___	b	promise
3	boast ___	c	talk too proudly about something connected with you
4	claim ___	d	guess the size, value, amount, cost, etc., of something
5	confirm ___	e	tell people new information
6	deny ___	f	say something is true
7	estimate ___	g	give reasons to support or oppose an idea, action, etc.
8	have doubts about ___	h	suggest a plan or action
9	hope to ___	i	say something is not true
10	insist ___	j	want something to happen
11	propose ___	k	say something must be done
12	swear ___	l	to say that based on evidence something is true

B Circle the correct option.

1 My friends often *boast / hope to / swear* about their good grades.
2 When will you *insist / announce / claim* your plans to sell the company?
3 I was happy that the report *confirmed / estimated / denied* my numbers were correct.
4 I know that John was at a concert last night, but he *insists / denies / proposes* it.
5 Jenny *denied / had doubts about / swore* she told me about the party, but she hadn't.

7.1 POSITIVE EXPERIENCES (PAGE 67)

A Circle the correct options. Sometimes both are correct.

1 In my job, I have a positive effect on people. They *are of use / value* what I do.
2 I'm proud of the work I do. It *makes a contribution / is an honor* to work for this company.
3 My job is a lot of fun. I *take pleasure in / am a good influence on* my work.
4 It's good to make a contribution – to feel that what you do is *beneficial / worthwhile*.
5 When people are scared, it makes a difference if you *devote your life / reassure* them.
6 Janelle is an excellent nurse and *is a good influence on / devotes her life to* others.
7 When you do a job well, you generally *get satisfaction out of / reassure* it.
8 I want a job that has a positive effect on the world. I want to *make a contribution / make a difference*.

B Complete the sentences with these expressions. Sometimes more than one answer is correct.

devoted their lives to	get satisfaction out of	make a contribution	make a difference
reassure	take pleasure in	value	was beneficial
was of use	was worthwhile		

1 I enjoyed working on the construction of the new hospital. I felt it ________________ for my city.
2 Thanks for your help. I always ________________ the career advice you give me.
3 My sister and her husband have ________________ helping others.
4 If we hire you, how can you help the company? How will you ________________?
5 I often help people in trouble, and of course, I ________________ that.
6 Don't worry. Let me ________________ you everything will be fine.

7.2 MAKING PURCHASES (PAGE 68)

A **Complete the conversation with the correct words.**

be foolish	convinced me	look ridiculous	makes financial sense
practical	purchase	regret a purchase	

Marcy I think we should [1] ______ these snowboards.

Jason Yeah, the salesperson [2] ______ it's cheaper than renting them.

Marcy It really [3] ______ . We snowboard a lot in the winter, so it's [4] ______ .

Jason But I'm not sure about these bright colors. I don't want to [5] ______ in front of our friends.

Marcy I think they're really cool, but I don't want you to [6] ______ that was kind of expensive. Why don't we go home and look at some other options online?

Jason Good idea. There's no reason to [7] ______ and make a quick decision.

B **Circle the correct option.**

1 Owning an environmentally friendly car has a lot of *appeal / sense*, and I *convince / encourage* you to consider getting one.

2 For me, buying new clothes *is not worth the money / looks ridiculous*. I get bored with them after a couple of weeks, and I always *regret the purchase / urge you to buy them*.

3 My sister *regrets / urged me* to a buy a laptop, but I think this tablet *has potential / is foolish*, too. It's cheaper and will do everything I need it to.

8.1 DESCRIBING NEATNESS AND MESSINESS (PAGE 76)

A **Circle the correct option. Sometimes both options are correct.**

1 We've *put the files in alphabetical order / folded the files* so they can be found easily.

2 Someone has *arranged the towels / hung up the towels* neatly.

3 He left his papers *all over the place / tangled up*.

4 She carefully *lined up / threw* the books on the shelves.

5 My dad *hung up his tools / put his tools in a pile* on the wall of his garage.

6 I keep telling my kids to *throw in / put away* their clothes.

7 All the dishes *are organized / are disorganized* neatly in the cupboard.

8 Your computer cables are all *jumbled up / tangled up*.

B **Complete the paragraph with these expressions. Sometimes there's more than one correct answer.**

arranges	disorganized	fold	hangs up	jumbled up
leaves … all over the place		lines up	organized	puts away
tangled up	throws … on			

Leo and Ed are roommates, but they have completely different habits. Leo is [1] ______ . He always [2] ______ his clothes neatly in the closet, and he [3] ______ his shoes side by side on the floor. But Ed is completely [4] ______ . His clothes are always [5] ______ , and he [6] ______ them ______ . He doesn't [7] ______ them, but just [8] ______ them ______ the floor.

8.2 TALKING ABOUT PROGRESS (PAGE 78)

A **Circle the correct option.**

1 My friend studied really hard, and *effectively* / *as expected*, she did well on her exams.
2 He does everything very quickly and *with ease* / *little by little*.
3 If you want to work on that project, you will have to do it *efficiently* / *on your own time*, not during work hours.
4 I researched the subject *thoroughly* / *smoothly*, but I still had trouble writing my essay.
5 It's a wonderful feeling to complete a project *successfully* / *steadily*.
6 I felt relaxed because I was allowed to work *with difficulty* / *at my own pace*.

B **Put the words in parentheses ( ) in the correct place in each sentence. There's sometimes more than one correct place.**

1 I have to do this because it's easy to make mistakes. (little by little)
2 We read the instructions but couldn't find the information we wanted. (thoroughly)
3 Just work on it, and don't worry about the schedule. (steadily)
4 How can we manage this project? (effectively)
5 If you want to complete this, that's fine with me. (on your own time)
6 It's amazing that you can work in this noisy office. (efficiently)
7 I completed the project, and I didn't enjoy it at all. (with difficulty)
8 Everything went, so we were all very pleased. (smoothly)

9.1 LUCK AND CHOICE (PAGE 86)

A **Complete the sentences with the correct expressions.**

be in the right place at the right time	chance encounter
deliberate decision	determination
fate	believe my luck
path	was fortunate

1 A(n) ________________ with a famous singer set me on a ________________ to study music.
2 Sara believes in ________________ . She says it's the reason she met her boyfriend, but I just think she happened to ________________ .
3 Joaquin made a ________________ to study law. He'll need a lot of ________________ to finish his degree.
4 I ________________ to get the last two concert tickets. I can't ________________ !

B **Circle the correct options.**

1 College was a *life-changing experience* / *fate* for me.
2 Laura got a *path* / *lucky break* when she was asked to appear on a reality TV cooking show.
3 Seeing my cousin at the mall was a *right place at the right time* / *coincidence*.
4 Gavin studied biology, but he *wound up* / *was fortunate* being a gym teacher.
5 She made a *chance encounter* / *deliberate decision* to cancel her trip when she heard about the storm.

9.2 COMMENTING ON MISTAKES (PAGE 89)

A **Circle the correct options.**

1 Now I realize it was a bad *side / move*. It was a dumb *mistake / thing* to do.
2 My clothes were totally wrong for the party. I found myself in an *awkward / incompetent* situation, but I could see the *bad / funny* side of it.
3 I tripped over a bench because I wasn't *watching / learning* what I was doing. I don't text while walking now, but I learned that the *silly / hard* way.
4 Her dog bit me, which was *incompetent / unfortunate*. It *was my own fault / kicked myself* because I accidentally scared it.
5 It was a *hard / silly* mistake. And I made it because I was in too much of a *hurry / move*.

B **Complete the sentences with the expressions in the box.**

dumb thing to do	incompetent at	kicked myself	learned that the hard way	
found myself in an awkward situation		sees the funny side	too much of a hurry	unfortunate

1 Because I was quite ________________ math, I decided not to become an engineer.
2 I couldn't remember the company director's name, so I ________________.
3 I left my phone outside. Phones don't like rain! I ________________.
4 I tried to carry six glasses. It was a ________________.
5 Out of everyone in the restaurant, I was the one hit by the flying tomato! I was so ________________.
6 At the airport, I realized I'd forgotten my passport. I could have ________________!
7 Take your time. You're always in ________________.
8 He's a pretty positive guy. He usually ________________ of things.

10.1 DESCRIBING CHARACTERISTICS (PAGE 98)

A **What are the sentences describing? Write the correct expression.**

a look	a match	build	features	look-alikes

1 Tom is very tall and has a lot of muscles. ________________
2 Mike and Joey aren't related, but people think they're brothers. ________________
3 I love the clothes my Aunt Larisa wears, and she always has a trendy hairstyle. ________________
4 Mario has dark eyes, a small nose, and a wide mouth. ________________
5 Jim and Cara are great for each other. They have a lot in common and get along well. ________________

B **Circle the correct options.**

1 My brother and I have similar features and *likeness / characteristics*, but our interests are completely different.
2 You have to complete the form with your name, contact information, and *feature / gender*.
3 My dog Charlie is a *male / female*, and he's very shy.
4 The *features / similarities* between Isabel and her cousin make them seem more like sisters.
5 John is a very independent *individual / match*. He always does what he wants, even if it's not popular.
6 Lara has a medium *build / look*, while her sister is really tall and slim.

10.2 DESCRIBING RESEARCH (PAGE 100)

A **Circle the correct options.**

We did a [1]*survey / calculation* of our customers two months ago. One of the marketing staff then [2]*analyzed / demonstrated* their profiles and [3]*calculated / identified* ten customers who could become our special advisers. We want them to [4]*examine / survey* our menu and give their [5]*survey / assessment* of which dishes no longer interest people. In return for their help, we will give them cooking classes, including [6]*demonstrations / analysis* and hands-on lessons. In addition, the manager has [7]*examined / calculated* that we can afford to pay them $50 each for their time.

B **Complete the sentences with the correct words. Sometimes there's more than one correct answer.**

analyze	assessed	assessments	calculations
demonstrations	examined	identify	surveys

1 Would you please ________________ this sales report and let me know if it's reliable?
2 I carefully ________________ the printer, but I didn't see anything wrong with it.
3 We watched a couple of interesting ________________ of how to interview new graduates.
4 I've ________________ the information and am going to start writing my essay this afternoon.
5 We found out later that most of his ________________ were wrong.
6 Unfortunately, the results of both customer ________________ were unclear.
7 Can you ________________ one or two employees who have the potential to be managers?

11.1 DESCRIBING CONSUMER GOODS (PAGE 108)

A **Complete the sentences with the correct words in the box. Sometimes there is more than one correct answer.**

authentic	counterfeit	deadly	fake	fireproof
genuine	inferior	legal	second-rate	sophisticated

1 Is this watch real or not? If it's a copy, it's a very ________________ one.
2 Don't buy that phone. It's made of cheap, ________________ materials, which won't last.
3 Your purse is ________________ . It's definitely made by our company.
4 Is it ________________ to copy designer clothing if you openly say it's not real?
5 One of the chemicals used in this hair dye is dangerous. In fact, it's ________________ . Throw it away!
6 I got a(n) ________________ $5 bill in my change yesterday. I took it to the bank, and they gave me a real one.
7 This blanket is made of ________________ material and is very safe for your child's bed.

B **Circle the correct options.**

My friend says she doesn't mind if goods are [1]*counterfeit / sophisticated* as long as they're cheap. But it's an [2]*inferior / illegal* trade, so that's why I prefer to buy [3]*fake / genuine* goods. Besides, I don't like [4]*second-rate / original* stuff.

I bought some [5]*fireproof / inferior* gloves because I often have barbecues in the summer. But it turned out they weren't [6]*a deadly / an authentic* product. The design was [7]*imperfect / original* and had many problems. To me, this was a [8]*fake / legal* issue because of the risk of injury, so I went to the police.

11.2 DEGREES OF TRUTH (PAGE 110)

A **Complete the sentences with the expressions in the box. There is one you won't use.**

controversial	dishonest	inaccurate	misinformation
suspicious	trustworthy	urban legend	white lie

1 I never believe what Joe tells me because he's ________________ .
2 I told Julie a ________________ because I didn't want to hurt her feelings.
3 I don't believe the ________________ about the clown statue that came to life.
4 Making clones of animals is a(n) ________________ issue.
5 That news article is ________________ . Over 21 million people live in Mexico City, not 11 million.
6 I always post articles on social media from ________________ sites because I want to inform people about the truth.
7 Donna's story is ________________ . I don't think she was in Los Angeles. I wonder where she *really* was!

B **Cross out the word that doesn't work in each sentence.**

1 Although the information is true, that article is *biased / inaccurate / controversial* because the author is friends with the person she interviewed.
2 Did you really think the story of a man owning a 200-pound cat was real? It was just *a hoax / a white lie / a rumor.*
3 Janice's story sounds *suspicious / exaggerated / trustworthy.* I don't think she really was lost for *15* hours!
4 That photo is *accurate / misleading / false.* Sharks can't live in lakes.
5 *Misinformation / Urban legends / Rumors* are entertaining as long as they don't harm anyone.

12.1 SKILL AND PERFORMANCE (PAGE 118)

A **Circle the correct options.**

My friend Tasha is [1]*talented / analytical* in many creative fields. She's very [2]*trained / artistic*, even though she's never taken an art class. She paints, draws, and is an excellent photographer. I like her paintings the best because they're so [3]*imaginative / determined*. She's also very [4]*athletic / musical* and is [5]*a skilled / an intellectual* piano player. Her father taught her how to play when she was three. Even though she's [6]*technical / gifted* in these creative areas and finds math difficult, she wants to be an engineer. She's [7]*determined / musical*, but I don't think it's a [8]*logical / competent* choice.

B **Complete the sentences with the correct words.**

analytical	athletic	competent	intellectual	technical	trained

1 Josh isn't a(n) ________________ life coach, but he gives very good life advice.
2 Sarah likes her science classes because she has a very ________________ mind.
3 You have to be a(n) ________________ person to be able to run a marathon.
4 I need help with some ________________ problems on my computer.
5 My accountant is very ________________ , but I prefer to keep track of my budget myself.
6 ________________ games that require skill and knowledge make you smarter while you play them.

12.2 DESCRIBING EMOTIONAL IMPACT (PAGE 120)

A **Circle the correct options. Sometimes both are correct.**

1 I'm so happy! You've really *brightened up my day / made my day.*
2 I didn't like that movie. It *was a real downer / took my mind off my problems.*
3 His wonderful speech *stressed me out / left a lasting impression on me.*
4 Thanks so much! Your party *raised my spirits / got me down.*
5 The doctor was great. She *put my mind at rest / ruined my day.*
6 Seeing the new art sculptures in the park *did me good / captured my imagination.*

B **Cover exercise A. Complete the sentences with the verbs in the correct form.**

be brighten capture do get leave raise ruin stress take

1 He says his work is ________________ him out right now.
2 You need something to ________________ your mind off your problems.
3 The things he said ________________ a lasting impression on me.
4 It will ________________ you good to get out of the house for a while.
5 Failing my exam yesterday ________________ a real downer.
6 You can ________________ up people's lives with just a smile.
7 The speaker's ideas really ________________ our imagination last night.
8 This cloudy, rainy weather is ________________ me down.
9 Going out to dinner and a movie should ________________ your spirits.
10 That bad news ________________ my day yesterday.

PROGRESS CHECK

Can you do these things? Check (✓) what you can do. Then write your answers in your notebook.

UNIT 1

Now I can …	Prove it
☐ talk about facing challenges.	Use four words to describe how someone you know deals with challenges.
☐ talk about present habits.	Write three things you do every day using three different forms.
☐ describe annoying things.	Think of a tech item you don't like. Use four words to say why.
☐ talk about past habits.	Write five things you used to do ten years ago. Use three different forms.
☐ discuss issues and agree strongly.	Complete the conversation with words that are true for you. **A** *As for* ________ *, I think* ________ . **B** *Overall,* ________ .
☐ write an opinion essay.	Look at your formal essay from lesson 1.4. Find three ways to make it better.

UNIT 2

Now I can …	Prove it
☐ talk about exploration and research.	Complete the sentences. **1** *I think travel to outer space* ________ . **2** *Exploring the ocean floor* ________ . **3** *We need to preserve* ________ .
☐ use comparative structures.	Compare living underwater in a submarine to living in outer space in a spacecraft. Use these words: *endangered, habitat, plant life, poisonous, territory.*
☐ talk about life forms in different environments.	Write five "amazing facts" about the animal, plant, and sea life in your country.
☐ use superlative structures and ungradable adjectives.	Use superlative structures to describe the amazing facts you wrote above.
☐ exchange important information.	Someone wants to visit your country for the first time. Give them some important information to help plan the visit.
☐ write a description of an area.	Look at your description from lesson 2.4. Find three ways to make it better.

UNIT 3

Now I can …	Prove it
☐ describe personality.	Describe two people you know. How are their personalities different?
☐ use relative clauses.	Complete these sentences. *My [family member], whose* ________ *, is* ________ . *Winter is a time when* ________ .
☐ talk about things I love or hate.	Write about a sight, sound, or smell you love and one you hate. Say how they make you feel.
☐ use present participles.	Complete the sentences with present participles and your own ideas. *I'm just sitting here,* ________ . *Animals* ________ *are* ________ .
☐ make and respond to requests.	Write a short conversation where one person makes a request and the other person refuses at first but finally agrees.
☐ write a personal statement for a job application.	Look at your personal statement from lesson 3.4. Find three ways to make it better.

PROGRESS CHECK

Can you do these things? Check (✓) what you can do. Then write your answers in your notebook.

UNIT 4

Now I can …	Prove it
☐ talk about my support team in life.	Write about two people you know and describe how they support you.
☐ use *so*, *such*, *even*, and *only* to add emphasis.	Write four sentences describing how easy, hard, or fun your daily life is. Don't forget to add emphasis.
☐ make decisions.	Write three sentences about how you assess ideas. Use *weigh the pros and cons, constructive, point out.*
☐ use reflexive pronouns and pronouns with *other/another.*	Write three sentences with examples of reflexive pronouns. Write one sentence with a form of *other* and one with *another.*
☐ discuss advantages and disadvantages.	Write about the pros and cons of job sharing.
☐ write a summary.	Look at your summary from lesson 4.4. Find three ways to make it better.

UNIT 5

Now I can …	Prove it
☐ talk about dealing with emotions.	Write sentences using each of these expressions once: *anxiety level, be scared to death, calm down, regain control.*
☐ use real conditionals.	Complete the sentences with your own ideas. *If I decide to travel, I'll* ________ . *I might* ________ *if* ________ .
☐ express willingness and unwillingness.	Complete the sentences. *I have no desire to* ________ . *I'm dying to* ________ .
☐ use alternatives to *if* in conditionals.	Write four sentences about communicating with people. Use *as long as, unless, even if, only if.*
☐ consider and contrast ideas.	Write about the pros and cons of studying online.
☐ write an online comment with examples.	Look at your comment from lesson 5.4. Find three ways to make it better.

UNIT 6

Now I can …	Prove it
☐ talk about fame.	Give definitions of these words: *broadcast, get hits, raise awareness.*
☐ use narrative tenses.	Look back over the last five years of your life. Describe how you came to be in your English class now from that point in your life. Use narrative tenses.
☐ use reporting verbs.	Which reporting verb means: Say something is not true? Say you plan to do something? Say you want someone to do something?
☐ use reported speech with modals.	Change these sentences to reported speech. Julian announced, "I'll be famous some day!" A website claims, "The owner of Amazon is the richest man in the world." My sister insisted, "We can sing well."
☐ make assumptions.	Imagine your friend took a vacation abroad. Write six assumptions about what their trip was like. Then write their reply to each one. Imagine some of your assumptions were totally correct, some were partly correct, and some were incorrect.
☐ write an interesting story.	Look at your story from lesson 6.4. Find three ways to make it better.

PROGRESS CHECK

Can you do these things? Check (✓) what you can do. Then write your answers in your notebook.

UNIT 7

Now I can …	Prove it
☐ describe positive experiences.	Write three sentences about something you get satisfaction out of, something you take pleasure in doing, and something that you value.
☐ use gerunds and infinitives after adjectives, nouns, and pronouns.	Write three sentences about how you spend your free time, how you waste time, and how people often spend weekends in your town.
☐ talk about purchases.	Write two sentences about a practical purchase you've made and two sentences about a foolish purchase.
☐ use infinitives after verbs with and without objects.	Complete the sentence with your own ideas. *Last year, I persuaded* __________ .
☐ bargain for a purchase.	Write down two expressions each for (1) bargaining, (2) accepting an offer, (3) rejecting an offer.
☐ write a for-and-against essay.	Look at your essay from lesson 7.4. Find three ways to make it better.

UNIT 8

Now I can …	Prove it
☐ describe neatness and messiness.	Write four sentences using each of these expressions: *put sth in alphabetical order, arrange sth neatly, be jumbled up, put away.*
☐ use modal expressions with *be*.	Complete the sentences. *We're supposed to* __________ . *Don't worry. He's bound to* __________ .
☐ talk about progress.	Complete the sentences. *These days,* __________ *is going smoothly.* *I* __________ *with difficulty.*
☐ use future forms.	Write two predictions and two plans about your future.
☐ suggest and show interest in ideas.	Write your response to a suggestion to have a pool party this weekend. Then write another suggestion.
☐ write a complaint letter.	Look at your complaint letter from lesson 8.4. Find three ways to make it better.

UNIT 9

Now I can …	Prove it
☐ talk about luck and choice.	Complete the sentences: *I don't believe in* __________ . *Good things happened to me because of* __________ .
☐ use unreal conditionals.	Complete the sentence: *If I could* __________ *, I* __________ .
☐ comment on mistakes.	Complete the sentences to match the comment. *Recently, I* __________ *. That was a bad move.* *Yesterday, I* __________ *. I wasn't watching what I was doing.* *Once, I* __________ *, but luckily, I saw the funny side of it.*
☐ express wishes and regrets.	Complete the sentences about small things you regret. *I wish I could* __________ . *If only I* __________ . *I wish I hadn't* __________ .
☐ reassure someone about a problem.	Complete these expressions of reassurance. *It's no use* __________ . *What are you* __________ ?
☐ write an article with tips.	Look at your article from lesson 9.4. Find three ways to make it better.

PROGRESS CHECK

Can you do these things? Check (✓) what you can do. Then write your answers in your notebook.

UNIT 10	Now I can ...	Prove it
	☐ describe people's characteristics.	Write three sentences about the features, build, and look of a well-known person.
	☐ use gerunds after prepositions.	Complete the sentence: *I believe in* ______.
	☐ describe research.	Describe some analysis you would like to do on the grocery shopping habits of your class. How would you go about the research and what would the research demonstrate?
	☐ use complements of verbs describing cause and effect.	Write four sentences. Use each of these verbs once: *enable, keep from, let, protect from.*
	☐ give my impressions.	Complete the sentences about what your friends are doing or thinking about. *I have a hunch that* ______. *I get the impression that* ______.
	☐ write a professional profile.	Look at your professional profile from lesson 10.4. Find three ways to make it better.

UNIT 11	Now I can ...	Prove it
	☐ describe consumer goods.	Write sentences with these words: *authentic, fireproof, illegal, second-rate.*
	☐ use passive forms.	Complete the sentences with passive forms and your own ideas. *This fake watch was* ______. *One day, goods will* ______ *by* ______.
	☐ talk about degrees of truth.	Write sentences with these words: *accurate, dishonest, exaggerated, hoax.*
	☐ use passives with modals and modal-like expressions; use passive infinitives.	Complete the sentence: *Fake purses shouldn't* ______ *online.*
	☐ express belief and disbelief.	Write two expressions each for expressing belief, some belief, and disbelief.
	☐ write a persuasive essay.	Look at your persuasive essay from lesson 11.4. Find three ways to make it better.

UNIT 12	Now I can ...	Prove it
	☐ talk about skill and performance.	Write three sentences. Use a pair of words in each sentence: *analytical/logical, athletic/trained, musical/artistic.*
	☐ use adverbs with adjectives and adverbs.	Complete the sentences with an adjective or adverb and your own ideas. *I sing especially* ______. *Soccer is an athletically* ______ *sport.*
	☐ describe emotional impact.	Write four sentences. Use each of these expressions once: *get me down, leave a lasting impression on me, make my day, stress me out.*
	☐ make non-count nouns countable.	Complete the sentences. *My teacher gave me two* ______ *advice.* *How many* ______ *clothing are you taking?* *Are you free for a(n)* ______ *basketball?* *Everyone needs a(n)* ______ *kindness.*
	☐ describe my ambitions.	Complete the sentences with your own ideas. *I'm determined to* ______. *I'm confident that* ______. *But I can't say for sure that* ______.
	☐ write a review of a performance.	Look at your review from lesson 12.4. Find three ways to make it better.

PAIR WORK PRACTICE (STUDENT A)

1.3 EXERCISE 3C STUDENT A

1 **Discuss smartphones with Student B. Give your opinions about the issues below.**

Issues:

- easy or difficult to set up?
- large enough screen?
- good camera?
- enough battery life?
- usefulness of pre-installed apps?

2 **Listen to Student B's opinion about laptops. Say if you agree strongly or give your own opinion on the issues.**

2.3 EXERCISE 3B STUDENT A

1 **Student B will ask you for advice about buying a backpack. Use the information below to advise them.**

The backpack should:

1 be comfortable (very important)
2 be light
3 be the right size for you
4 have a waterproof cover
5 have a belt to go around your waist

2 **Then ask Student B for some advice about what kind of clothing to take on a skiing trip. Also ask about what kind of gloves to take. Your hands get cold easily, and you're worried about this.**

3.3 EXERCISE 3C STUDENT A

1 **Ask Student B for a favor:**

Conversation 1

You want them to be your guest at a company party this weekend.

2 **Listen to Student B, and for each refusal, use these cues to respond:**

- the people are nice and very friendly
- there will be good food, games, and music
- bring nephew; some coworkers have kids; kid-friendly activities are planned; he'd love it

3 **Student B is going to ask you for a favor. Listen and use the cues below to respond.**

Conversation 2

- refuse; you don't really like dancing
- refuse again; you're too shy; you'd be embarrassed
- refuse again; it's probably too expensive
- accept in the end

4.3 EXERCISE 3B STUDENT A

You're going to discuss open-plan offices (offices where all employees work in one big room). Tell your partner these advantages and disadvantages. Listen to their ideas.

Advantages:

- makes teamwork easier and increases creativity
- encourages people to work harder because they see others working

Disadvantages:

- is so noisy that it's difficult to work
- others can hear your work calls

5.3 EXERCISE 3C STUDENT A

1 **Imagine you like swimming. Tell your partner about its good and bad sides. Say how certain you are.**

+ Being in water keeps you cool.
+ A swimsuit is usually pretty cheap.
+ It doesn't hurt your knees and ankles.

– Chlorine from the water is hard on your skin.
– You have to pay to use the pool.
– You can get an ear infection.

2 **Now listen to your partner. They will tell you about the good and bad sides of running.**

3 **Compare your sports.**

PAIR WORK PRACTICE

6.1 EXERCISE 4A STUDENT A

A **You're going to tell a story about becoming famous quickly. Read the story quickly. Then read it again and underline key points. Pay attention to verb tenses. Then tell your partner the story in your own words.**

K-Pop Rocks

South Korean band Monsta X started in 2015 and became instantly famous for their synchronized choreography and unique mix of hip-hop, pop, and electronic dance music. The band had formed when its members participated in a TV talent show. Their first U.S. performance was in Los Angeles in 2015, but it was their first studio album with the title song *Beautiful* that reached number one in the Billboard World Albums chart in March 2017. In April 2018 their Japanese single *Spotlight* received an official gold certification by the Recording Industry Association of Japan. Now almost everything they do goes viral; the fans want to know everything. Like, did you know that the band leader Shownu loves dancing, is a good swimmer, and can pick things up with his toes? And Wonho, the lead singer and dancer, has acrophobia (fear of heights).

B **Give your opinion of the stories.**

7.3 EXERCISE 5 STUDENT A

Conversation 1

Read the information. Then use these arguments while bargaining to get the best price from Student B.

Situation: You want to sell your mountain bike for $175 (your opening price can be higher).

- It's very strong and reliable.
- You've only used it for a few months. It has no damage.
- It's a popular model. Mountain bikers love it.
- You can throw in a lock for free.

Conversation 2

Situation: You want to buy a couch from Student B. Find out the price and bargain hard to get the best deal.

9.3 EXERCISE 3C STUDENT A

Conversation 1

You and Student B are close friends.

Problem: You forgot your eight-year-old nephew's birthday, and he's really upset. Tell your friend about it and ask for advice.

Conversation 2

You are a professor. Student B is your student.

Listen to Student B's problem and give advice. Reassure them, using expressions that are appropriate for your relationship.

10.3 EXERCISE 5A

Discuss the gyms, giving your impressions of each. Decide which one you'd each like to join, and why.

	Gym 1	Gym 2	Gym 3
Cost	Programs for all budgets	Student discounts	Pay by month or by year
Location	Two locations: uptown and downtown	Six convenient central locations	One convenient central location
Classes	50 classes a week: yoga, dance, swimming, diet and weight loss	Boxing, karate, judo, personal training	Fitness classes, 8 large studios, personal trainers, athletic training
Equipment	Weights, running machines	Weights, running, and cycling machines	modern equipment, wall/rope climbing
Social area	Wi-Fi, healthy snack bar	TVs, Wi-Fi, café and juice bar	Café, lounge, TVs, Wi-Fi
Pool	Large changing rooms	✗	Clean changing room, spa
Hours	Open daily 8:00 a.m. to 10:00 p.m.	Open 24/7	Open 6:00 a.m. to midnight

PAIR WORK PRACTICE (STUDENT B)

1.3 EXERCISE 3C STUDENT B

1 **Listen to Student A's opinions about smartphones. Say if you agree strongly or give your own opinion on the issues.**

2 **Discuss laptops with Student A. Give your opinions about the issues below.**

Issues:

- size OK?
- weight OK?
- fast enough?
- enough battery life?
- usefulness of pre-installed software?

2.3 EXERCISE 3B STUDENT B

1 **You want to buy a new backpack. Ask Student A for some advice. Also ask about using the backpack in the rain. You're concerned that stuff inside it will get wet.**

2 **Then Student A will ask you for advice about what kind of clothing to take on a skiing trip. Use the information below to advise them.**

Things you'll need:

1 a ski jacket (very important): thick, waterproof, strong

2 snow pants

3 ski goggles to protect your eyes (large sunglasses)

4 a warm hat

5 ski gloves: thick, waterproof, long enough to cover your wrists

3.3 EXERCISE 3C STUDENT B

1 **Student A is going to ask you for a favor. Listen and use the cues below to respond.**

Conversation 1

- refuse; you don't know anyone
- refuse again; you don't think you'd enjoy it
- refuse again; you might have to take care of your ten-year-old nephew that day
- accept in the end

2 **Ask Student A for a favor:**

Conversation 2

You want them to join the dancing class you teach (decide the kind of dancing).

3 **Listen to Student A, and for each refusal, use these cues to respond:**

- it's really fun; they will love it
- dancing will make them more confident and outgoing
- it's not expensive; you'll give a big discount

4.3 EXERCISE 3C STUDENT B

You're going to discuss open-plan offices (offices where all employees work in one big room). Tell your partner these advantages and disadvantages. Listen to their ideas.

Advantages:

- can encourage introverted employees to interact
- can save the company money

Disadvantages:

- people tend to waste more time because it's easy to talk to others
- can cause stress, especially for employees used to having a personal office

PAIR WORK PRACTICE

5.3 EXERCISE 3 STUDENT B

1 **Listen to your partner. They will tell you about the good and bad sides of swimming.**

2 **Now imagine you like running. Tell your partner about the good and bad sides of your sport. Say how certain you are.**

+ It's a good way to get outdoors.
+ You don't have to pay to use sports facilities.
+ You can listen to music while you're running.

– In hot, cold, or wet weather, it's not much fun.
– Good running shoes can be expensive.
– It can be hard to find quiet routes without people and traffic.

3 **Compare your sports.**

6.1 EXERCISE 4A STUDENT B

A **You're going to tell a story about becoming famous quickly. Read the story quickly. Then read it again and underline key points. Pay attention to verb tenses. Then tell your partner the story in your own words.**

DIY Style

Wengie has been entertaining her friends for years, but she's only been a famous YouTuber for a short time. She was born in China and has lived in Australia since she was a child. She started writing one of Australia's top blogs, called the Wonderful World of Wengie, in 2011. She later started a YouTube channel that now has more than 11 million viewers. Her videos have gotten over 50 million hits. She gives tips on fashion and makes videos showing people how to make DIY (do-it-yourself) projects, such as colored pencils and holiday gifts. She had worked in a business office before she became a famous blogger and YouTuber. She gave up a well-paying job to follow her dream. Now she makes appearances around the world and is worth almost $2 million.

B **Give your opinion of the stories.**

7.3 EXERCISE 5 STUDENT B

Conversation 1

Situation: You want to buy a mountain bike from Student A. Find out the price and bargain hard to get the best deal for yourself.

Conversation 2

Read the information. Then use these arguments while bargaining to get the best price from Student A.

Situation: You want to sell your large couch for $200 (your opening price can be higher).

- It's in excellent condition, almost new.
- It's large and seats three people comfortably.
- It's a very stylish dark-gray color. The material is very strong.
- You can throw in three pillows for free.

9.3 EXERCISE 3C STUDENT B

Conversation 1

You and Student A are close friends.

Listen to Student A's problem and give advice. Reassure them, using expressions that are appropriate for your relationship.

Conversation 2

You are a student. Student A is your professor.

Problem: You have failed two tests recently. You are worried about the future of your studies. Tell your professor about it and ask for advice.